EVERYTHING'S COMING UP PROFITS

THE GOLDEN AGE OF INDUSTRIAL MUSICALS

B.F.Goodrich

1966 SALES MEETING

O. K. LYNN, BFG'S GENERAL MANAGER OF DEALER SALES.

W. B. FLORA, BFG GENERAL MANAGE OF RETAIL SALES.

EVERYTHING'S COMING UP PROFITS

THE GOLDEN AGE OF INDUSTRIAL MUSICALS

Steve Young and Sport Murphy

Blast Books
NEW YORK

Edited, designed, and digital imaging and prepress by Laura Lindgren

Blast Books gratefully acknowledges the generous help of Otis Fodder and Donald Kennison.

Library of Congress Cataloging-in-Publication Data

Young, Steve
  Everything's coming up profits : the golden age of industrial musicals /
Steve Young and Sport Murphy. — First edition.
      pages   cm
  Includes bibliographical references and index.
  ISBN 978-0-922233-44-1 (alk. paper)
  1. Industrial musicals—History and criticism. I. Murphy, Sport. II. Title.
  ML2054Y68 2013
  781.64809—dc23   2013020047

Published by Blast Books, Inc.
P.O. Box 51, Cooper Station
New York, NY 10276-0051
www.blastbooks.com

Printed in China

10 9 8 7 6 5 4 3 2 1

Contents

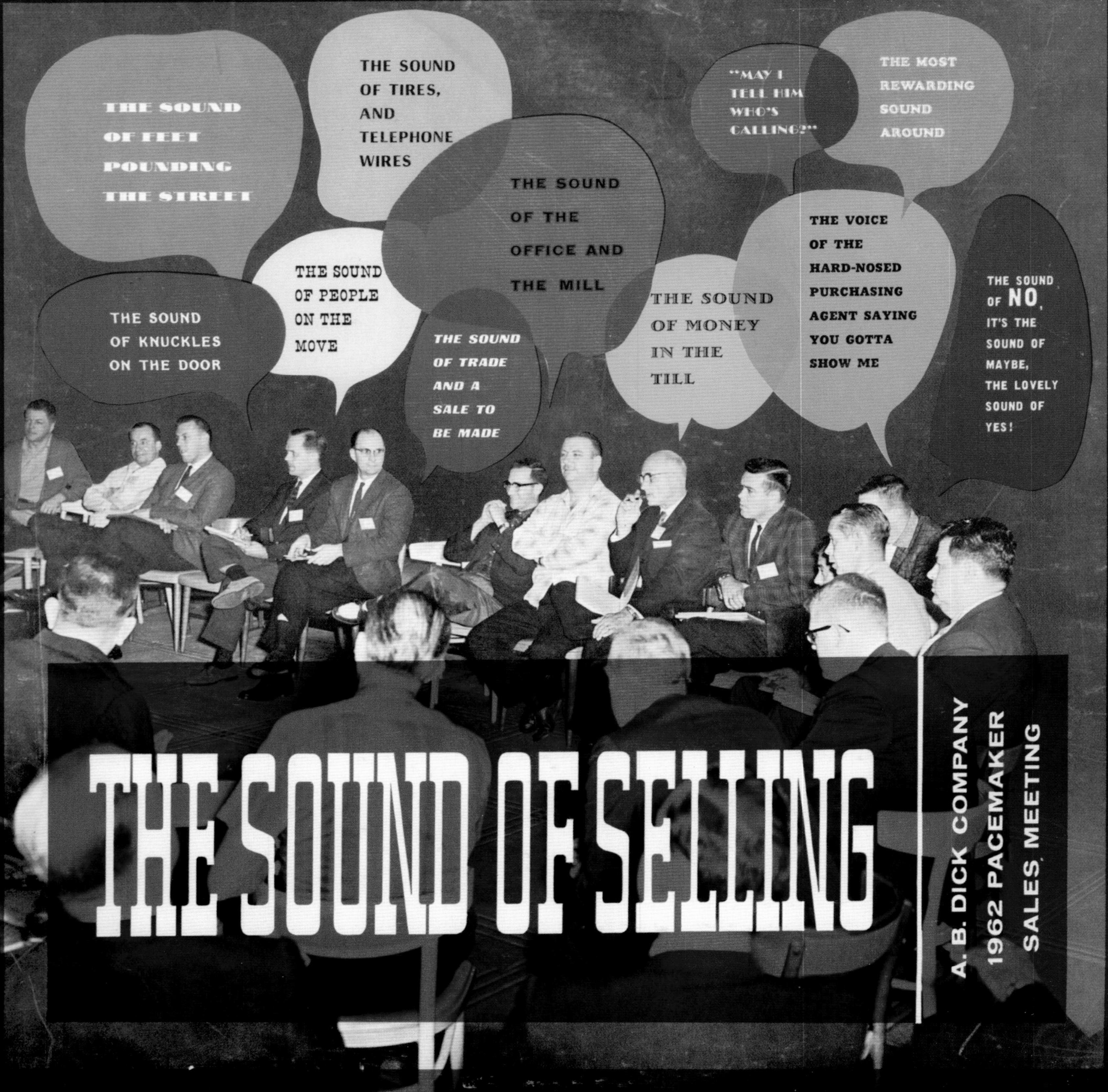
THE SOUND OF FEET POUNDING THE STREET
THE SOUND OF TIRES, AND TELEPHONE WIRES
"MAY I TELL HIM WHO'S CALLING?"
THE MOST REWARDING SOUND AROUND
THE SOUND OF THE OFFICE AND THE MILL
THE SOUND OF PEOPLE ON THE MOVE
THE SOUND OF KNUCKLES ON THE DOOR
THE SOUND OF TRADE AND A SALE TO BE MADE
THE SOUND OF MONEY IN THE TILL
THE VOICE OF THE HARD-NOSED PURCHASING AGENT SAYING YOU GOTTA SHOW ME
THE SOUND OF NO, IT'S THE SOUND OF MAYBE, THE LOVELY SOUND OF YES!
THE SOUND OF SELLING
A. B. DICK COMPANY
1962 PACEMAKER
SALES MEETING

Introduction

You know what musicals are even if you're not a fan. And you're familiar with industry, even if in postindustrial America it's not what it used to be. But if you're like most people, the phrase "industrial musical" will elicit only a look of blank puzzlement.

Your look is about to change from blank puzzlement to amazed delight, with perhaps a flicker of horror.

Corporate musical motivation goes back nearly a hundred years. By the 1920s companies such as IBM were holding meetings at which employees sang familiar songs with rewritten lyrics praising the company and its leaders. But it wasn't until after World War II that three trends converged to produce the industrial musical.

First, postwar America was an economic juggernaut. The rising middle class wanted stuff, lots of stuff, which American corporations were eager to supply. By 1955 U.S. industry was turning out two-thirds of the world's manufactured goods.

Second, within these humming companies, management was turning to new psychological methods to keep the workforce happy and productive. Selling a endless river of soap, typewriters, cars, and appliances could be a depressing grind. Conventions and sales meetings became increasingly common as a way to let "the man in the gray flannel suit" blow off steam while building esprit de corps and introducing new products and selling strategies.

Third, starting in the 1930s, Broadway and movie musicals had become increasingly mainstream entertainment. Even unions and labor organizations began producing slick musicals to educate and inspire their membership. And by the late 1940s the advent of long-playing 33 rpm records allowed for a show's soundtrack to be enjoyed at home.

The conditions were ripe for a perfect storm of business-themed musical theater. Corporate America realized it had the means, the motive, and the opportunity to stage full-blown musicals that would educate and entertain the sales force. Give 'em an instructive story laced with catchy tunes and inside jokes, maybe a couple sexy ladies—it was an experience much more memorable than listening to a guy with horn-rimmed glasses droning at a podium.

With the amount of money the big corporations had to spend, top-notch talent was within reach. Both established and up-and-coming composers, singers, dancers, and other creative types were happy to take these gigs. The word spread that industrials were a great way to pay the rent, make connections, and practice your craft between "real" shows or while you waited for your big break.

Although the effect of these shows on the sales force may have been hard to quantify, by the 1960s they'd fanned out from the initial beachhead of the car companies into

GENERAL ELECTRIC
PRESENTS

GO FLY A KITE

FIFTH ELECTRIC UTILITY EXECUTIVES CONFERENCE
WILLIAMSBURG, VIRGINIA
SEPTEMBER 19-21, 1966

I knew none of this in 1993 as I regarded a record album titled General Electric Presents *Go Fly a Kite*. The look on my face was blank puzzlement, I'm sure.

I was the writer in charge of "Dave's Record Collection" on *Late Night with David Letterman*. We played clips of unintentionally funny records — ideally, something like William Shatner singing — and Dave would deliver a quip. It was up to me to scour New York City's used record stores for material. That's how I came to be holding a copy of the hefty GE double album, a souvenir of the Fifth Utility Executives Conference in Williamsburg, Virginia, September 1966.

Listening to the records, I was surprised to hear an elaborate musical play about the electric power industry, with a plot about Ben Franklin meeting a modern utility executive, and electricity-related subplots involving beatniks, witches, and hillbillies. There was a love song expressed through electrical jargon and a peppy number called "PDM Can Do," about Power Distribution Management. Well done — amazingly well done, in fact — but obviously ridiculous. Perfect for mocking on late night television. Little did I realize that this album was just the tiny, tuneful tip of an invisible showbiz iceberg.

Record store "miscellaneous" bins yielded more corporate oddities: *Diesel Dazzle*, a 1966 musical about selling and servicing GM diesel engines. *My Insurance Man*, a 1968 show put on at a Continental Insurance meeting. *Music from AM Route 66*, the 1966 American Motors Automotive Announcement Show. All were pressed in minuscule quantities, intended for the ears of company insiders only.

By now two things were happening. I was becoming dimly aware that this might be an actual genre. And God help me, I was walking around Manhattan humming songs about

a wide range of industries. Surely some of the momentum was due to the novelty and prestige of putting on a show just as big as anyone else was doing. But industrial show vets attest to the power of a song to bring tears to the eyes of hardened salesmen and middle managers, especially if the message affirmed the value of their daily battles and the glory they could bring to themselves, their families, their company, and America. A souvenir record could re-create the magic and reinforce the message back home — though the extra expense of making a recording meant that these souvenirs were always the exception rather than the rule.

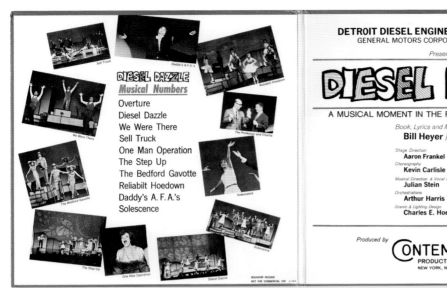

DIESEL DAZZLE
Musical Numbers

Overture
Diesel Dazzle
We Were There
Sell Truck
One Man Operation
The Step Up
The Bedford Gavotte
Reliabilt Hoedown
Daddy's A. F. A.'s
Solescence

SOUVENIR RECORD
NOT FOR COMMERCIAL USE

DETROIT DIESEL ENGINE DIVISION
GENERAL MOTORS CORPORATION

DETROIT DIESEL

Presents

DIESEL DAZZLE

A MUSICAL MOMENT IN THE PURSUIT OF SOLESCENCE!

Book, Lyrics and Music
Bill Heyer / Harold Beebe

Stage Direction
Aaron Frankel

Choreography
Kevin Carlisle

Musical Direction & Vocal Arrangements
Julian Stein

Orchestrations
Arthur Harris

Scenic & Lighting Design
Charles E. Hoefler

Produced by
CONTEMPO!
PRODUCTIONS, INC.
NEW YORK, NEW YORK

DAVID B. MARSHALL
Executive Producer

selling cars, insurance, and diesel engines, because many of the songs were *really good*. The less ambitious shows relied on song parodies and couldn't rise above a certain level of hokey charm. But the top-shelf examples, with catchy original melodies and improbable lyrics belted out by pros, were a revelation.

I'd grown up knowing nothing about musical theater, but I was hooked. This was no longer for the *Letterman* show; now it was personal. I began cold-calling record stores, going to record shows, and networking with dealers and collectors, who often needed a lot of explanation before they understood what I was looking for. Then eBay came along, freeing up the contents of America's closets, basements, and attics. The initial handful of records multiplied and started to fill up shelves.

Twenty years after I first encountered *Go Fly a*

Kite, I've acquired hundreds of extremely rare records. I've tracked down and interviewed many composers and performers. I've made great friends, including artist–writer–musician–bon vivant Sport Murphy, who brings his range of talents to bear on the subject here with fantastic results. I've received an unexpected education that touches on musical theater, business, and American

About the Cast

MICHAEL FESCO began his theatrical career at the Brussels World Fair with the New York City Center productions of Carousel and Wonderful Town. Since then, he has appeared on Broadway in Goldilocks, New Faces of '62, Irma La Douce, and the musical revue From A to Z.

CHUCK GREEN is currently featured on the Jimmy Dean Show; he has also appeared on Omnibus, the Sid Caesar Show, Hallmark and the U.S. Steel Hour. On Broadway, Mr. Green was featured in West Side Story and Here's Love.

DAVID HARTMAN played Rudolph, the German Headwaiter, in the original Broadway cast of Hello Dolly for two years. This season he was the seafaring Oliver in The Yearling, and has appeared in My Fair Lady, and on major television shows.

EDWARD J. HEIM has been a featured dancer on Broadway in I Had A Ball, Bells Are Ringing, and By The Beautiful Sea, in which he played the role of Lenny. Mr. Heim's dance partners in theatre and television include Gwen Verdon, Carol Lawrence, Chita Rivera, and Carol Burnett.

ROBERT R. KAYE was last seen on Broadway opposite Liza Minelli in Flora The Red Menace; he played the title role in the national company of Li'l Abner. His most memorable moment was a White House performance in Brigadoon before the late President John F. Kennedy. Mr Kaye has appeared on the Bell Telephone Hour and the CBS Workshop.

MARIE LAKE played the lead in New Girl In Town, on Broadway, replacing Gwen Verdon. Miss Lake has been a regular on The Entertainers and the Garry Moore Show.

BOBBI LANGE studied voice at the Paris Conservatory of Music, and has sung the lead roles in Madame Butterfly, Rigoletto, La Boheme, and other operas. On Broadway this season, she played in Half A Sixpence and The Yearling.

HAL LINDEN played opposite Judy Holliday in Bells Are Ringing, and was Barbara Harris' leading man this season on On A Clear Day You Can See Forever. In between have been assignments in Wildcat, Subways Are For Sleeping, Something More and What Makes Sammy Run.

DIESEL DAZZLE

A MUSICAL MOMENT IN THE PURSUIT OF SOLESCENCE!

APRIL 27, 28, 29, 30, 1966

McGREGOR MEMORIAL AUDITORIUM DETROIT, MICHIGAN

history. And I've become passionate about sharing and celebrating these ephemeral works we were never supposed to hear.

It wouldn't be fair to dangle these astonishing artifacts in front of you without allowing you to hear the music. In fact, it would constitute torture, as defined by the 1949 Geneva Conventions Protocol IV, which bans musical theater teasing. We have therefore set up a companion website, industrialmusicals.com, where you can hear many of the greatest hits.

So check in, drop off your suitcase in your room, and then get back downstairs. The meeting's about to start, and we've got some very special entertainment prepared. You may find yourself stunned, amused, exhilarated, and even a bit frightened, but we think you'll agree: there's no business like business show business!

—Steve Young

RARITY RANKINGS

This book is not intended primarily as a record collecting guide, but for readers curious about the scarcity of these records, each entry is ranked on a scale of 1 to 4:

1 only one or two copies known—good luck finding one in this lifetime
2 just a handful of known copies, rarely turns up
3 scarce but turns up occasionally
4 relatively common for an industrial show (though still rare by most other standards)

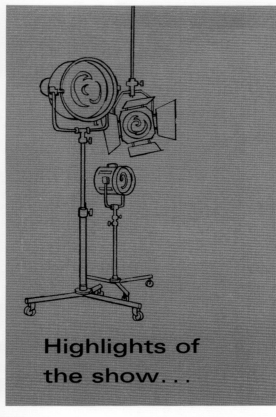

Highlights of the show...

Detroit officially recognized the gathering of the "Men From Fruehauf" to the city with this announcement on the marquee of Cobo Hall.

Fruehauf representatives from all over the U.S. and Canada, and affiliates from several foreign countries attended the presentation.

The team of F.R.U.E.H.A.U.F. "agents," providing security for their products, included heroic "OO-F," wily "Mr. Elderly," and winsome "36-24-36."

The "R.O.T." agents, attempting to steal Fruehauf's secrets, included "Dr. Quincy Crawtail," bumbling "Artemus Q. Whiffle," and not-so-motherly "Mom."

Tank-Trailers of many types were among the units that appeared in a dramatic stage setting representing a full-scale truck stop.

Vans for numerous applications participated in the all-day "parade" — and narrowly escaped destruction by the villainous R.O.T. agents.

Among the various types of specialized hauling equipment viewed in the parade was this Stainless Steel Van, with the most trouble-free floor lift built.

Hoist-type Dump-Trailers also passed on parade. The disclosure of the superiorities of these units helped to demoralize the counterspies.

The new interior and exterior design of the "possum belly" Livestock Van was one of the many recent product innovations announced in the show.

By the end of the spectacle, even the scurvy R.O.T. crew unanimously agreed that "THE MEN FROM F.R.U.E.H.A.U.F. ARE THE GREATEST!"

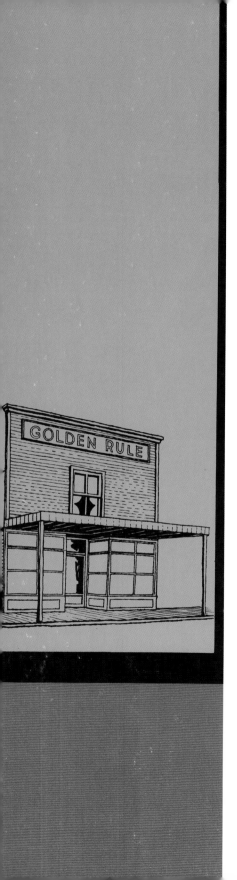

Preface

In the 1970s my family moved from Brooklyn to Long Island. It was an easy hour's drive, but for a kid who wore handmade Bonzo Dog Band T-shirts and Alice Cooper eye makeup; it was banishment to the Gulag...or at least the Pointless Forest. Mom assuaged my trauma in a thousand empathetic ways, including regular treks to thrift shops, where we'd sift through stale-smelling racks and bins for what fortune might provide. I can still hear Dad groaning with mock disapproval as we hauled each day's catch into the house and up to my room: disintegrating George Ade paperbacks, personalized bowling shirts, strings of cheap plastic Chinese lanterns, home "limbo party" kits, and the real treasure: armfuls of vinyl records. Of such raw materials were the mutant sensibilities of a suburban exile formed.

In this private alter-culture, where Charles Ives and Rahsaan Roland Kirk passed for superstar names and the likes of the De Paur Infantry Chorus and Josef Marais and Miranda served as daily fare, the mainstream seemed more and more irrelevant. Well, not exactly true; it had an oblique relevance, via those rare, screwy records by and for American corporations, never meant for civilian use: production library albums, generic radio jingle collections, and, one mythic afternoon, a curio entitled *Penney Proud*.

What on earth was THIS? Sumptuous as *Man of La Mancha* in style and execution, except the songs, rather than

invoking Impossible Dreams, applied the same grandiosity to Mundane Realities, like...uh...credit cards. This introduction to industrials led to an intermittent, often frustrating search for similar finds. Stuff turned up, though, as stuff will. Through subsequent decades, as I pursued my own musical picaresque, I'd occasionally slip favorites like "Up Came Oil" and "May I Have Your Penney Charge Card, Please" into band sets. Along the way, I made the odd buck or two writing and recording songs for public service films and serving as hired vocalist on "employee motivational" recordings. Such work fostered a respect for the artistry involved in industrial LPs without demystifying any of their beguiling bizarreness.

When eBay arrived to drain this singer-songwriter's scant finances, my patient searches for industrials usually led to disappointing outbids, invariably by the same competitor. I eventually contacted the bastard directly. "Dave's Record Collection," unsurprisingly, had been my favorite *Letterman* segment, but now the bitter realization dawned that I'd been bidding against the deep pockets of Worldwide Pants. Sure, I could've nursed a grudge; instead, Steve Young and I became friends. People talk about a special bond—a kind of unspoken *knowing*—between people who've shared intense experiences like armed conflict or Olympic team competition...it didn't take long for Steve and I to implicitly understand that both of us had an apparent interest in old souvenir LPs of sales meetings.

Steve, like *Penney Proud* itself, concealed a singular strangeness behind a facade of deadpan normalcy. He'd gone much further than I, undertaking a long project of interviewing the creators of these shows, diligently ferreting out the genre's history, and accumulating a vast archive of albums. Thus, even more surely than Leo Guild was the ideal author of Hedy Lamarr's autobiography, Steve Young was the only man to pen the saga of industrial musicals. Likewise, Laura Lindgren, who designs ravishing books as naturally as you or I might make annoying throat-clearing noises, has expertly culled a bright bouquet from what, let's face it, can be some pretty weedy sources. I, for one, would have rejoiced simply to *find* such a book, provided the price was right or I got a free review copy. Instead, I've actually helped write it.

As a complement to Steve's erudition and wit and Laura's artistic excellence, my contribution takes two forms. First, here and there throughout these pages, I've focused on specific songs and album covers in a manner such as you might experience if you were to join us at the private social club I run on Long Island, the School Yard Gents. There, over fine scotch, Serrano ham, and the evocative stench of burning peat, we sometimes listen to these numbers, and a sense of the conversation they inspire may be gleaned from my short essays here, without the lame comments from all the other bores in the room.

I've also made a few comic strip pages based on behind-the-scenes tales that the performer John Russell has generously shared with us, all about his long career in the industrials racket. This is the guy who sang "Up Came Oil"! We hope these comics do fair justice to John's charming accounts of what it was like to make a living dancing about architectural supplies. We also hope that our efforts here (along with the abundant supplementary content you'll find at industrialmusicals.com) will entertain you, sure, but mainly that the result sells and sells some more, propelling Steve, Blast Books, and myself toward new, exalted heights of profit.

— Sport Murphy

THE MUSIC FROM "FORD-I-FY YOUR FUTURE"

Years ago, when I found this record, I showed it to a friend, who marveled at the wonderful cover. Then he turned it over and his eyes widened. "Sheldon Harnick and Jerry Bock?!" Those names didn't mean anything to me at the time, but I've come a long way since then.

By the late 1950s the songwriting team of Bock and Harnick was starting to get noticed. They wrote the songs for the Broadway musical *Fiorello!*, about the former New York City mayor, which opened in November 1959. They later went on to huge success with *Fiddler on the Roof*. But like many Broadway strivers, they paid the bills at first by writing industrials such as this 1959 Ford Tractor & Implement Division show. The presentation via closed-circuit telecast was unusual, and Sheldon Harnick recalls another innovation: Ford planted crops months in advance that were harvested by the new tractors as part of the show.

There are only four songs on the one-sided record, but they're all pretty entertaining. "Golden Harvest" revs up the sales force.

> *Gonna be a golden harvest in 1959!*
> *Gonna be a lot more buyers to sign that*
> *   dotted line!*
> *With the new Ford tractors, the future's*
> *   looking fine!*
> *Now's the time to roll your sleeves up,*
> *So if you rise and shine,*
> *Gonna be a golden harvest in 1959!*
>
> *Turn your tractors and implements*
> *To a bumper crop—of dollars and cents!*

Strangely, the back cover description of "Golden Harvest" seems to have been written in English, translated into Chinese, and back into English: "It's rollicking type of music is exciting yet meaningful. This is a sales story—and a story of selling—told in a chanting and singing style." Also, Jerry Bock's last name is misspelled as "Brock."

Other songs include "The Answer Is Ford" and "Any Speed for Any Need," about the new Select-O-Speed transmission, and the impressive "More Power to You," featuring a spiraling-upward section listing endless farm tasks and the happy solution:

> *More power to you! With the*
> *   Powermaster,*
> *The Workmaster, and the Power Major too!*
> *More power to you! You provide the*
> *   tractors*
> *That do more than any other tractors do!*

Though Sheldon Harnick contributed new lyrics to some song parody industrials, *Ford-i-fy* was the only industrial show he did with Jerry Bock, the only one he worked on with original music, and the only one to be recorded. The clunky liner notes finally get one point across correctly: "The original music, designed to tell a product story, is a fine example of combining 'Broadway' musical talent with industry."

RARITY: 3

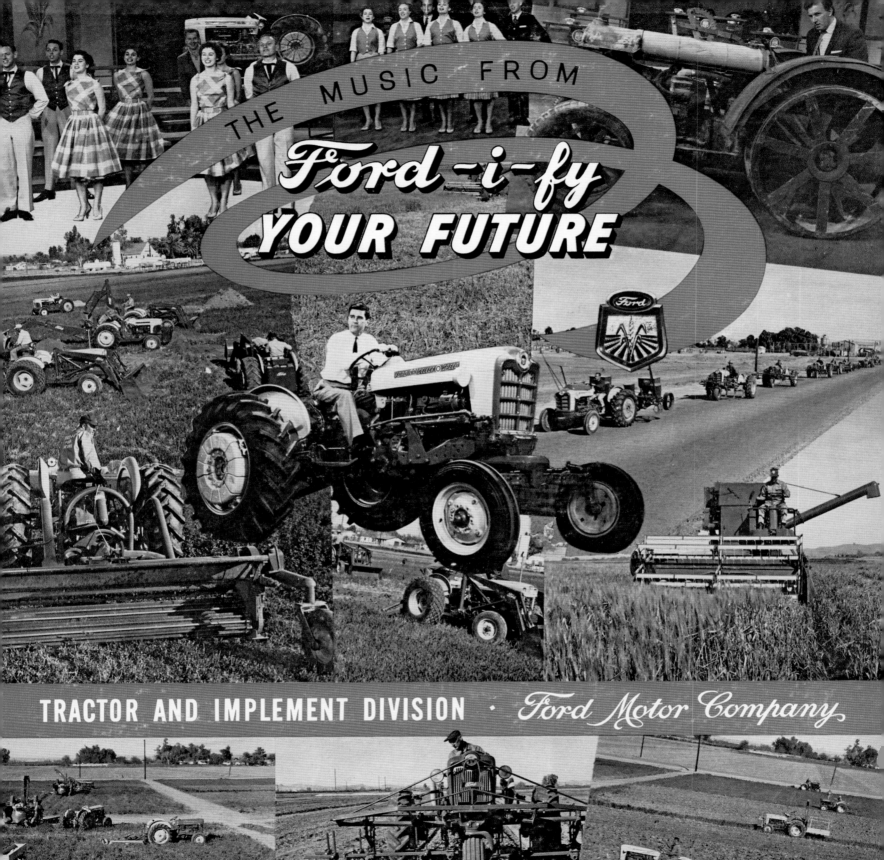

THE MUSIC FROM

Ford-i-fy
YOUR FUTURE

TRACTOR AND IMPLEMENT DIVISION · *Ford Motor Company*

ACTORS 'N' TRACTORS

When Bock and Harnick crafted the score for 1959's *Ford-i-fy Your Future*, they withheld none of the pizazz that earned them a Pulitzer for their musical *Fiorello!* that same year. From the Select-O-Speed testimonial "Any Speed for Any Need," with its counterintuitively slow, strolling tempo, to the optimistic hoedown "Golden Harvest," Jerry and Sheldon were firing on all cylinders on this one, brief as it is.

"More Power to You" concludes the '59 Ford show's quartet of classics, a deft microsuite heralding the unprecedented efficiency and economy of Ford's Workmaster, Powermaster, and Power Major tractors.

First we're forced to confront a merciless analysis of the Sisyphean "work of the world." With "Twelve Days of Christmas" relentlessness, we're reminded of the "...mowing, towing, bailing, nailing, seeding, breeding, spreading, shredding, clipping, stripping, shaking, raking..." that swallows up one's precious earthly time, sunrise to sunset, just before deliverance from all that ticktock torment arrives via a rollicking big swing title chorus, all customary self-laudatory claims inclusive.

As we see in other shows, especially ones dealing with humongous farm machinery, the contrast of dreary labor and glad relief, courtesy of the corporation's benevolent innovations, is

something of a standard template. But isn't kvetching about such things tantamount to complaining that Road Runner is forever thwarting Wile E. Coyote? The pleasure is, of course, in the variations within.

Take, for example, the superb kick-line finale of "More Power to You":

Let's hit the sunny trail to Yuma/
Let's jump the gun on the consum-ah!

Right there's your difference between a mere tuneful contemplation on the promotion of backhoe loaders...and the elusive realms of Art.

So, four songs, one side, no waiting: there's efficiency and economy for you. And with such jubilant inspiration at their fingertips, it's no surprise that, very soon indeed, Messrs. Bock and Harnick would no longer need to wonder about what it would be like to be biddy biddy rich, aidle-diddle-daidle-daidle men.

—SM

THE BIG CHANGE

Standard Oil of Indiana commissioned this ambitious 1957 show to address a problem: too many managers were running themselves ragged micromanaging rather than delegating. Much of the show concerns an overworked manager and his secretary, Miss Hopkins, who reads him his schedule in "Busy, Busy Day."

There's a personnel meeting at nine o'clock,
A training meeting at ten,
Mr. Jones is in from Chicago, you must see him, but when?
Mr. Gilson out on Main Street is giving us no peace,
He's coming in to talk about relinquishing his lease!
I'm the one to do the job, I can handle it right!
I will do it if it takes me day and night!

Meanwhile, customers deliver musical demands for convenient station hours, top-quality products, and fair prices. "The Advisory Committee" bemoans the lack of long-range planning and management's unhealthy obsession with something called Report 216. And in "The Man with High Hopes," a station owner mourns the departure of an experienced field rep.

On the day he said goodbye,
they replaced him with a guy
Who seemed lacking in experience and judgment.
When it came to merchandising,
or an item such as pricing,
It seemed to us that we were showing him!

Still, he's a very fine young man,
and he helps us all he can,
But as a salesman, he doesn't have the time
To go much into detail as to how we ought to retail
All the products that we sell — it's a crime!

What a mess!

The way forward was presented metaphorically. Most of side 2 is a parable set in the land of Princelvania, a beautiful but inefficient kingdom where well-intentioned King Claude strangles the economy due to his insistence on running everything himself. In the end the problems are straightened out, and a bright new day dawns for Princelvania and Standard Oil.

Although this record is uncredited, when I tracked down Lloyd Norlin in conjunction with another show, he fessed up to several others, including *The Big Change*. According to Lloyd, the show was presented at the Great Northern Theater in Chicago at 8 a.m. and was a huge hit. That evening at a gala reception, company brass announced that a cast album and a film version would be recorded, thrilling the performers, who would now be paid twice more. The recording features a crew of talented vocalists and a punchy orchestra with a sound very similar to the other shows Lloyd wrote in the late '50s for the production company Wilding. Lloyd was hired to write four more shows for Standard Oil, although all that seems to have survived is one song from 1958. Meanwhile, Lloyd was also cranking out shows for Ford.

RARITY: 3

Born in 1918 in South Dakota, Lloyd Norlin had a long, successful musical career and was an accomplished songwriter by the time he earned a master's degree in music. In 1942 he received an Academy Award nomination for his song "Out of the Silence," from the film *All American Co-Ed*. His first industrial was for Chicago's Marshall Field's department store in 1951. As the musical director for Wilding Pictures in Chicago for several years, he produced a string of industrials that made it onto vinyl, including the '57 Ford car and truck shows, the '57 Standard Oil show, the '59 Ford show, and the 1960 *Pepsi Power Phase Two* show, the liner notes of which mention that by this point he'd composed more than 250 industrial show tunes.

A 1965 show for Hamm's beer is so far the last of Lloyd's industrial shows to be found on a souvenir record, although he continued to write industrials into the 1980s. He also won Emmy awards in the 1970s, contributed to off-Broadway shows in Chicago, and had a song performed at Mount Rushmore during the 1976 Bicentennial.

I had the pleasure of speaking with Lloyd several times in the 1990s. He passed away in 2000, gratified that collectors were beginning to find and enjoy his industrial work.

TURN AND FACE "THE BIG CH- CH- CHANGE"

In 1957 (era of the International Geophysical Year, eventually celebrated in song by Donald Fagen), Standard Oil presented a swank seventy-fifth anniversary TV special featuring performances by the likes of Duke Ellington, Tyrone Power, Kay Thompson, and Jimmy Durante, plus an animated cartoon by Ronald Searle. It was a heady year for music: Monk and Coltrane played together at Carnegie Hall, Bernstein and Sondheim premiered *West Side Story*, and Sullivan said of Presley, "This is a real decent, fine boy…you're thoroughly all right."

Far away in Liverpool, a young fellow named Paul McCartney introduced himself to one John Lennon, who'd just performed with his "skiffle" group, the Quarrymen. One can almost hear Paul telling his new friend, "Nice sound, mate…know anything by Lloyd Norlin?"

Unlikely that Lennon did, as Norlin's songs for *The Big Change* were rather sub rosa to all but a lucky corroboree of sales managers who demanded an original cast album as keepsake of their '57 conference (alas, the film version of *The Big Change* has not yet surfaced, though *Midwest Holiday*, a 1952 Wilding Picture Productions travelogue, also produced for Standard Oil, exists, along with other Wilding films for Oldsmobile, Chrysler, GE et al., in the Prelinger Archives). How those Standard Oil managers must have felt when they finally laid eyes on the album cover!

Sometimes with LPs, you just fall in love with one as an object, music aside, and *The Big Change* cover is one lovely object. Its asymmetrical design with south-central trapezium motif seems at once elegant and playful, an impression enhanced by the title copy, set in B. Altman Impromptu script typeface, with quotation marks adding a further splash of buoyant savoir faire. Here is a cover design full of champagne and bright laughter, the kind of album cover you want to just grab hold of and take on a giddy hansom cab ride under a twinkling night sky. Sleek lamination makes it a dandy substitute Colorforms board.

—SM

"The Big Change" means

1. Delegate responsibility—then coach.
2. Let's function as a "team" toward a common goal.
3. More customers—more completely served.
4. Develop new selling and merchandising ideas.
5. Don't be afraid to "break" with tradition.
6. Develop long range plans.
7. Don't move from crisis to crisis.
8. First manage yourself.

We are most pleased to forward to you a recording of the music from "The Big Change."

Sales Promotion and Advertising Department

music from

"The Big Change"

STANDARD OIL COMPANY

1957

sales management conference

written and produced by
WILDING PICTURE PRODUCTIONS INC.
Chicago, Illinois

ORIGINAL MUSIC AND LYRICS

HIT TUNES

from the
1957 FORD INTRODUCTION SHOW

Overture
Happy New Year 1957
Got to Have a Car
☆ Ford Has Done it Again
☆ It's a Beautiful Car

☆ It's Fun to Drive a Ford
☆ We're the Station Wagon Set
☆ The Belle Song
☆ The Best Ford of Our Lives
☆ All Aboard for Arizona ☆ Finale

HIT TUNES FROM THE 1957 FORD INTRODUCTION SHOW

Ford was one of the "low-priced three," but its shows sounded better than that. The 1957 model year saw a double-barreled attack: separate Lloyd Norlin shows for the car and truck lines, both recorded and pressed on souvenir discs. *Hit Tunes from the 1957 Ford Introduction Show* isn't quite as ambitious as the Oldsmobile shows of the era, going for a revue of unrelated songs rather than a full plot, but it has some memorable melodies, fine production values, and a few appealingly weird touches.

If you're not familiar with the '57 Ford, "It's a Beautiful Car," according to the designers in the Styling Rotunda. "We're the Station Wagon Set" includes a surprisingly risqué moment.

> *Delivering flowers every day, I feel*
> *   qualified to say,*
> *It's the greatest thing for work I've ever*
> *   found.*
> *And at night it's great for parkin', you can*
> *   do a lot of sparkin',*
> *A mighty handy car to have around!*

"The Belle Song" is an unusual picture of the Ford-Chevy-Plymouth rivalry, with two women personifying the Plymouth Belvedere and the Chevy Bel Air. They're always "on the make, to hoodwink any sucker we can possibly take," and aren't above sniping at each other.

> *Now I come from that sturdy old Chrysler*
> *   stock!*
> *—And she's still got a shape like a*
> *   Plymouth rock!*

The guys resist the slutty come-ons of the Belles.

> *To us your appearance is plain, even*
> *   shady,*
> *'Cause we have a date with a beautiful*
> *   lady!*
> *And over the highway she'll reign,*
> *She is Ford's brand-new Fairlane!*
> *   (The Fairlane? Hah!)*
> *   (A little new paint and a lifted face,)*
> *   (Don't kid us, she's not in the race!)*
> *Fairlane is gonna surpass you! (Yeah?)*
> *Fairlane is gonna outclass you! (Huh!)*

The audience must have roared at the climax of "Ford Has Done It Again" as Chevy takes another not-for-public-consumption hit.

> *From bumper to bumper, completely*
> *   new — the '57 Ford!*
> *From top to bottom, the same is true — the*
> *   '57 Ford!*
> *Here's the greatest new car today,*
> *Here's the car that will lead the way,*
> *And BEAT THE HELL OUT OF*
> *   CHEVROLET —*
> *Ford has done it again!*

Although the '57 Chevy is an icon today, at the time Ford actually eked out a rare sales victory over its archrival. Chalk it up to the beautiful, longer, lower '57 Ford — and the show's potent combination of snappy boosterism and station wagon sex.

RARITY: 3

CAST OF CHARACTERS

(not in order of appearance)

From the *Milwaukee Journal*, May 7, 1955

D. P. Brother & Co., and others like them, aren't kidding around. Theirs is no college type show, designed to compete with Broadway. They're out to sell cars, and, if a show is going to help, they'll do a show. But it'll be the car first, the show second.

That's all right with the actors who do the show. It's perfect for them. They get 10 weeks of work, at full Actors' Equity scale, and maybe do seven or eight shows. They get taken to New Orleans, for example, for four days. While there, they have to do one show. The rest of the time is their own, and they're getting paid every minute.

So, when Brother announces auditions for a new Olds show, they are swamped with the cream of the Broadway crop. It's a lot better than clerking in a department store between Broadway parts.

Most of the other automobile makers have similar shows. So do the bigger manufacturers of refrigerators, TV sets, furniture, even ice cream…it's a trend that everybody seems to like — the organizations that produce them are thriving, the concerns that sponsor them seem to feel they're worth while, the actors who participate are delighted, the salesmen who watch have fun. Nobody objects.

ONCE IN A LIFETIME

You probably know about the Edsel. Launched with great fanfare in 1957 for the '58 model year, it was a disaster for parent company Ford. The Edsel wasn't really new or revolutionary compared to other cars on the market. It looked funny, and buyers couldn't tell whether it was a step up or down from Mercury. To make matters worse, a recession arrived in late '57. The Edsel was a car that nobody needed. It limped into 1959 with a reduced lineup and was killed off shortly after the '60 models were announced. Today "Edsel" is synonymous with "flop."

The show's very good, though.

The 10-inch disc has six uncredited songs. The three on side 1 build anticipation, with a promise of success in "Howdy Partner," and the pleas of "Adam and Eve," the first Edsel buyers, for a car that gives them performance, economy, luxury, room, and style. "We're in the Market" is a refreshingly frank look at the cynicism of car buyers. A man and woman sing of their "muddled mind and jaundiced eye" caused by car companies' confusing claims, counterclaims, and hyperbole.

> *They're all the smartest, sweetest,*
> *loveliest, fleetest,*
> *Lowest, classiest, the unsurpassiest,*
> *Finest, chic'est, the latest.*
> *But how can they all be the greatest?*
> *We listen and stare and shop and*
> *compare and roam,*
> *And all we want is to buy a car and drive*
> *the hell home.*

Finally the car is revealed, and in "This Is the Edsel" the audience is assured

> *A whole new market is ready to bloom*
> *now,*
> *The world will make room now,*
> *For a car so fine.*
> *They'll say, this is the Edsel, make it*
> *mine!*

"Once in a Lifetime" tells the newly recruited dealer force that they've made the right choice by grabbing this rare opportunity. A dealer and a salesman sing of their limitless prospects, and then the dealer's wife chimes in.

> *The life of a wife of an Edsel dealer is a*
> *very exciting life!*
> *Overnight and suddenly, everyone wants*
> *to talk to me,*
> *A neighborhood celebrity is an Edsel*
> *dealer's wife!*

With a crisp, brassy orchestra and solid performances, the show certainly sounded convincing, and the dealers must have left the auditorium beaming. But the lyrics of "We're in the Market" turned out to be prescient. The car-buying public cast a jaundiced eye on the Edsel propaganda, shrugged, and turned away. The dealer on the album cover probably wishes he'd done the same.

RARITY: 3

ONCE IN A LIFETIME

*the complete musical score
from the Edsel Dealer Announcement Show*

Howdy Partner

Adam and Eve

We're in the Market

This Is the Edsel

Once in a Lifetime

Green Light

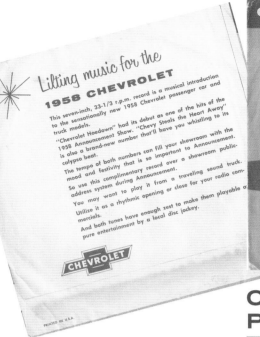

CHEVROLET PRESENTS 2 TOP TUNES FOR 1958

This 7-inch disc with two songs represents industrial giant Hank Beebe's first recorded corporate work, produced by the Jam Handy Organization, for decades a leader in business training materials, including industrial shows. (Hank also wrote the '57 Chevy announcement show, which has not survived.) Calypso was the hot new sound, and Chevy jumped on the trend with "Chevy Steals the Heart Away," complete with "Day-O, Chevrolet-O" background vocals and semi-convincing accents. The flip side goes country with the truck song "Chevrolet Hoedown."

Take a look at the new front end,
Built so strong it'll never bend!
Twirl your partner 'round the block,
Chevy's solid, built like a rock!
It's never gonna quiver like Zeke's old
*   flimsy flivver!*

Unusually for industrial show material, both songs were cleared for public use, with the back of the sleeve noting "Both tunes have enough zest to make them playable as pure entertainment by a local disc jockey." Another tip: "You may want to play it from a traveling sound truck." Yes, I may want to do that. Let me think about it.

RARITY: 2

THE BIG BONUS

The Big Bonus, Lloyd Norlin's 1958 follow-up to '57's *The Big Change*, yielded only one song on a 10-inch disc. Nothing is known about the plot of this Standard Oil show, but "I Love a Salesman" has a salacious subtext. Three women sing pleadingly:

A salesman, send a helpful salesman,
Send one who's got a lot of vigor and vim,
A salesman, send a helpful salesman,
Just like a dealer needs him, that's how
*   much we need him.*

Oh hurry, tell the guy to hurry,
To wait until we're old and gray and past
*   our prime*
Would be a crime.

Here's hoping the ladies convinced the salesman to give them the big bonuses they yearned for.

RARITY: 1

THE THEME IS FORD

Lloyd Norlin's '57 Ford show songs turned up again two years later, half a world away, on a 10-inch souvenir disc of the 1959 Australian Ford introduction show. Minor lyric tweaks reflect Down Under model variations such as Consul and Zephyr. The Aussies proved a bit timid in one regard: "Beat the hell out of Chevrolet" becomes "In spite of Chrysler or Chevrolet."

RARITY: 2

THE CAR: BUICK '59

A minor announcement show example, with a batch of song parodies and bare-bones sung introductions of the flamboyantly finny new models: "Invicta! Invicta! Invicta!" "LeSabre! LeSabre! LeSabre!" This live recording on red vinyl is mysterious, devoid of credits and song titles. It may have had a very limited pressing just for top Buick brass.

RARITY: 1

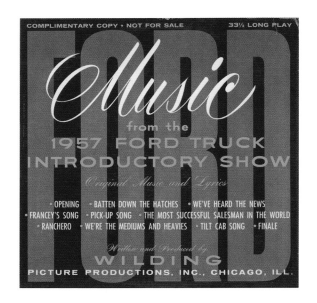

MUSIC FROM THE 1957 FORD TRUCK INTRODUCTORY SHOW

The fraternal twin of Lloyd Norlin's '57 Ford car show is a one-sided disc with ten songs, including "Ranchero," about the new hybrid car-pickup, and "We've Heard the News," in which potential truck buyers, including a surprisingly hip-sounding landscaper, sing their needs and concerns.

The privet hedge, the flowering shrub,
The evergreen, they buy my grub.
When I roll up to a rolling lawn,
My landscape truck must look real gone!

"Francey's Song" encourages the truck salesmen:

Oh, the boys I know who make the dough
And don't just gaze at the stars
Are the combination salesmen
Selling trucks as well as cars...

Oh, trucks are more than power and weight
Or the size of the differential.
There's the big reward in the profit stored
In the extra sales potential!

Befitting the utilitarian nature of trucks, many of the song titles, like the title of the show itself, are no-frills: "Pick-Up Song," "Tilt-Cab Song," "We're the Mediums and Heavies." But like the '57 line of Ford trucks, the songs are sturdy, well designed, and get the job done with style.

RARITY: 3

WORDS AND MUSIC FROM THE 1959 FORD CAR AND TRUCK INTRODUCTION SHOW

Lloyd Norlin also wrote the '58 Ford show, but all that survives is a little "sneak preview" 78 rpm teaser record with a brief sample of an opening number and a reminder to mail in for tickets. For the '59 show, Lloyd was back, but just handling the music, with lyrics contributed by Tom Byrnes. The disc is packaged in an elaborate twenty-page booklet crammed

MUSIC TO SET THE MOOD
...FOR THE '59 FORD

Here is a record that you might want to play in your showroom at Public Announcement. It's gay and sprightly —and most appropriate.

On one side are variations on the theme of the Ford song for '59—"You're Ahead in a Ford All the Way" —played in a number of interesting tempos.

The reverse side contains all the music and words of the '59 Introduction Show.

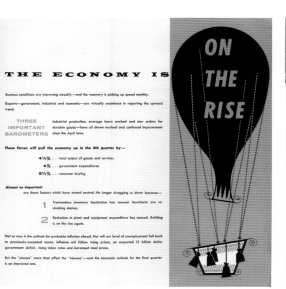

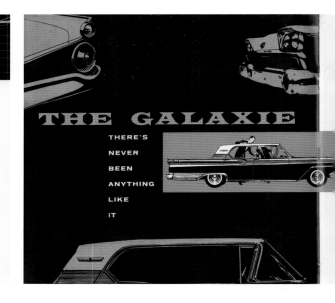

with selling strategies and data points for the new models. Although 1958 had been an off year, optimism reigned at the outset of '59, with "Here You Are" touting the low-priced Custom 300, and a dealer boasting "I'm in a Spot to Envy" because he has three different Ford convertibles to sell. "The Potential of the Influential" displays a curious blend of pre–feminist era condescension and grudging respect.

> *Oh, we're the prospects' wives, more*
> *important than you think*
> *For many a wife ignored has let the deal*
> *go down the sink.*
> *Our husbands choose the make of car,*
> *At least that's how it's been so far,*
> *But we decide between a car and no new*
> *car at all!*
> *So pay more attention, don't let us be*
> *ignored,*
> *It's easier to close a deal with the*
> *husband's wife aboard!*

In "A Matter of Proportions," a "gal who knows" sings

> *A car may ride nice and smooth on roads*
> *that are bumpy,*
> *But no one's gonna buy it if it's short,*
> *squat, and dumpy.*

That theory was already being disproven by VW and Rambler, and before 1959 was over each of the Big Three would debut its own compact car.

RARITY: 3

THE MIGHTY "O"

A late 1953 souvenir record of "The first all-musical announcement show in Oldsmobile's history," *The Mighty "O"* is the earliest industrial show in my collection. And it's no half-baked prototype: it's got a story, a big orchestra and cast (including a young Bob Fosse), sets, costumes, choreography, and the climactic new car reveal that was the hallmark of automotive introduction shows for decades.

The plot concerns the crew of an aircraft carrier with top secret "rockets," a reference to Oldsmobiles, since Olds was famous for its Rocket engine. Girlfriends appear in a dream sequence and later show up on board as

BEST BUY FOR STYLE VALUE ECONOMY

THE CUSTOM "300"

If most car buyers mean what they say in conversation, in print, in surveys—we have the volume sale car of the year in our '59 Ford Custom 300 series!

Here is a model which delivers what people have said Detroit can't build—a stylish, full-sized, adequately powered, comfortable sedan that gives better than 20 miles per gallon, is economical to maintain—and delivers for less than $2,000.

There is a pent-up demand for such a car. Proof lies in the increased market penetration by Rambler and foreign cars. But these cars are compromises. Now you have the real thing!

You can meet '59's continued strong buying accent on economy with the fine performing Mileage Maker 6 in the Custom 300. It's the only modern "6" in the industry.

Last year you set an all-time Company record by delivering 52% of your Custom 300's with 6-cylinder engines. Never before had sales of "6's" exceeded "8's" in a series of Ford cars.

Sales of "6's" should be even higher in '59. For instance, you have a new sales pitch for the 6-cylinder automatic transmission buyer. He'll like the new first gear starts now possible with our new Fordomatic.

In styling, the Custom 300 doesn't look up to anything in the industry. It has the smooth, flowing, balanced proportions of all '59 Fords. For an added styling touch there is a DELUXE TRIM KIT consisting of flowing chrome "birds" for the rear quarter panels, fender ornaments, sun visors, arm rests, cigar lighter, horn ring, etc.

Viewed from any angle—style, economy, performance—the Custom 300 is a true Value Leader, not only of our line but of the entire industry.

And to further its saleability, it will be the most competitively priced car in the industry.

Display it proudly—and sell it confidently. The Custom 300 is a money-maker for '59!

IT'S MUSIC TO THE EYES...

THE '59 THUNDERBIRD

They loved the '58—and they'll go wild for the '59!

That's the new Thunderbird—smarter (if possible), trimmer looking, more sophisticated!

There's never been a traffic-builder like the Thunderbird. And carry-over from the tremendous public acceptance of the '58 should get your '59 Thunderbird sales off to a flying start.

Everyone has "The Word"

It will benefit from the millions of dollars worth of tie-in copy lavished on it in '58 and '59 Ford advertising. The "Thunderbird luxury"..."Thunderbird styling"..."Thunderbird power"... message has penetrated virtually every populated spot in America.

The '59 T-Bird's own advertising schedule hits luxury market living rooms from Walla Walla to West Palm Beach.

What's Ahead Profit-Wise?

Your own washout sheets will tell you the 4-passenger Thunderbird has been a profit producer without peer. National average unit gross (with trade-in at wholesale) has consistently averaged over $600.

Sharper studies in 4 principal markets showed its per-unit gross was $140 higher than the Lincoln Capri. And it came to within $41 of the Cadillac "62".

...And Unit-Wise?

—an adequate supply to meet your ordering and stocking requirements.

For 1959 the Ford Division will set up sales potentials and monthly sales objectives by dealer.

Production planning has been geared to meet these volumes.

Watch for the Thunderbird Guide

Your dealership's sales potentials and objectives will be explained to you when retail orders for January are taken.

At that time you will receive a Thunderbird guide, a valuable fact-packed book that will

1 Explain and define the broad market which the Thunderbird is designed to penetrate.

2 Outline plans to help you reach and sell that market

3 Detail Ford Division's promotional plans for pre-selling that market in '59.

Meanwhile a considerable share of your sales solicitation efforts for the '59 could well be directed toward owners of General Motors' products. Trade-in of GM units is running 40%—and getting higher every month! Use your luxury car owners' list to reach these willing prospects with the Thunderbird style and product story.

Market analyses show the Thunderbird has appeal for every price buyer. Forty-six percent of sales are to owners in the low price field; 31% to medium-price owners and 17½% to drivers of luxury-type cars.

Seems as if everyone wants the Thunderbird. Let's sell it to them!

PRODUCT

WELL, THAT'S THE STORY...

You've read about the policies, plans, programs and promotions to help you launch the handsome new '59 Ford on a successful and profitable sales year.

You know you have a car designed for today's market. More than anything competition can offer, it fills the three concepts which buyers say they want in a car—low price, economy and compactness.

You've seen the sound marketing strategy—sales planning, sales training, advertising and promotion—which will introduce the '59 line and keep it in the public eye throughout the year.

And you've read about the improved economic climate in which you will be selling.

With these important elements—

...a product the buyer has asked for

...sound plans to help you sell it

...prospects able to buy

—the result can only be more sales and profits with the '59.

TO GIVE YOU THAT

New Ford Feeling...

YOUR 1959 FORD CAR AND TRUCK INTRODUCTION SHOW BRINGS YOU...

THE YEAR OF THE SALESMAN

THE CAST

DONALD CLARKE — Appeared as soloist with New York Philharmonic at Carnegie Hall, and Philadelphia Orchestra in Victor recordings. Lead tenor roles in numerous light operas and musical comedies.

WALTER FARRELL — In Broadway production of Shangri-La. Appearances with New York City Center Opera Co. Night club appearances in New York and Las Vegas. TV credits include Godfrey and Gleason shows.

HAL HACKETT — Played lead with George Raft in motion picture, Train to Auburn. TV includes Schlitz Playhouse, Private Secretary, Robert Montgomery Show. Stage roles include principal part in Kismet on Broadway.

JOSEPH MACAULAY — Seven successive full seasons at Kansas City Starlight Theater; ten years with St. Louis Municipal Opera; seven years with Detroit Civic Light Opera Co. Many Broadway musicals and operettas.

WILLIAM MacCULLY — Scores of stock theater appearances in such productions as Mikado, Desert Song, Plain and Fancy, Student Prince. Has sung with various opera companies and concert groups. Guest soloist on TV and radio.

MAYBIN HEWES — Has appeared in several Broadway shows. Played summer circuits in Detroit, Chicago and the East Coast. Many TV appearances including Jack Paar Show, Ed Sullivan Show, the Show of Shows.

DOROTHY IRWIN — On Broadway in The Pajama Game as Poopsie; Happy Hunting with Ethel Merman; New Girl in Town. TV credits include Robert Montgomery Theater, Studio One, the musical spectacular, Bloomer Girl.

JANET MELDIN — Broadway role in Sweethearts with Bobby Clark and ingenue lead in The Red Mill. On the musical stage regularly in The King and I, Carousel and others. Toured with An Evening with Beatrice Lillie.

GLORIA SMITH — Began dancing with Detroit Civic Light Opera. In number of Broadway shows. Danced lead in Top Banana and others. On Ed Sullivan's show. Assistant choreographer on Omnibus and TV spectaculars.

BETTY JANE WATSON — Lead in New York version of Oklahoma for three years, and in London. Broadway shows include As the Girls Go, South Pacific, Annie Get Your Gun. Many appearances with Ed Sullivan and at supper clubs.

THE YEAR OF THE SALESMAN

OLDSMOBILE

presents

A MUSICAL
ANNOUNCEMENT
SHOW

The Mighty

O!

Starring the **NEW 1954**
"ROCKET" OLDSMOBILES

Recorded for Oldsmobile's "Rocket Pilots" by the Original Cast, Chorus and Orchestra

stowaways; meanwhile, rumors fly about the amazing new '54 Rockets.

The music appears to be mostly original, with occasional nods to the 1905 hit "In My Merry Oldsmobile" and "Anchors Aweigh." The orchestra motors smoothly through songs such as "Demonstration Blues" in which the girls complain

He calls me up at half past eight
To tell me, baby, I'm gonna be
*   late,*
'Cause he's got a date
*   to demonstrate an 88 —*
There goes our date!

In "What Does It Take to Make a Rocket," the boys affirm the need for intangibles like spirit and know-how but also that

It takes Rocket engine power, it takes
*   power steering too,*
It takes power brakes,
*   the kind that makes*
That pedal ease come true.
It takes years-ahead-in-styling, it takes
*   room and comfort too,*
Power to pass 'em by! Autronic Eye!
And all-'round better view!

Though it sounds like the monster in a '50s horror movie, the Autronic Eye was a GM gadget that automatically dimmed high beams when it detected another car's headlights. There's no record of the Autronic Eye becoming self-aware and rampaging until destroyed by the military.

Other fun songs for car buffs include "Panoramic Windshield," about the new windshield design, "Longer, Lower, Lovelier," sung by the three ladies, and "The Mechanic's Song," in which one of the ladies reveals her tomboy side.

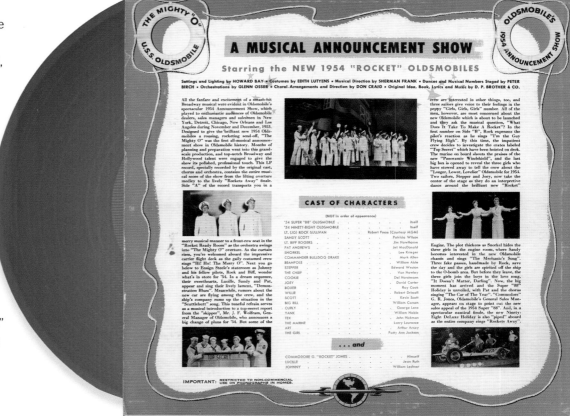

Gee, I love these clothes that I'm wearing,
So chic in a sleek dungaree.
Know how to care for a bearing,
What a task with a gasket can be.
Makes no differential to me...
Let me hear you whisper Quadrajet, baby,
Lovey-dovey things like piston pins and
*   piston rings...*

The new kind of announcement show was here to stay for Oldsmobile. In the years ahead, its advertising firm D. P. Brother would produce many more, though not always on the nifty translucent red vinyl. Meanwhile, the splashy spectacle of the corporate musical was catching on across American industry.

RARITY: 2

1000 AND ONE!

No album cover or Playbill has turned up for *1000 and One!*, Oldsmobile's 1955 announcement show, but a 1955 newspaper article fills in some details: the show was based on the 1953 Broadway hit show *Kismet* and cost $250,000 to tour around the country for ten weeks. The cast of seventeen included Chita Rivera, and choreography was by future Tony winner Carol Haney, who'd be back for several other Olds shows. In "I Can't Make an 88," a Genie is frustrated:

I can squeeze lemon out of thin air!
Ask for lady — lady is there!
Peroxide, pronto! New color hair!
But I can't make an 88!
   [chorus] Takes years and years of
     know-how,
   Takes engineering whiz,
   You don't snap your fingers and say
     "Oldsmobile!"
   And there she is!

"The Power Song" and "Hot Number" enumerate the selling points and new features, and "Have You Heard?" previews the advertising blitz that will accompany the rollout of the '55s on November 19, 1954. Mark your calendars!

RARITY: 1

MERRY OH-H-H!

The '56 Oldsmobile show, *Merry Oh-h-h!*, yielded only one song on a 78 rpm disc, "The Car Is the Star of the Show."

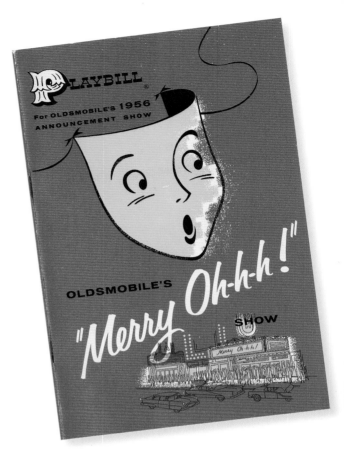

Our star was not born; she's built!
Our star may wear makeup of green or gilt.
And that star on the door is no mirage,
The number-one dressing room is...a
   garage?!
She gets grease, not greasepaint, no first-
   night panic,
Her wardrobe mistress is called
   "mechanic."

Chita Rivera was back, along with the future "Riddler" Frank Gorshin. The Playbill also notes that in the show finale, the costumes were made of Super 88 upholstery fabric — a fashion innovation that apparently didn't catch on.

RARITY: 1

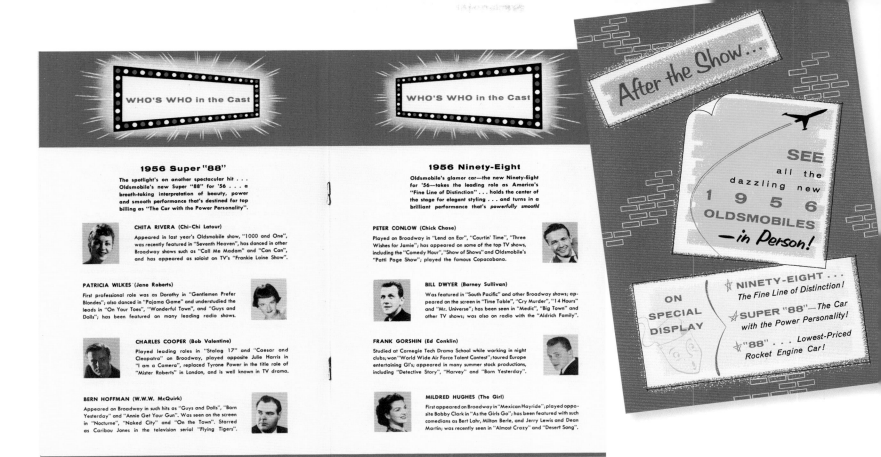

WHO'S WHO in the Cast

1956 Super "88"

The spotlight's on another spectacular hit . . . Oldsmobile's new Super "88" for '56 . . . a breath-taking interpretation of beauty, power and smooth performance that's destined for top billing as "The Car with the Power Personality".

CHITA RIVERA (Chi-Chi Latour)

Appeared in last year's Oldsmobile show, "1000 and One", was recently featured in "Seventh Heaven", has danced in other Broadway shows such as "Call Me Madam" and "Can Can", and has appeared as soloist on TV's "Frankie Laine Show".

PATRICIA WILKES (Jane Roberts)

First professional role was as Dorothy in "Gentlemen Prefer Blondes"; also danced in "Pajama Game" and understudied the leads in "On Your Toes", "Wonderful Town", and "Guys and Dolls"; has been featured on many leading radio shows.

CHARLES COOPER (Bob Valentine)

Played leading roles in "Stalag 17" and "Caesar and Cleopatra" on Broadway, played opposite Julie Harris in "I am a Camera", replaced Tyrone Power in the title role of "Mister Roberts" in London, and is well known in TV drama.

BERN HOFFMAN (W.W.W. McQuirk)

Appeared on Broadway in such hits as "Guys and Dolls", "Born Yesterday" and "Annie Get Your Gun". Was seen on the screen in "Nocturne", "Naked City" and "On the Town". Starred as Caribou Jones in the television serial "Flying Tigers".

1956 Ninety-Eight

Oldsmobile's glamor car—the new Ninety-Eight for '56—takes the leading role as America's "Fine Line of Distinction" . . . holds the center of the stage for elegant styling . . . and turns in a brilliant performance that's powerfully smooth!

PETER CONLOW (Chick Chase)

Played on Broadway in "Lend an Ear", "Courtin' Time", "Three Wishes for Jamie"; has appeared on some of the top TV shows, including the "Comedy Hour", "Show of Shows" and Oldsmobile's "Patti Page Show"; played the famous Copacabana.

BILL DWYER (Barney Sullivan)

Was featured in "South Pacific" and other Broadway shows; appeared on the screen in "Time Table", "Cry Murder", "14 Hours" and "Mr. Universe"; has been seen in "Medic", "Big Town" and other TV shows; was also on radio with the "Aldrich Family".

FRANK GORSHIN (Ed Conklin)

Studied at Carnegie Tech Drama School while working in night clubs; won "World Wide Air Force Talent Contest"; toured Europe entertaining GI's; appeared in many summer stock productions, including "Detective Story", "Harvey" and "Born Yesterday".

MILDRED HUGHES (The Girl)

First appeared on Broadway in "Mexican Hayride"; played opposite Bobby Clark in "As the Girls Go"; has been featured with such comedians as Bert Lahr, Milton Berle, and Jerry Lewis and Dean Martin; was recently seen in "Almost Crazy" and "Desert Song".

After the Show . . .

SEE all the dazzling new **1956 OLDSMOBILES** —in Person!

ON SPECIAL DISPLAY

★ NINETY-EIGHT . . . The Fine Line of Distinction!

★ SUPER "88"—The Car with the Power Personality!

★ "88" . . . Lowest-Priced Rocket Engine Car!

THIS IS OLDSMOBILITY

No recording of the '57 announcement show *Three for All!* has been found, but Olds was back on dealer turntables in '58 with *This Is Oldsmobility*, starring Bill Hayes and the future "Mrs. Brady" Florence Henderson. In 1957 Florence was a successful young Broadway actress who'd already starred in *Oklahoma!* and *Fanny*, but now she was married and pushing her first child in a stroller around midtown Manhattan. A producer named Frank Egan spotted her and asked if she'd be interested in a short-term gig like an announcement show. She ended up doing four of them. Florence notes that she did drive Oldsmobiles in her private life. Why not? She got to borrow them for free.

Much of *This Is Oldsmobility* centers around a romance plot, but there are some automotive goodies: the new air-ride-suspension-inspired "Floating on Air," which Florence sang from a specially rigged car seat that was lifted out of the car by a crane and flown out over the audience. Other numbers include "This Is Oldsmobility," a boast about how the new

ADMIT ONE

Tuesday Oct. 1—8.30 p.m. Masonic Temple Detroit

1958 OLDSMOBILE ANNOUNCEMENT SHOW

"This is OLDSmobility!"

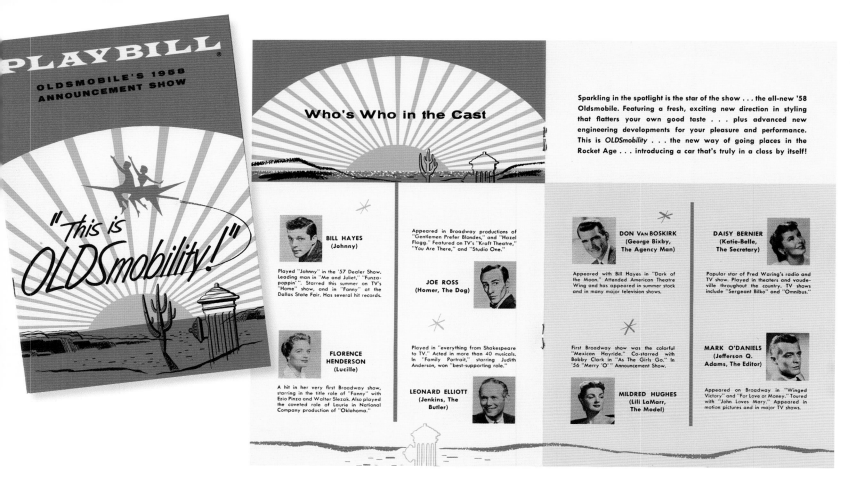

Olds is going to be heavily advertised in top magazines, and "Back to Rockport, Indiana," which has no automotive content but allows Florence to sing about her actual hometown. Like the '54 and '55 shows, this one was pressed on translucent red vinyl.

RARITY: 4

GOOD NEWS ABOUT OLDS

The stars stars of the '58 show, Florence Henderson and Bill Hayes, were back for Oldsmobile's '59 show, which was an adaptation of the 1927 musical *Good News*, about a college girl tutoring a guy so he can pass a class and stay on the football team. The music is a powerful combination of Broadway glitter and industrial nuttiness. Arranger Luther Henderson (no relation to Florence, though they were sometimes mistakenly booked in the same hotel room) contributed a snappy original song, "Magnify You, Minimize I."

You gotta see that car through your
  customer's eyes,
Think of what you'd want when it's YOU
  who buys.
Magnify product, dramatize style,
Itemize features, and all the while,
You magnify "you" and minimize "I."

Who's Who at OLDS U.

FLORENCE HENDERSON (Lucille) Most Popular Girl! Leading lady in Oldsmobile's 1958 Announcement Show, after graduating first in her class from the Broadway sensation "Fanny" where she played opposite Ezio Pinza. Played coveted role of "Laurie" for 2 years in "Oklahoma," National Co. Starred in U.S. Steel TV dramatic shows this year; teamed with Bill Hayes in rave-notice nite club tour.

BILL HAYES (Johnny) Big Man on Campus! Enrolled at Olds U. for 1957 Announcement Show, took top honors again with smash hit performance in 1958. Popular leading man on Broadway in such successes as "Me and Juliet", "Funzappoppin' ". A versatile vocalist, he has many hit records to his credit. During '57-'58 vacation scored in U.S. Steel Hour triumphs, toured nation with standout nite club act.

FRANK FONTAINE (Coach Savoney) Coach of the Year! Played center attraction for such standout clubs as New York's Copacabana; Chicago's Chez Paree and Palmer House; Las Vegas' Riviera; and Miami Beach's Fontainebleau and Americana. Regarded as one of the real "pros" of the comedy game today. Has been a frequent guest on TV. Enters the coaching ranks for the first time at Olds U.

1-Trudy Carole
2-Bob McClure
3-Ann Barry
4-Howard Lear
5-Jean Pierce
6-Jonathan Bush
7-Jeannine Masterson
8-Barbara Anne Quaney
9-Robert Lane
10-Genevieve Owens
11-Lee Cass
12-Nora Reho
13-Shellie Farrell
14-Tom O'Steen
15-Robert Sands
16-Ed Pfeiffer
17-Dick Gain
18-Patricia King
19-Frank Fontaine
20-Betty Rhodes
21-Bill Hayes
22-Wisa D'Orso
23-Jim Hutchison
24-Hugh Lambert
25-Patricia Marand
26-Florence Henderson

PATRICIA MARAND (Pat) Broadway lead in "Wish You Were Here" and "Pajama Game". Also one of the nurses in the Broadway hit, "South Pacific". Played "Marsinah" in "Kismet", and "Laurie" in European tour of "Oklahoma". Appeared often on TV.

WISA D'ORSO (Babe) Applauded for appearances in the famous "Ziegfeld Follies", also toured extensively with the Esther Williams "Aquacade". Has danced on many top TV shows, including General Motors' memorable 30th Anniversary Spectacular.

LEE CASS (Professor Kenyon) Appeared most recently in original Broadway production of "Most Happy Fella". Also featured on TV in NBC Opera Company, can be heard on Columbia recordings of the music from "Oklahoma", "Desert Song".

HUGH LAMBERT (Beef) Danced on Broadway in such hit shows as "Hazel Flagg", "Wonderful Town", and "Can Can". Has appeared on television in many major shows. Appeared in Oldsmobile's successful 1957 Announcement Show, "Three for All!"

JIM HUTCHISON (Bobby) Featured in "Steam Heat" number in the Broadway sensation "Pajama Game" with the brilliant Carol Haney. Recently appeared with Ethel Merman in "Happy Hunting". Lists many appearances on major TV shows.

BETTY RHODES (Flo) Hails from the West Coast and is a graduate of the University of Southern California. Appeared in "Joyride" at the Huntington Hartford Theater in Hollywood. Was recently seen on the Jack Paar "Tonight" show on television.

CREDITS

Scenery by IMPERIAL SCENIC STUDIOS, INC. • Lighting Equipment by CENTURY LIGHTING, INC. • Costumes executed by RAY DIFFEN STAGE CLOTHES • Sound by KURTIS SOUND SYSTEMS • Men's "After Six" formal wear by RUDOFKER • Jewelry by CORO • Dancing Shoes by CAPEZIO • Athletic equipment by ALEX TAYLOR, INC. • Hosiery by JESSIE ZIMMER • Gloves by VAN RAALTE • Hats by EVE SHELLEY • Handbags by LEWIS PURSES.

The other highlight is "Talk About a Rocket." In a lengthy fever dream of rapid-fire patter backed by percussion, Bill Hayes plays a student trying to convince his professor of the appeal of the 188 new features of the '59 Olds.

Why, there's so much room inside,
That a witch could ride on a broom inside,
And I wouldn't be surprised if a DC-7
Mistook such elegant space for heaven!
Gracious, man, it's spacious!
There's more shoulder room, head room,
  leg room,
Your knees never hit your chin,
Like when you curl up in those small
  foreign cars,
Like pickles in a jar!

The pretty red vinyl is gone, and no copies have turned up with a cover, though a bonus 7-inch '59 "Party Platter" record with two songs has a swell photo sleeve.

RARITY: 3 (12-inch record), 2 (7-inch "Party Platter")

For "record" sales let Florence Henderson and Bill Hayes make your next sales meeting a **PLATTER PARTY**

spin this original cast recording of
★ "MAGNIFY YOU . . . MINIMIZE I"
★ "TALK ABOUT A ROCKET"
2 SELLING SONGS FROM THE OLDS HIT SHOW OF 1959 — GOOD NEWS!

USE THIS RECORD AGAIN AND AGAIN AS THE ROUSING START TO YOUR SALES MEETINGS!

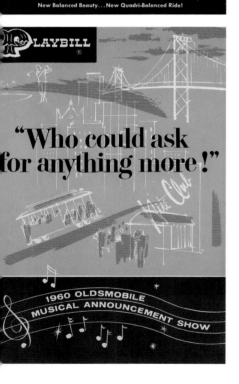

THE OLDS FOR '60 MUSICAL: "WHO COULD ASK FOR ANYTHING MORE!"

The Oldsmobile dealer show from late 1959 stars Florence Henderson and Bill Hayes for the third straight year. Much of the score consists of several mostly straight Gershwin classics such as "'S Wonderful," "Embraceable You," "Bidin' My Time," and "I Got Rhythm," used with permission of George Gershwin's estate. We also get hardcore selling: the excellent "Don't Let a Be-Back Get Away," again by Luther Henderson, finds Florence instructing Bill on how to help indecisive customer Mr. Van Snuff (comedian and character actor Jack Gilford) finally pull the trigger.

> *(I'll be back!) Why ya' leavin'?*
> *(I don't know, thought I'd go, I'll be back!)*
> *Before you go, I'd like to know*
> *   where did I fail?*
> *Is it something I said, is it something*
> *   you read,*
> *The product, the price, why did I lose*
> *   this sale?*
>
> *(It WAS something you said, that it only*
> *   comes in red!)*
> *My product comes in red, white, black,*
> *   or blue!*
> *(I like black!) That's MY favorite!*
> *(Can't decide, let it ride, I'll be back!)*

Of course, persistence pays off, and Mr. Van Snuff finally buys a gleaming new 1960 Olds, presumably in black.

RARITY: 3

W. T. GRANT'S 50TH ANNIVERSARY GOLDEN OPPORTUNITY SONGS

This 1956 red vinyl disc from the defunct department store chain is noisy and mushy despite the "Fine Sound" claim of the label. Composer Michael Brown, from whom we'll be hearing much more in the '60s, performs his own songs, including "W. T. Grant Work Song," a version of his "Manager's Work Song," which he adapted for various retail chains. A few other tracks such as "Fifty Golden Years" and "Come and Go with Grant's" mention the company but are short on detail. Some songs, such as the striking "Case of the Blues" and "Quiet, Please, It's Sleepy Time Down South," demonstrate Michael's range as a songwriter but have no industrial content. Maybe more material about how to run the business would have been appropriate: when Grant's declared bankruptcy in 1976, it was over $1 billion in debt, making it the biggest American retail failure to date.

RARITY: 1

Theme Center . . .
Contemporary Collection, 1957

The entrance way to five imaginative kitchens designed and decorated by the editors of five of America's most popular magazines and exhibited at Appliance Park, Louisville, Kentucky.

IT'S A GREAT NEW LINE!

Like Westinghouse, GE apparently felt its appliance introductions were as exciting as new car announcements, warranting a fall '56 rollout of the '57 line for dealers. This 10-inch souvenir record packs in twenty short songs by John McGee, with a lot of filler and reprises, though the music has a good sound. For sheer hilarious lameness, it's hard to beat "The Dishwasher and the Disposall."

The dishwasher and the disposall
They're moving up!
The dishwasher and the disposall
Go, go, go, go, up, up, up!

The one track that scores a direct hit is "I've Got a Wide Range of Features." Backed by a brassy orchestra that deftly switches between full blast and delicate tickle, an unknown female vocalist sings in character as a new GE range:

I've got a wide range of features,
Some are old and some are new.
I've got the new circuit breaker,
And the tele-cook lights too.
On my new automatic units, things cook
*   themselves!*
My oven's got a take-off door and
*   reversible shelves!*

It's a great new line, and briefly a great record.

RARITY: 1

THE SHAPE OF TOMORROW

This autumn 1957 "musical introduction to 1958 Westinghouse appliances" features a plot about J. W. Butterfield, Inc., a Westinghouse store so snobbish that "We only condescend to sell to upper-crusted clientele." The modern cover, sparkling music by John Wyman, and a very entertaining book and lyrics by industrial rookie Herb Kanzell (who also directed) make this dealer show a blue chip item. Fun trivia: because he got to be both a performer and choreographer for *the shape of tomorrow*, cast member Buff Shurr turned down a small role in *West Side Story*.

Martyn Green, a veteran Gilbert & Sullivan performer, headlined the cast. Kanzell wrote him a song called "Nightmare," in the vein of "The Nightmare Song" from *Iolanthe*.

Why does the business of kitchen utilities
Cause hypertension to make me feel
*   ill at ease?*
Why do I feel that I'm falling apart at
*   the seams?*
Doctor, do some enlightening, explain
All my frightening dreams!

Chuck Green, an industrial mainstay well into the '60s, battled his way through pages of range features in the exhausting "Easy as A, B, C."

The C in ABC is for the cleaning ease that
*   Westinghouse makes trouble-free!*
With plug-out surface units, oven heaters
*   as well*
The wonderful new no-drip top's
*   convenient, do tell*
All this plus adaptable new styling
*   throughout*

Are reasons why with Westinghouse
*   we shout*
That our ranges are easy to look at, easy
*   to live with,*
Easy to see why they excel!
Sell up, sell down, the choice is sellably hot
Stock all six ranges, show the features
*   they've got!*

While Chuck staggered away to catch his breath, Marilyn Ross belted out a similarly dense number about refrigerators, "Tomorrow — Today."

The new Cold Injector sends a jet-stream
*   of air*
To bring colder temperatures to all the
*   foods there*
The cheese server, butter server,
*   meat keeper too*
Make sure your foods stay fresh and stay
*   in view*
And here on the front is the magnetic
*   door,*
But don't run away, because there's
*   plenty more!*

There's a jaunty song about advertising campaigns called "You Gotta Let Them Know" and a delightfully weird calypso-inflected song about historical figures such as George Washington and General Pershing, who were unhappy despite their success because "He Got No Westinghouse Franchise."

I also got no Westinghouse franchise, but I got this Westinghouse record, and that's plenty.

RARITY: 2

N GREEN as
Butterfield

MARILYN ROSS as
Stephanie

ILLEBRAND as
e I. Tower

EDGAR POWELL as
Hialeah Herman

ORIN as
Neussbaum

CHUCK GREEN as
Bill Brown

HURR as
sley

ADRIENNE ANGEL as
Mitzi

Y WESTON as

DOROTHEA MAC FARLAND as
Susie

HACKENBERG as
Mate

HELEN ELLIS as
Space Mate

ECCE PROMO

Full of "character" voices and unabashed attention to flat-out selling, "You Gotta Let Them Know" modestly embodies much of the doofy charm that got us addicted to industrials in the first place. This strutting little primer on getting the word about Westinghouse Electric Appliances out to the consumer predates *How to Succeed in Business without Really Trying* by a few years, but it plays so much like lesser Loesser, it could be passed off as something sung by the craven ad execs to whom Bobby Morse posed such a threat.

The repeated directive "hit 'em hard, hit 'em often, hit 'em right between the eyes" might seem rather aggressive, but a jaunty soft shoe tempo keeps things from getting scary, and we can dig the lyric as a time capsule of old-school promotional techniques. Floor and window displays, Sunday supplements, and billboards are all cited, along with the newer mass media avenues that Westinghouse was so early to exploit with its massively successful broadcasting division, known as Group W by the early '60s.

Of special interest to pop culture aficionados are lyrical references

to *Studio One*, the company's flagship anthology TV series, and its popular spokesmodel Betty Furness, who famously demonstrated the company's appliances and assured the viewer "You can be sure… if it's Westinghouse." *Studio One* is best remembered for original teleplays such as *Twelve Angry Men*, but some of us, knowing that no kinescope of *the shape of tomorrow* will ever satisfy our hopeless yearnings, at least have this album to console us.

—SM

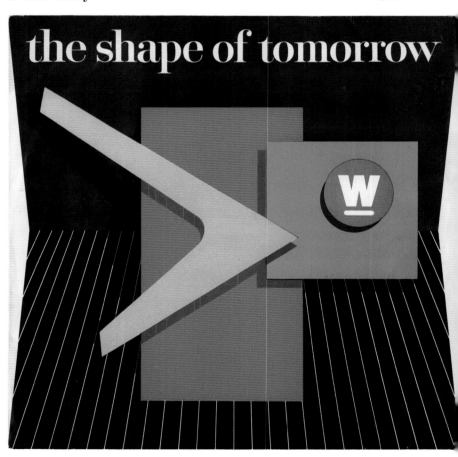
the shape of tomorrow

Perfume, oils, and fats.
Boil them all together till the stuff
    saponifies,
But if you want to make the soap the
    whole world buys...

Then we're off and running through an industrial show tune subgenre that turns up occasionally: a musical listing of all the important executives. It's labored and tedious, but sort of stupidly awesome. And big bonus points for being the only known song lyric to mention saponification, the conversion of a fat or oil into soap.

RARITY: 2

THE COLGATE CANNONADE FOR 1955

Another red vinyl disc with poor sound quality, this record's got three Colgate-Palmolive meeting songs by Peter Cadby. The material falls well short of greatness, but there are a couple moments of charm, and the cannons on the label are cool.

Side 1 consists of a musical medley touting various Colgate-Palmolive products, including Veto deodorant, Rapid Shave shaving cream, Palmolive soap, and Florient room deodorizer. It's not bad, but it just sounds like a long multipart commercial. Side 2 has a pair of songs that are the same except for different intros, one for soap sales and one for other toiletry articles. "The Colgate Soap Sales March" begins

Any dope can make some soap
In kettles or in vats,
All you need is caustic soda,

A SOUVENIR RECORDING OF THE FIRST ANNUAL SEWING FASHION FESTIVAL 1956

A contemporary newspaper article notes that this show was part of "the grand sew-off in the Singer National Sewing Contest." The music was by Ken Hopkins, with lyrics by Lee Gilmore and Ken Hopkins. The plot involves dressmakers' dummies coming to life and subsequently finding love with a pair of lonely night security guards. (Worry about how reproduction will work is brushed off with one guard's assertion that he's "human enough for both of us.") Most of the single-sided disc is taken up by lush, impressive songs about love yearned for and found, but there's a bit of propaganda on the topic of sewing your own clothing, in "The Dress Makes the Woman."

A Souvenir Recording of the First Annual SEWING Fashion Festival 1956

NEW YORK COLISEUM JUNE 11 - 17

The rose on the rosebush looks just fine,
But it won't look right on the ivy vine.
So here's the rule I wish to stress,
The dress makes the woman
When the woman makes the dress!

This ultra-rarity has a couple interesting distinctions: the star was Edith Adams, better known as Edie Adams, an Emmy and Tony winner as well as the wife of Ernie Kovacs. One of the male leads was Bill Heyer, who was a performer before he joined forces with composer Hank Beebe in the '60s to write a long string of top-tier industrials and other projects.

RARITY: 1

1

CHECK-IN

2

3

39

40

COLUMBIA RECORDS NATIONAL SALES CONVENTION 1957

Here we have an unconventional take on convention songs. Unlike most other companies, Columbia Records didn't need to hire performers—they had a roster of stars at the ready. So at its Miami Beach meeting, the entertainment consisted of live performances by Columbia hit makers of the day: Johnny Mathis, Marty Robbins, the Hi-Lo's, Mel Tillis, Frankie Laine, Ray Price, Erroll Garner, Ray Conniff and His Orchestra, and several others spread over two discs.

There's a bit of business involving a supposed audition by a young up-and-comer who briefly plays piano and is then revealed to be Leonard Bernstein. A cringe-inducing moment is the introduction of the Mexican group Trío Los Panchos, who according to the emcee "also brought in a shipment of

COLUMBIA RECORDS NATIONAL SALES CONVENTION 1957

*Americana Hotel
Miami Beach,
Florida*

2

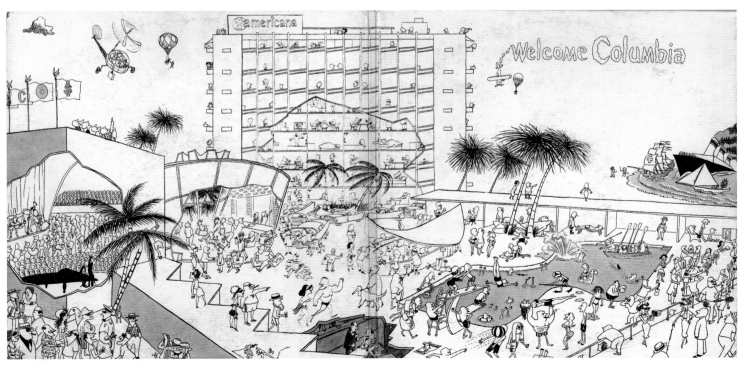

18

19

20

marijuana which helped pay for this." Big audience laugh!

So no original songs about the record business, but this is a cool bit of music history with fine sound quality, ultra-obscure live performances by some big names, twenty-three pages of photos, and a panoramic cover by the famous cartoonist Arnold Roth. Among the many amusing details is what appears

to be Columbia stalwart Mitch Miller having dinner in the basement.

RARITY: 1

FASHIONS

YOUR FUTURE IS SOUND   TAKE STOCK IN YOUR FUTURE

WE ASKED A SEASONED VETERAN OF THE INDUSTRIAL CIRCUIT HOW IT FELT TO PERFORM "IN THE TRENCHES!" SO PULL UP A CHAIR AND ENJOY AN INSIDER GLIMPSE AS JOHN GETS "CHOKED UP" RECALLING A GIG THAT LEFT ITS CAST **UTTERLY EXHAUSTED!**

THE **JOHN DEERE** TRACTOR SHOW WAS AT DAWN.

IT WAS IN **KANSAS CITY** AT THIS HUGE AUDITORIUM.

IT WAS A SMALL CAST, JUST **FOUR** OF US.

AND WHEN WE GOT THERE, THEY'D **STARTED** THE ENGINES...

... OF ALL THESE **TRACTORS** & **HARROWERS** & SO ON.

ALL THESE **GIANT** MACHINES, WHICH WERE NOW SITTING THERE **IDLING.**

Welcome John Dee. Sales Con.

We have som very exciti entertainm and inform

IT WAS LIKE GOING INTO A **GAS CHAMBER.**

ONE OF THE GIRLS ACTUALLY **THREW UP** BEFORE WE HAD TO GO ON.

so withou further a

The 1960s

THE BATHROOMS ARE COMING!

She's free, she's free
From bathroom oppression she's free!
She's free, she's free
No more bathroom hazards to see!

This one's a monster. Most people who've had any exposure to industrial shows have heard of the 1969 American-Standard show *The Bathrooms Are Coming!*, which has been percolating as an underground cult favorite since the 1990s. It's a mother lode of eye-popping visuals, warped pseudo-feminism, and crazily catchy, improbable songs by Sid Siegel.

The front cover has several puzzling elements — a caveman with a toilet? a monk and gospel-themed outhouses? a hillbilly swilling moonshine? — and the back hints at the nuttiness ahead: "The story began with the introduction of a mythical Greek goddess Femma, the epitome of all women's attitudes, reflections, and desires, and the leader of all women's movements. In the play, women implore Femma to start a bathroom revolution." There's also a reference to "the Cornell research," a 1966 study by a Cornell professor that called for a rethinking of the ergonomics and design of bathrooms. The study, "The Bathroom: Criteria for Design," was sponsored by — guess who — American-Standard.

The show, including both live and film elements, was staged in Las Vegas at American-Standard's "Distributor Principals' Conferences." In addition to dazzling distributors with its new product line, American-Standard tried to suck up with a number called "The Distributors."

We deal in bathrooms, in all kinds of
*   bathrooms,*
In every way, every day,
Big ones and small ones and wide ones
*   and tall ones,*
It's like we say — they all pay.
Our shelves are all full, yes, we're ready,
The line doesn't change, but it's steady.
We're good distributors, kindly
*   distributors, give us praise,*
We carry our customers ninety days.
We may be conservative, but it pays!

Outmoded bathrooms, beware: American-Standard is on the warpath. A shyster plumber reminisces about inferior plugged-up plumbing in the sarcastic "Bring Back Those Glorious Years." A modern woman complains about her cramped, outmoded bathroom in "Look at This Tub."

Look at this tub! LOOK AT THIS TUB!
It's dangerous and certainly a hazard!
It's positively lower than substandard!
Everything here is lower class,
Why, I could slip, I could fall right on
*   my . . . nose.*

Several songs convey the crucial data about the new bathtubs and showers, all aimed at women. In "Proximatics," two vocalists describe motion-sensor tub and shower controls. "Spectra 70," introducing a two-headed shower unit, has a loopy pseudo-rock sound and startling lyrics.

A Souvenir Album

Music from
The Bathrooms are Coming!
AN ORIGINAL MUSICAL PRESENTED BY AMERICAN-STANDARD

33⅓ RPM
AMC 2371

SIDE I

1. It's Revolution
2. The Distributors
3. Bring Back Those Glorious Years

4. Behind Every Man Is A Woman
5. Proximatics
6. Ultra Bath Dream

AMERICAN STANDARD

A Souvenir Album

Music from

The Bathrooms are Coming!

AN ORIGINAL MUSICAL PRESENTED BY AMERICAN-STANDARD

This album recreates the music from the presentation made by American-Standard at its 1969 Distributor Principals' Conferences, January 6 and 10, 1969

MATT   MARK   JOHN

GAME OF THRONES

Plumb Loco

Even before your ears encounter marvels like "Look at This Tub!" and "My Bathroom," the colorful montage of photos on the cover of American-Standard's 1969 Distributor Principals' Conferences LP indicates that this is no ordinary distributor principals' conference souvenir album.

Like a travel brochure from some exclusive vacation resort for the profoundly incontinent, dreamlike images of toilets and tubs abound, all velvet-draped, columnated, and fit for a porcelain goddess. And there she is, our Lysistrata of the loo, gazing with regal, vacant grace as if deciding which opulent *salle de bain* she will choose for this morning's ablutions.

Her female comrades all share her narcotized, *Redbook* sorta mien, but get a load of their male counterparts: a filthy, drunken hillwilliam; a Cro-Magnon, knock-kneed with mictuatory desperation; a creepy monk loitering by a quartet of outhouses designated for—get this—the authors of the four biblical Gospels! This is the kind of stuff that got *Laugh-In*'s sister show *Turn-On* canceled during its first broadcast. Could the songs actually rise to this (American) standard?

What a relief to discover that they actually surpass it. Here American-Standard dealt us a royal flush, with concept, design, and content representing the high-water mark of industrial show quality.

Dear John

Many's the industrial musical devotee who first encountered the genre through "My Bathroom," a fulsome ode to Milady's pissoir, and it's understandable; there's a built-in hardy-har-har quotient to the very idea of a sincere, impeccably rendered love song to the smallest room in the house that makes this song a mix-tape must.

Any neophyte's first impulse upon hearing it is to gasp "What were they THINKING?" but the truth is, they were thinking exactly what you are. As any delve into the industrial repertoire soon reveals, the composers and lyricists of these shows were no song poem-esque suckers, accidentally crafting musique brut with a dollar and a delusion. The best of these artists were worthy successors to Cole Porter and Dorothy Fields, slipping in as much wit and intentional satire as possible whilst ably serving the client's banal demands.

Unlike Brian Wilson and Gary Usher, who sidestepped the onanistic subtext of "In My Room" with all that humbug about "dreaming" and "scheming," Sid Siegel isn't shy about innuendo. But he keeps it just subtle enough to make you feel slightly creepy for noticing and embeds it in a soaring paean to freedom and individuality with a genuinely memorable melody. All that, performed with ravishing sincerity by an actress with fantastic pipes, results in an incontrovertible triumph.

—SM

On your drywall, a utility shelf, its use as good as gold,
For books and kits, martinis too! A safety bar to hold!
For cigarettes, a storage shelf with lots of room to spare
For soap, shampoo, and bubble bath,
And your rubber teddy bear!

Were people really smoking and drinking in the shower in 1969? I honestly can't tell if it's a joke.

"The Ultra Bath" introduces a luxurious new tub, a lady's fantasy.

Then to add to your satisfaction, another added attraction:
A lovely whirlpool action, it's a vision to behold.
The Ultra Bath, the Ultra Bath, you'll be bathing in luxury,
You will find it so heavenly, the Ultra Ultra Bath.

Like many industrials, *Bathrooms* not only covers the product information but steps back to look at the big picture. The amazing "My Bathroom" is a tribute to a modern woman's relationship to this vital part of the house.

My bathroom, my bathroom, is a private kind of place.
Very special kind of place.
The only place where I can stay
Making faces at my face.
My bathroom, my bathroom, is much more than it may seem.
Where I wash and where I cream.
A special place where I can stay
And cream, and dream, and dream, and dream, dream.

Hypnotic, beautiful, and weird, "My Bathroom" is the cherry on top of a luscious industrial sundae. Forty-plus years later, *The Bathrooms Are Coming!* continues to astonish and delight.

RARITY: 3

SEAGRAM
1965 DISTRIBUTOR MEETING
SIDE ONE
3059 A
COMPATIBLE STEREO CAN BE PLAYED ON ANY PHONOGRAPH
Brand New Breed
100 Pipers
Overture
Dress Right, Dress
Seagram Look
CREATED & PRODUCED BY
CONTEMPO!
PRODUCTIONS, INC.
NEW YORK

"You'll drink it and you'll like it!" says the narrator. Arrogance? Nah, it's confidence that animates Seagram's "The Sure One," a nearly eight-minute leviathan celebrating the company's Seven Crown whiskey, fundament of that iconic drunken-uncle cocktail the 7 and 7. This epic fourth movement of the "Seagram Symphony" from the 1965 show ("crescendo con blendo") struts along over an assertive walking bass for most of its duration before bongos kick in and contrapuntal chaos erupts, presumably as the firewater takes effect.

Though the singers suspiciously stumble through some of the lyrics, lushwells take heed: true sophistication eschews intemperance; this slight awkwardness is likely due to the rush-job nature of the recording session, and most of its participants were probably hardly even buzzed that early in the day.

Alongside tempting invitations to enjoy this most versatile of blended whiskies in a variety of mixed drinks, the piece includes a Victor Lundbergian father-to-son cautionary aside, noting that the "privileges of manhood" depend upon a "sensible and moderate" approach to swilling the product. Whether burgeoning womanhood boasts any such privileges remains undisclosed, but that swoony soprano gliding over the double-time choristers would indicate that some sisters are pourin' it for themselves.

If you're like me, perusing period magazine adverts while listening to industrial albums, you'll observe that, while contemporary magazine ads for pricier Crown Royal invoked prestige and elegance (a velour-bagged gift for only "very dear friends"), Seven Crown was presented as an everyday quaff for corduroy-jacketed party guests, bright-eyed tennis players, and gun enthusiasts, all described in this song as "the sure ones" ... a breed of born winners who, knowing good whiskey, insist upon the Sure One whenever and wherever they gather.

About those gun enthusiasts, by the way, the song assures us that "Liquor always comes later ... after the guns are cleaned and racked." Sure.

—SM

THE SEAGRAM DISTILLERS DISTRIBUTOR MEETING

Don't be fooled by the bare-bones graphics and utilitarian title; the modest packaging houses a great show. Most of the creative team from *Diesel Dazzle*, including the songwriting team of Hank Beebe and Bill Heyer, also worked on this 1965 show, and the excellent orchestra and cast bring the material to vivid life. Producer David Marshall says Seagram hadn't initially planned to produce a souvenir record of this show. But the audience response was so raucous that the company hastily rented a studio in Miami the day after the meeting, and the show was laid down in one take.

With baby boomers just hitting the drinking age, Seagram wanted its people to pursue the "Brand New Breed."

Every eight seconds
Another one of us comes into your market!
Every eight seconds, opportunity beckons!
Opportunity you'd better be ready for!

Oh yes indeed, if you want to succeed,
Aim your brand at the brand-new breed.
Opportunity knocks—on the rocks!

Seagram touted its upmarket image with "Seagram Look."

It's the handsomest building in all
  New York!
A plea for moderation on Father's Day!
That's it! That's it! That's part of the book
We could write about the Seagram Look!
It's that quality touch in the ads you see,
Type, models, photography!
That's it! That's it! That's part of the book
We could write about the Seagram Look!

THE SEAGRAM DISTILLERS DISTRIBUTOR MEETING

MIAMI, FLORIDA
MARCH, 1965

Another number, "100 Pipers," presents a freshly concocted legend about the scotch delivered in a fairly convincing brogue. Seagram was so pleased that it used the lyrics in a two-page *Life* magazine advertisement, netting Beebe and Heyer a nice extra payment.

Side 2 consists of "The Seagram Symphony," with four "movements" describing in song the advertising campaigns planned for Seagram's VO, Gin, Crown Royal, and Seven Crown from February through November of '65. All are great, with typical Beebe and Heyer wit and style, but the real stunner is the fourth movement, a lengthy odyssey of varying themes and tempos, cascading fragments of advertising copy, bravura vocals, and a needle-pinning performance by the high-revving orchestra. In the last second, as the final notes die away, you can faintly hear one singer gasp for breath. No wonder the Seagram people were on their feet hollering at the show's end.

RARITY: 3

HAMM'S '65 · BURSTING WITH FRESHNESS!

The hundredth anniversary show for Hamm's, the St. Paul–based brewery, yielded a souvenir record on translucent blue vinyl, evoking the "land of sky blue waters" slogan. Side 2 is all commercials, but side 1 has uncredited show songs by Lloyd Norlin. "You Gotta Show the Merchandise" is one of Lloyd's trunk songs, used in many shows, but he did knock out

some Hamm's-specific numbers such as "The Young Adults," exhorting the sales force to capture baby boomers just reaching the drinking age; "The First 100 Years," a musical history of the company; and "We've Got Everything Going For Hamm's."

We'll have everyone going for, everyone
* asking for*
Hamm's beer—this year!
The only aluminum can will do its share!
With this fresh combination, how can you
* help but thrive?*
We've got everything going, everything
* going,*
For you and Hamm's in '65!

Aluminum beer cans? What a crazy idea. I'm not surprised it never caught on.

RARITY: 2

CLUTCHIN' THE ESCUTCHEON

Here's a cover that sorta just sits there, seemingly indistinguishable from other audio "souvenirs" like college marching band records or foreign-language documentaries about the funeral of some dignitary. Nothing there but a coat of arms, the ordinary logo of an everyday brand of garden-variety beer.

But if, ferinstance, it was about fifteen years after that Schmidt's marketing meeting, and you were a young person...the kind of colt who might, of a Thursday evening, scour every pair of unwashed trousers in the room for loose change until accumulating the buck ninety-nine required to score a six of Schmidt's from, say, the 7-Eleven up on Motor Parkway. Were this the case, you might well recognize that same coat of arms on the label of one of those blessedly affordable "brewskis." On such a night, you might idly examine its details in some wistful mood of mild curiosity. And what then?

You'd note a few standard crest images: a lion, an eagle. Yeah. Then the self-explanatory bundles of barley and hops: makes sense...it's beer. You'd likely wonder for a moment, "Why the winged helmet? What's with that thing that looks like an obscure Hebraic Aleph-Bet character being

pecked by a bird?" Then, while twisting the cap off that hard-earned bottle, you'd turn to your friends—let's call them Tony, Tom, and Jim—and say, "Hey, fellas, let's listen to that weird album I got at the Salvation Army thrift store yesterday." You'd drop the stylus into the side 1 groove of *Penney Proud* and take a swig of your Schmidt's.

And you'd never look back. Well, actually...

—SM

EDWARD A. GARDINER
Chairman

Just prior to Prohibition we achieved one of our dreams: We became the number one brewery in Philadelphia. We were a three plant operation then, comprised of the Robert Smith, Peter Schemm and Schmidt breweries. We produced a total of 300,000 barrels. When Prohibition came along, we became a one plant operation trying to survive through the noble experiment. This year, for the first time since 1919, we became a three plant operation... we not only are once again number one in Philadelphia, but we became the first brewery in Pennsylvania ever to brew more than two million barrels in one year. Much of our success and growth we owe to the closeness we have experienced with our distributors, many of whom have been with us through this wonderful era of growth.

CARL E. VON CZOERNIG
President

"I want to express my heartfelt thanks for your combined efforts toward helping Schmidt's pass the two million barrel mark in 1964. Our total increase came to a record 260,000 barrels—the largest single year increase in the history of our company. Over the past few years we have developed a moving upward trend. We plan to support this trend to the hilt in 1965. With the new Cleveland plant, a multi-million dollar improvement program at all three plants, plus a $1 million dollar increase in advertising and merchandising... Schmidt's is 'Go' for 1965 ... we don't only want your greatest combined efforts put forth in 1965 to support what we call a winning team, but we also want you to benefit both volume-wise and financially so that we can build an even stronger combination team for the future. From any point of view, Schmidt's is today facing the brightest outlook it has had for many a year."

THOMAS McCONNELL, 3rd
Executive Vice President

All indications point to a good year both for our industry and our company in 1965, except one: the exception is that 1965 is an odd-number year, which means that most of the State Legislatures will meet. The greatest collection ever of tax proposals and restrictive measures affecting our industry will be tossed into the hoppers of the 47 State Legislatures that will convene this year. USBA was organized for the purpose, among others, of alerting our industry to unsound and unfair proposals but USBA cannot defend the industry alone. You as salesmen can do much by fostering and maintaining a good relationship of confidence in each other and a realization by our distributors that we consider them an essential part of the Schmidt family. If all segments of our industry work together we can successfully resist unfair taxation and regulations; if we don't pull together we'll all suffer.

CHARLES S. STRICKLER
Vice President Treasurer

"1964 was an excellent business year, with most industries recording new highs. The Brewing Industry also had an excellent year, with its largest sales increase in more than 20 years—about 5 percent or 5 million barrels to a record total of 98 million barrels. Rather surprisingly, this excellent year was not shared equally by the major companies. Schmidt's increase of more than 13 percent was the third largest among the leaders. Consumer preference for convenience in packaging was reflected in the sales level of the 12 oz. non-returnable bottle. With the population explosion favoring our industry, and assuming general business conditions remain strong, our company conceivably could reach 3 million barrels by about the end of this decade."

W. SIMMS SHARNINGHAUSEN
Vice President Secretary

There has been much speculation and concern about beer concentrate and reconstituted beer. As of now two points are clear: Beer concentrate is still in the experimental state and, it is subject to severely limiting regulations. Only brewers can concentrate beer, and can reconstitute it only in the same plant where it was concentrated, in a plant already owned by the brewer, or export it. The fact that the word is "Reconstituted" must appear on the label in type at least as large as the word "beer" on the label. As far as we know, many brewing interests will bring legislation to restrict further beer concentrate and its reconstitution. It is expected that one bill will be re-introduced which will prohibit the shipping of concentrate from one of a company's plants to another.

WILLIAM A. HIPP
Vice President Production

"The increasing demand for Schmidt products, the acquisition of a new plant, and the constant desire for better facilities have resulted in a rather ambitious program for 1965. The company's executive committee has wisely seen fit to approve an investment of $3.8 million for plant improvements and new production facilities at our three plants. The most spectacular project is the 40,000 barrel capacity stockhouse. Equipped with 20 stainless steel tanks, this five-story building will be the most modern of stockhouses... unique and revolutionary in design... there is no other in existence like it."

WILLIAM T. ELLIOTT
Vice President Marketing

"As a long range goal, we're heading for the top ten and over three million barrels within the next five years ... we honestly believe we are capable of it ... if everyone holds up his end and accepts his share of the responsibility. In this effort we must share equally... it must be a completely combined effort. It isn't you on one side and us on the other—it's both on the same side. I contend that brewery and wholesaler interests are so mutual that there is no problem in their relationships. At least I'm confident this exists in our combined attitudes."

JOHN G. STROMMER
Marketing Department Coordinator

"There is much activity by many breweries to put draught beer in the home with portable coolers and home refrigerator dispensers ... we at Schmidt's do not want to get into a marketing program that will by-pass the tavern ... the traditional draught beer outlet. To Schmidt's, draught beer always has been the birthright of the tavern ... its season for being. Unfortunately, the present trend can only result in siphoning-off customers and profits from the tavern. Remembering that draught beer is the only exclusive item taverns have to sell, we have prepared a booklet to demonstrate that serving draught beer in the tavern ... and more specifically Schmidt's draught beer ... can be profitable."

LINCOLN W. ALLAN
Advertising Manager

"Never before have we had such supreme confidence in the fact that what we are doing is right. We now have research methods for measuring and evaluating the results of our advertising. We now know exactly who our best customer and prospect is—how he thinks—what he feels—how he lives. We know how to reach him—what words to use—what media to use ... and we have research to measure the results of our efforts. In short, Schmidt advertising is no longer a hit or miss proposition."

WILLIAM A. RICE
Merchandising Manager

"Well rounded ... is the best way to describe this year's point-of-sale and merchandising program. Solid in illumination, with the addition of an 'On Tap' display and a 'Sparkling Gold Beer' sign added to the other favorites ... the globe and the clock ... we are now in a position, with proper installation, to dominate on-premise accounts. For merchandising materials, we have put together the most versatile units ever designed ..., units that can be used individually or collectively to form mass merchandisers. With a 'food and beer belong together' theme for the first and last third of the year, and a dimensional nautical motif for the summer months, we've touched all bases for making this year 1965 the most promising for both customer and consumer appeal. Used wisely, they will mean extra profits for all!"

HENRY B. KING
President U.S.B.A.

In the last 30 months, I have traveled almost a quarter of a million miles in 40 states and 16 countries and visited about every brewer and a thousand or more wholesalers. All in our industry are living under an atmosphere of controls. This year, we can expect 7500 proposed pieces of legislation directed at restricting, limiting or inhibiting the normal role of our industry. The USBA will fight this legislation. The aim of USBA is to keep open the channels of distribution.

In 1965, the USBA will also initiate trade relations programs with Hotel, Restaurant, Grocery and Tavern Associations to stimulate an awareness of the profitability of beer. Schmidt's is aiding us in these programs.

SOUVENIR ALBUM 1965 MARKETING MEETING

A low-budget outing from Schmidt's, a now defunct Philadelphia brewer, consisting of labored skits and song parodies recorded live. This clunky show is saved from complete irrelevance by two factors: the brilliantly corny "Beer on Tap," a chanted recitation of draft beer statistics interspersed with tap dancing, and the array of Schmidt's executives pictured on the back cover. The go-go '60s? Not here!

RARITY: 2

THE OLD PRO INTRODUCES...

A circa-1964 Falstaff beer show on a 7-inch disc, with only a plain paper sleeve and no credits, but it sounds very much like the work of Lloyd Norlin. (Sadly, Lloyd had passed away by the time this record turned up.) The Old Pro, a Falstaff advertising character who sounds like a drunk, belligerent Mr. Magoo, introduces songs such as "Please Don't Forget about Me," a female beer customer's plea for her share of sales attention, and "Old Buddy," a grim, oddly compelling spoken-word piece in which

a narrator recounts the miseries of the route salesman, including parking tickets, cranky tavern owners, collapsing cardboard cases, and broken glass. The salesmen get a musical merchandising lesson in "Be Shelf Conscious."

> *Be shelf conscious, I said shelf conscious*
> *You've got to think of display!*
> *Be shelf conscious, always shelf conscious*
> *If you want your business to pay.*
> *Get that Falstaff up to the eye level, that's*
>   *the buy level,*
> *Spelled B-U-Y!*
> *Don't let competition grab the best position*
> *You never get ahead by acting shy!*

Apparently competition grabbed the best position. Falstaff declined rapidly in the late '60s and early '70s and became extinct in 2005.

RARITY: 2

THE GOLDEN SIXTIES

Hank Beebe, who either alone or with partner Bill Heyer wrote many of the best industrials preserved on vinyl, has an uncredited solo 1960 entry here for Brunswick's bowling equipment that proves he can get strange as well as tuneful. At first "There's Nothing Like a Sale" seems perfectly conventional:

> *There's nothing like a sale to get me*
>   *feelin' fine,*
> *There's nothing like that signature on the*
>   *dotted line!*
> *For raisin' up my spirit, I've never seen*
>   *it fail,*
> *There's nothing in this world like a sale!*

But the suit-wearing, sample-case-carrying singer is identified as "Willie Loman, the

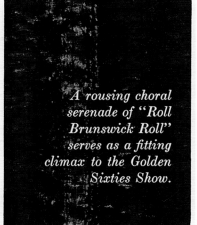

A rousing choral serenade of "Roll Brunswick Roll" serves as a fitting climax to the Golden Sixties Show.

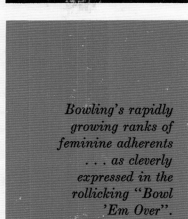

Bowling's rapidly growing ranks of feminine adherents . . . as cleverly expressed in the rollicking "Bowl 'Em Over".

character made famous in the play *Death of a Salesman*." You know, the salesman whose life is so empty and dysfunctional that he kills himself. Way to motivate the team!

The show has a college theme, with the audience referred to as "alumni," back at Brunswick Bowling College for homecoming. The crowning of Miss Brunswick leads into "Gold Crown Line," presented by Jam Handy regular Wayne Sherwood. Much of it is chanted patter backed by skittering percussion.

> *So this golden topper is the crowning*
> *glory of the finest line of bowling*
> *equipment it'll be your pleasure and*
> *privilege to see! Even folks who aren't*
> *lovers of the game will take off their*
> *hats with a hey-hey-hey, askin' how did*
> *bowling ever get that way? Well, you know*
> *the answer is the Gold Crown Line from*
> *BBC! That's B for bright, B for beautiful,*
> *C for customized!*

(BBC also stood for the Brunswick-Balke-Collender Company, the full name of the company until it became just the Brunswick Corporation later in 1960.) This odd, frenzied jabber eventually resolves into a train-themed song.

> *On the Gold Crown Line,*
> *the places it'll take you are really fine!*
> *Like Greater Salesville, Higher*
>   *Profitstown,*

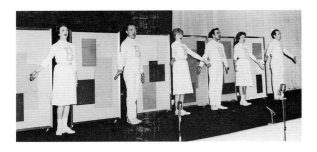

*Upper Bracketsburg! I tell you, the
scenery's fine
When you ride that Gold Crown Line!*

"Bowl 'Em Over" is a musical playlet about
two dopes, George and Morty, who call up two
dames, Flo and Marge, to go bowling. Thanks
in part to Brunswick's new cluster return that
speeds up the game, Flo and Marge have so
much fun bowling that they don't want to move
on to anything more romantic!

"Class Will Tell," with a dual college class/
high class premise, explains new features
such as Telefoul, Telescore, and upgraded
lockers: "Class will *sell!*" In "Brunswick Colors
on Parade," the cast unveils six dazzling new
ball colors. "Roll, Brunswick, Roll," reminiscent
of "Blow, Gabriel, Blow," sums it all up, and
Brunswick's coach sends the team out onto
the field to fight. It's a nicely done show with
enough weirdness to make you take off your
hat with a hey-hey-hey.

RARITY: 2

DIESEL DAZZLE

Once you see that title, you can never un-see
it. *Diesel Dazzle*. The two words perfectly evoke
the collision of the two worlds contained in the
phrase "industrial show."

The title, the graphics, the gatefold cover
with show photos, the souvenir program—
it's all enough to make this 1966 Detroit Diesel

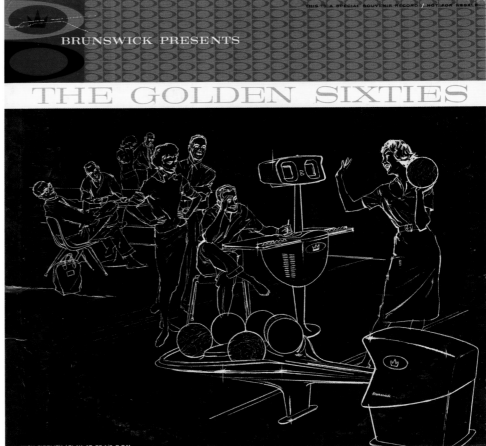

Engine Division of General Motors show a
notable example of the genre. But it's the songs
that send *Diesel Dazzle* into the stratosphere.

*Dazzling sales, dazzling growth!
That's where the future lies!
Detroit Diesel men, they've got both!
They've got Diesel Dazzle in their eyes!*

*Excuse us if our prosperity's showing
It means Cummins is going
The bottom is what they'll eventually be at
As we at
Detroit Diesel Dazzle!*

DIESEL DAZZLE

A MUSICAL MOMENT IN THE PURSUIT OF SOLESCENCE

BILL SHIRLEY has played and sung on stage virtually every leading tenor role in American musical comedy and light opera repertory. He can be heard as the singing voice of "Freddy" in the Warner Brothers film, My Fair Lady.

PAT TURNER has performed in London's Drury Lane Theatre, the Brussels and New York World's Fairs, and was featured in eight Broadway musicals, including Can-Can and I Can Get It For You Wholesale.

BERYL TOWBIN has appeared in nine Broadway shows including the King And I, Bells Are Ringing, Plain And Fancy, and Family Affair.

BERNIE WEST was hailed for his performance as Dr. Kitchell, the songwriting dentist, in Bells Are Ringing on Broadway, the road and in the motion picture.

When the city began to throb!
We were there on the dunes and the
river bank
With the diesel to do the job!

The most stunning combination of diesel engines and musical theater may be "One Man Operation," a wife's lament about her overworked Detroit Diesel husband (with a knockout uncredited performance by Joan Marshall, wife of the show's executive producer, David Marshall).

Once he thought he could do it, but as
more business came
Rebuilding, selling, taking orders too
Workdays, holidays, they all became the
same
And it was night when his day was through.

He did it all alone
Keep books and tend the phone
Eighteen hours every twenty-four
But now the one man in my life
Is no one-man operation anymore.

Now he has two mechanics
A parts and service man
A girl to take the calls and keep the books
He spends weekends giving the children
all he can
And telling me how young his wife looks...

Several other great songs such as "Sell Truck" (the distillation of a four-hour talk by a Detroit Diesel executive, according to David Marshall), "The Step Up," and "Reliabilt Hoedown" (a barn burner about rebuilt engines) would have been the highlights of a lesser show.

Diesel Dazzle had four performances in April 1966, at the McGregor Memorial Auditorium in...Detroit, of course. Afterward,

The show was written by the Lennon and McCartney of industrial composers, Hank Beebe and Bill Heyer, who'd started writing shows together in 1961. The seasoned thirteen-member cast (including future *Barney Miller* star Hal Linden and future TV newsman David Hartman) is backed by a killer orchestra (including uncredited piano by Dick Hyman), and they power their way through numbers such as "We Were There," a brassy, finger-snapping boast about the crucial uses of diesel engines.

We were there when the thirsty desert
drank,

Daddy's A.F.A.'s

DIESEL DAZZLE
Musical Numbers

Overture
Diesel Dazzle
We Were There
Sell Truck
One Man Operation
The Step Up
The Bedford Gavotte
Reliabilt Hoedown
Daddy's A. F. A.'s
Obolescence

TRANSPORTS OF BLISS

DETROIT DIESEL

These days, it's a given that popular classics like "Fever" (Peggy Lee), "Hit the Road Jack" (Ray Charles), and "Blank Generation" (Richard Hell and the Voidoids) owe a fair debt to Ukrainian composer Mykola Leontovych's 1904 piece "Shchedryk," seasonally known as "Carol of the Bells." But only devotees of the industrial musical understand that this song form's characteristic descending bass figure, minor tonality, and swingin' cadence reaches its musical and sales-motivational apogee in one of *Diesel Dazzle*'s key numbers, the spectacular "We Were There."

The lyric ably hews to a common pattern in the genre: an episodic cataloguing of all the dire historical circumstances and dilemmas eventually answered by the corporation's benevolent application of can-do innovation (how such narratives looked onstage may be glimpsed in Union 76 service stations' lovably grubby in-house film *The Battery*, in which mankind's eternal desire for reliable automotive power is illustrated in crass burlesque vignettes set in the Stone Age, Ancient Rome, the Old West et al.).

But it's the music of "We Were There" that stuns, demonstrating the genuine brilliance of Hank and Bill, past all considerations of oddity and camp; it's a flat-out killer that would've stood out in even the most high profile Broadway production.

At first, finger snaps and that spare piano-bass figure seem to augur garden-variety Shchedrykspiel, but before the jaded listener can moan "Oh, Leontovych again?" a male vocal ensemble of uncommon smoothness begins crooning Detroit Diesel's proud saga, and for the next few magical minutes, Katy, bar the door! The orchestra cooks like Basie's crew finessing a prime Hefti chart, with special delectability in the low reeds. All the while, from slow-burn opening groove through climax after soaring climax, the singers—warm as the Ames Brothers, bright 'n' tight as the Hi-Lo's—propel us from barren deserts of yore straight up to Telstar's gleaming orbit on wings of dynamic optimism.

Once heard, "We Were There" is unforgettable; we latter-day listeners can only sigh and wish that we were indeed "there" among those lucky company reps who witnessed this stellar work blowing the roof off that long-ago sales conference.

—SM

Reliabilt Hoedown

the company was so anxious to reinforce the show's messages that management took the unique step of offering the souvenir record in both stereo and mono. Yes, you need both!

RARITY: 3

THE WIDE NEW WORLD WITH FORD

Somebody at Ford's Tractor and Implement Division liked shows. Three made it onto vinyl from 1959 to 1964. The Jam Handy–produced 1960 show's flimsy paper sleeve lists no credits, but the songs are by Hank Beebe, except for Harnick and Bock's "More Power to You," reprised from the '59 show. A skeptical farmer named Mr. Clayburn gets the hard sell in songs like "Hayin' Line Ahead of Its Time" and "You Can't Miss with Ford." "Tractor-Drivin' Man" is a stirring paean by a farmer to his new Ford tractor. By the end of the show, Mr. Clayburn is so enthralled by the line's features that he's moved to sing "Ford Can Do It!"

If there's a job to do, Ford can do it!
If there's a field to mow, Ford can mow it!
Baler, loader, backhoe, spreader,

"Wide
New Wonderful
World"

...CED FOR **THE T**...

LICENSE TO TILL

When those first golden rays o' dawn peek all shy over the horizon, why, a man can't hardly wait to put down his breakfast fork and get out there and plow. And just keep on a-plowin' from can to can't. It's a mighty feeling, and maybe you can achieve it sitting atop a Mahindra—anything's possible these days—but ask the man who owns a Ford.

The tractor-drivin' man who sings the hymn of pride and purpose "Tractor-Drivin' Man"—a "Follow That Dream" for the Dickies bib overalls set—would have us imagine tractor seats so comfortable that "forty winks could be stolen/with Select-o-Speed doin' all the controllin' " but, brother, nobody's gonna nod at the wheel during this number, at once so pastoral, so anthemic and so... maddening.

The piece's real earworm involves a tight posse of singers who repeat the title over and over, each iteration modulating skyward with the kind of chugging urgency library music composers once used to evoke busy city traffic. This vocal ground figure technique is relatively rare; it lent a Latin Quarter oomph to Eddie Maxwell and Jule Styne's unforgettable ode to the La Brea

Tar Pits, "Pico and Sepulveda." Spike Jones used it to deface David Raksin's "Laura" with a surrealistically apt chant of "Bromo-Seltzer! Bromo Seltzer!" Then there's the "Gone gone gone she been gone so long" of Chilliwack's chartbuster "My Girl" ...maybe the technique isn't that rare after all. Further study is needed to evaluate and eventually discard the claim.

In any case, as The Fall's Mark E. Smith sagely observed, "This is the Three Rs: repetition, repetition, repetition." The redundancy undertow gimmick nags at one's psyche like the "learn that poem... learn that poem" conscience-mantra that led Breezy Brisbane to forsake his truant ways in the *Our Gang* comedy "Readin' and Writin'." Here, after a brief oboe solo as honeyed as Edvard Grieg's Sabbath ham, it begins chugging: "Tractor-Drivin', Tractor-Drivin', Tractor-Drivin' Man!" Mesmerized, we long to climb up and ride that gleaming marvel of modern engineering and turn some furrows. Or, barring that, lift our highball glasses and pledge to sell some more goddamn Ford tractors to the man who will.

—SM

For industry and farm, Ford can do it better!

A good show, and certainly one of the top industrials involving a geodesic dome.

RARITY: 3

THE NEW WIDE WORLD OF FORD

Look at that cover. Yes, it's New York's Radio City Music Hall, with tractors, Rockettes, and a big cast sharing one of the world's great stages. This 1964 show was Ford Tractor's first Worldwide Dealer Conference, performed for more than 5,300 people from 120 countries. The liner notes boast that the Jam Handy production was "a stage presentation specifically created to be the most inspirational, enthusiastic business meeting ever presented."

Wilson Stone's stand-up-and-cheer songs such as "Straight Ahead with Ford" are among the most lavishly produced industrial show tunes ever committed to vinyl.

It's got the pull! It's got the might!
And when it starts in rollin', it's rollin'
right!
Steering wheel's connected to
The swingin'est tractor I ever knew
It's got the power to see you through!

Unlike some industrials, *The New Wide World of Ford* focused on the vision and the spirit rather than on product details. "Food, Fibre and Ford" explains to the audience how Ford is one of the three pillars of civilization.

Where you find abundant food that serves
a hungry land

I can tell you, you will find a tractor close
at hand!

What's the reason clothes we wear are
plentiful today?
One big factor is the tractor Ford has sent
our way!

Food, fibre, and Ford!
Three words that are birds of a feather!
Three basics that work together!
Food, fibre, and Ford!

"The Mark of Precision" has a suave, slightly menacing feel, almost as if we've stumbled into a James Bond film in which 007 has quit the secret agent business to sell tractors. Jam Handy regular Wayne Sherwood (uncredited, as is the whole cast) belts out the image-building message.

This is precision, the sound of precision,
The mark of the leader today
Men with fresh vision who look for
precision
In tractors that speak of today
Look to Ford to show the way!

The back cover has quotes from attendees, including this one from an unnamed Austrian: "This was the most beautiful day of my life." Your first reaction might be to giggle. But imagine you're a tractor dealer from some rural corner of Europe, flown to New York City, wined and dined, and plopped down in Radio City Music Hall, where an over-the-top spectacle with dancing girls tells you you're the linchpin of mankind's existence. How could it not bowl you over? Plus, the new line of tractors does look fantastic.

RARITY: 3

THE NEW
WIDE WORLD OF FORD

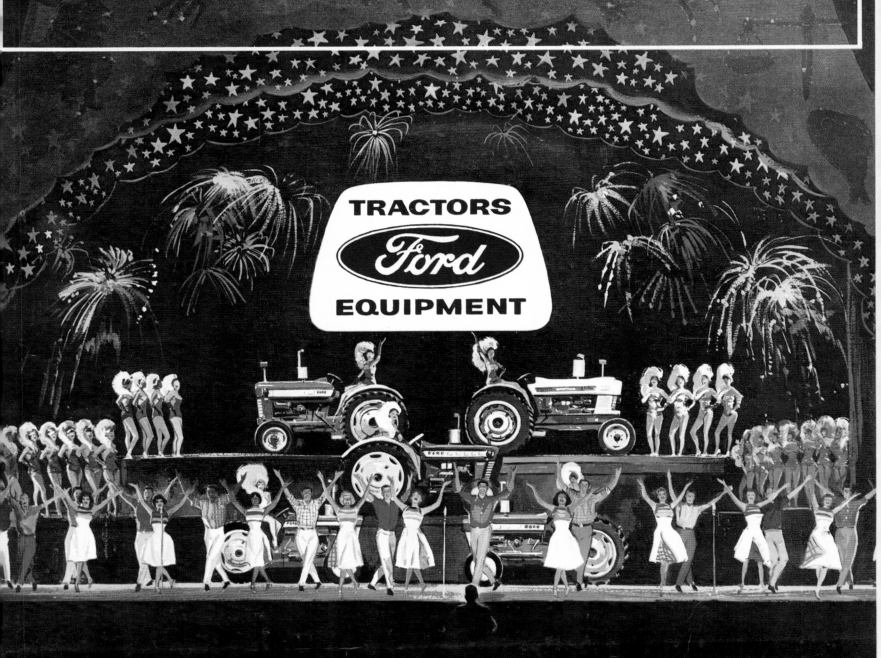

TRACTORS
Ford
EQUIPMENT

THE MAN FROM F·R·U·E·H·A·U·F

This 1967 convention souvenir record from the Trailer Division of the Fruehauf Corporation has a lot going for it: that "bomb" on the cover is actually the record label peeking through a die-cut window. There's a plot spoofing the '60s secret agent show *The Man from U.N.C.L.E.,* with secret agents 00-F and 36-24-36 foiling truck trailer corporate espionage. We're treated to many pages of photos and captions describing the show, the convention exhibits, and more than two dozen models of tankers, hoppers, vans, dumpers, bulk haulers, and more. The music is cool and jazzy. So what's missing? Songs. There are no actual songs. But it's so cool I had to put it in the book.

An enclosed letter from Fruehauf executive Bob Malcomson exhorts branch managers to give the record to each salesman to take home "and listen to once again either in private or along with his family. To fully appreciate all that is recorded will take several listenings." Good luck with that, Bob. "Mommy, *please* make Daddy stop playing that record!"

RARITY: 1

SELLING HELPS, MONEY-MAKING IDEAS for your

SALES DEVELOPMENT MEETING FRUEHAUF DIVISION

May 10, 1967

TO: All Branch Managers & Distributors

YOU WERE THERE:

-- at Cobo Hall, Detroit, Michigan, earlier this year when the 1967 FRUEHAUF NATIONAL SALES CONVENTION featured the greatest transportation line in history -- and the greatest array of selling tools in our business.

Much that was significant was said, and heard, and seen. In fact, too much to remember in its entirety unless you are blessed with the power of total recall. For this reason, we have prepared a special album and record which we feel captures some of the high-lights and excitement of the convention. Perhaps "reviewing" the convention once again will call to mind some important point that will help make your job -- and each of your salesmen's jobs -- easier and more profitable.

Our suggestion is that you play the enclosed copy of the record at the next sales meeting at your branch. Then, give a copy of the album and record (a sufficient quantity has been shipped to your attention) to each man after the meeting to take home and listen to once again either in private or along with his family. To fully appreciate all that is recorded will take several listenings.

Those of us here who have heard the recording hope it renews your "convention enthusiasm" just as it has ours.

Good listening, and good selling:

Bob Malcomson

1967 FRUEHAUF NATIONAL SALES CONVENTION FEATURES GREATEST TRANSPORTATION LINE IN HISTORY AND THE GREATEST ARRAY OF SELLING TOOLS IN OUR BUSINESS!

EXTERIOR POST AND SMOOTH PANEL COUPLABLE CONTAINERS—With sliding couplers and automatic retracting anti-nose-dive supports.

EXTERIOR POST CONTAINER—Lines, mounted on adapter frame. Hat channel door reinforcements. Meets USASI stand

DROP FRAME PLATFORM—Level rear deck. Underslung F2 Suspension. Inside or outside stake pockets. Rugged and versatile.

25-TON CARRYALL—Constructed of tri-ten Oak floor raised above frame for maneuver of metal track vehicles.

INSULATED ALUMINUM TANK—Quick and easy convertibility for hauling great variety of flam-mables and non-regulated commodities.

ALUMINUM GASOLINE TANK—With new, cally tapered ends. Payloads up to 51,00 Legally operable in most states.

SUPER CUBE VOLUME★VAN PLUS—13½" drop and 10:00x15 tires for longer fast hauls. Smooth, soft riding new L1 or L2 Safety Air Suspension.

CITY DELIVERY VAN—Built for grueling service, with rugged external bracing and durability features. Pre-paint available.

EXTERIOR POST MODEL F VAN—With all the features trailer users want most. Maintenance-saving design throughout. Fast delivery.

BEADED PANEL MODEL F VAN — Extra throughout. Aluminum pre-painted panel Select-A-Point tandem. Excellent lease pl

A pageant of stars . . .

★★★★★★★★★★★★★★★★★★★

HITTING A NEW HIGH

A 1966 British industrial for International Harvester, with music by Michael Sammes and lyrics by Herb Kanzell, who moved across the pond a few years after working on the great Westinghouse appliance show discussed in the previous chapter. The 45 rpm record has three brassy, good-sounding songs.

A, B, C, D, E, F, G, I - H
International H, A, R, V, E, S, T, E, R
All around the world, that's the modern
   way of spelling
Good tractors, equipment, good value,
   good selling!

The IH looks like a great choice if your farm is an infinite, featureless black void.

RARITY: 2

It was your show...
and the principal subject
was **YOUR** future!

Our 1967 National Sales Convention, in my opinion, was the most significant and successful in our company's history.

One reason for the great significance of this event was the introduction of our new Model F Vans. It's my firm belief that the new concept of design, manufacturing, and selling which they represent will revolutionize the trucking industry. Now, for the first time, a long-standing transportation need is filled by our development of a "universal" van of first-rate quality and value with the added advantage of quick delivery.

The main reason for the success of the meeting was your own interest in — and attention to — all the things we were able to show and tell you.

That's why I would like you to have this record album as a remembrance of a wonderful get-together, and a reminder of what we have accomplished and will continue to accomplish together.

W.E. Grace

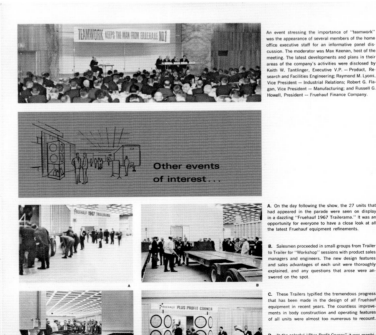

An event stressing the importance of "teamwork" was the appearance of several members of the home office executive staff for an informative panel discussion. The moderator was Max Keenan, host of the meeting. The latest developments and plans in their areas of the company's activities were disclosed by Keith W. Tantlinger, Executive V.P. — Product, Research and Facilities Engineering; Raymond M. Lyons, Vice President — Industrial Relations; Robert G. Flagan, Vice President — Manufacturing; and Russell G. Howell, President — Fruehauf Finance Company.

Other events of interest . . .

A. On the day following the show, the 27 units that had appeared in the parade were seen on display in a dazzling "Fruehauf 1967 Trailerama." It was an opportunity for everyone to have a close look at all the latest Fruehauf equipment refinements.

B. Salesmen proceeded in small groups from Trailer to Trailer for "Workshop" sessions with product sales managers and engineers. The new design features and sales advantages of each unit were thoroughly explained, and any questions that arose were answered on the spot.

C. These Trailers typified the tremendous progress that has been made in the design of all Fruehauf equipment in recent years. The countless improvements in body construction and operating features of all units were almost too numerous to recount.

D. In the colorful "Plus Profit Corner" it was graphically illustrated that the "Man From F.R.U.E.H.A.U.F." can realize valuable earning advantages from the creative handling of Service, Parts, and Accessories, of Tires and Batteries, and of Used Trailer merchandising methods.

YORK DIV. OF BORG-WARNER

BORG WARNER®

PRESENTS

"UP FROM THE VALLEYS"

SALES MEETING
ARUBA-1968

UP FROM
THE VALLEYS

Up from the Valleys from 1968 is the first of four known shows for the York Division of Borg-Warner, which made air conditioners. The songs are by Skip Redwine, and his shows are always a good bet, with impeccably produced music, clever lyrics, and small but thoroughly professional casts.

"Land of Opportunity" is an unusual glimpse into the mind of a less than ethical salesman.

If you're not too damn sincere,
When opportunity knocks, you'll hear.

We stretch the truth and stretch the
*   pocketbook,*
Stretch the flattery—
In this great big land of opportunity!

"I Love 'Em, But I Can't Sell 'Em" is an air-conditioner salesman's lament about the off-season.

I reason, same as the buyer,
Why buy till the temperature's higher?
But gimmicks and salesmanship, I have
*   got none*
So I just love 'em and don't sell a one.
I love the blowers deep inside
The filters fill me with such pride
I love the power, every volt,
Each tiny cog, each nut and bolt.

York to the rescue, with its off-season selling plan to help York salesmen climb "up from the valleys." More help comes in "The Lesson," a complete door-to-door cold calling script in song form.

Windows closed, the room is quieter,
We remove humidity.
Sell your house, you get a better price,
It's paying for itself, you see!
*   Can you recommend one model*
*   That'll do what it ought to do?*
Let's see, how about—the York
*   Champion 2!*

The song goes on to describe the external reset button, the horizontal coil, and the vertical air discharge fan and boasts a couplet enshrined in the Industrial Show Rhyme Hall of Fame:

Slow speed fan, enclosed compressor
Make the customer say "yessir"

The fantastically bleak cover: another reason this show makes me say "yessir."

RARITY: 2

MILLION DOLLAR OPPORTUNITY

The only known industrial performed on a cruise ship, the 1969 York show was remembered by cast member Georgia Creighton as "the boat show." She and fellow performer SuEllen Estey both recalled staggering back and forth on the stage and holding on to each other as the ship hit rough seas during the performance.

There are a few song parodies, but it's mostly original material by Skip Redwine. Once again the most memorable songs are the heavy-duty selling numbers, such as "Exclusively York's."

Many fast food enterprises, many schools
and factories
Find a double need arises, for air and
ice — they need both of these!
Our competitor says in a thin voice,
"We do this, but we don't do that!"
So for one operation, one invoice,
Well, York is where it's at!

"The Gift of Gab" is a cold calling script song in the vein of '68's "The Lesson," but instead of showing how to talk to homeowners, it's about how to approach business owners. Even if a factory already has air-conditioning, a York rep might be able to snag a service contract.

I ask who does the service, is it dealer or
the plant?

YORK DIVISION OF BORG-WARNER

BORG WARNER®

PRESENTS

"Million Dollar Opportunity"

SALES MEETING
CARIBBEAN CRUISE/1969

Is there a maintenance contract?
(That's a very important slant!)
Our service isn't good, but I just
haven't known what to do!
Then could I have a York dealer stop by
and talk to you?

Other numbers include "Aruba," dangling the prospect of a tropical getaway to salesmen who meet their quotas, and "The Mass Merchandisers," about sinister retailers selling inferior, cut-rate air conditioners. Bastards.

RARITY: 1

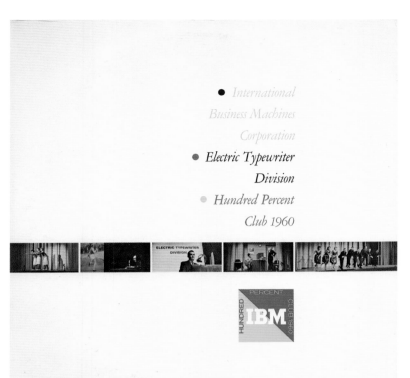

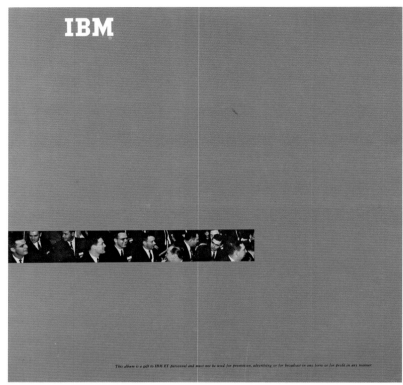

IBM ELECTRIC TYPEWRITER DIVISION HUNDRED PERCENT CLUB

Despite the substantial heft of this 1960 two-record set, it's largely forgettable. This is a live recording, with speeches about the updated Model 632 and the Executary PBX system to skip through, along with various comedy skits. Cynical salesman Jack Wilson keeps popping up to predict that he won't make his quota and therefore won't get to attend the annual meeting. Most of the song material consists of a recurring number by the Olympic Trio Girls.

> *Gotta go higher, be stronger, we gotta be swifter too!*
> *Because that's what the champs, the IBM champions do!*

Feh. If you get only one typewriter convention show, make it the Royal show, not this one.

RARITY: 1

MIDWESTERN REGION 1967 HUNDRED PERCENT CLUB

This IBM show is all song parodies, and the vocals are by the MWR Quintet, apparently a Midwestern Region in-house chorus. But the orchestra is sharp, the cover is a fun 1968 period piece, and the songs don't take themselves very seriously. Plus, the disc is translucent (if schmutzy) "Big Blue" vinyl!

In the opening medley, the salesmen who've met their 1967 quotas sing excitedly about their reward, the upcoming trip to Miami. Then the

bomb is dropped: no Miami trip this year; the winter meeting's in Chicago. That's the Chicago Hilton on the cover. Sorry, boys!

In the '60s, IBM was all about selling systems, and rhymes for the word *system* get a workout in songs such as "The Leading Salesmen."

> **We aid, abet, then we enlist 'em**
> **Sign 'em up and sell a system**
> **IBM, they can't resist 'em at all...**
> **The leading salesmen for IBM!**

The melodies are lifted from various sources, including *Thoroughly Modern Millie* and *How to Succeed in Business without Really Trying*. The show ends up being a lesson in how to sort of succeed in industrial shows by sort of trying.

RARITY: 3

OLYMPIC SALES POWER

A. B. Dick's 1961 meeting celebrated the 316 salesmen who had reached Pacemaker status in 1960. So there's a clue as to just how scarce this record is.

> **You did it! You did it!**
> **You made your quota, you won the race!**
> **You did it! You did it!**
> **You made your quota, you set the pace!**
> **You deserve a reward for all the work**
> **   you've done,**
> **And that's exactly why you're here,**
> **So just relax and have fun!**

Most of the 10-inch record is devoted to live recordings of speeches by company brass, so it's hard to take seriously the "relax and have

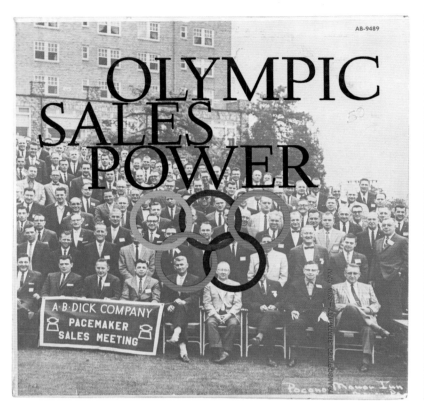

fun" lyric. Also hard to take seriously is the Olympic theme, with the '60 summer games seven months in the past. But the few musical segments by John McCarthy are crisply produced, if stuck in the generic set-the-pace-win-the-race mode.

A. B. Dick was known largely for mimeograph machines, the mainstay of copying technology until Xerox changed the game. The company managed one more show and souvenir record, but after that Xerox said "We'll *Take It from Here*."

RARITY: 1

THE SOUND OF SELLING

In 1962, A. B. Dick once again rewarded top salesmen with a meeting show featuring songs by John McCarthy. The album cover, like those of many industrial show records, occupies that strange twilight world somewhere between beautiful and ugly. The musical numbers again avoid any mention of the company's specific business or product, but the jaunty, xylophone-heavy "The Sound of Selling" is a champ of an industrial trunk song.

The sound of selling is a very exciting sound!
It's the most exciting sound around!
It's the sound of reluctant prospects,
Making excuses and stalling,

THE SOUND OF FEET POUNDING THE STREET
THE SOUND OF TIRES, AND TELEPHONE WIRES
"MAY I TELL HIM WHO'S CALLING?"
THE MOST REWARDING SOUND AROUND
THE SOUND OF THE OFFICE AND THE MILL
THE SOUND OF PEOPLE ON THE MOVE
THE SOUND OF KNUCKLES ON THE DOOR
THE SOUND OF TRADE AND A SALE TO BE MADE
THE SOUND OF MONEY IN THE TILL
THE VOICE OF THE HARD-NOSED PURCHASING AGENT SAYING YOU GOTTA SHOW ME
THE SOUND OF NO, IT'S THE SOUND OF MAYBE, THE LOVELY SOUND OF YES!
THE SOUND OF SELLING
A. B. DICK COMPANY
1962 PACEMAKER
SALES MEETING

*It's the sound of the little receptionist
saying,
"May I tell him who's calling?"*

"Here's Larry Aikens" is a nice example of
an executive introduction song.

*Here's Larry Aikens, good old Larry Aikens,
He's heard the sound of selling, and how!
Your field sales manager, field sales
manager,
Larry Aikens — take a bow!*

Take a bow, A. B. Dick Company! You're gone
from this world, but you left us the gift of music.

RARITY: 1

TAKE IT FROM HERE

Xerox had been around in various forms for
decades, but it became a household name only
with the introduction of its first plain paper
copier, the 914, in 1959. Four years later, sales
were soaring and about to take another gigantic
leap with the introduction of the desktop copier,
the 813. The autumn 1963 launch of the 813
was the occasion for this show.

Xerox was in the big leagues now and hired
Jam Handy, the company that produced shows
for Coke and Chevrolet, to mount an ambitious
production that featured live actors interacting
with elements on film. Wilson Stone's anthemic
songs, expertly executed by a big cast and
orchestra, focused on the broad themes of
success rather than the nitty-gritty of the
machines' features. On the title track a new
salesman, Charlie, sings of his limitless future
with Xerox. Later, in "Dream of Destiny," his
boss sings of the farsighted men who guided the
company through the lean years. Less grandiose
is "The Old Soft Sell," with the vaudeville team of

Xer and Rox explaining their selling techniques.
"Xerox's the Name," sung by uncredited Jam
Handy regular Wayne Sherwood, portrayed the
newcomer as a force to be reckoned with.

*Who makes the best line of copy machines?
Whose copies flowin' put dough in your
jeans?
There's only one champ in the copy hall of
fame,
And Xerox, Xerox, no one else but Xerox,
Xerox is the name!*

"Miracle" unveiled the revolutionary 813:

*A miracle! From research, a master design!
Most unbelievable of all their feats,
And more inconceivable: the market it
meets!*

A card I found tucked into a copy of the 10-
inch album conveys the company president's
hope that the recording will add to the
recipient's holiday cheer. Employees might
have preferred a cash bonus, but fifty years
later I'm glad they went with the record album.

RARITY: 4

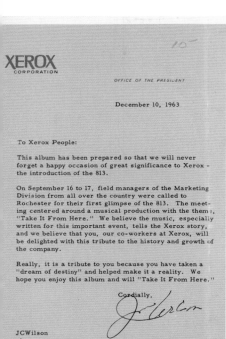

XEROX
CORPORATION

OFFICE OF THE PRESIDENT

December 10, 1963

To Xerox People:

This album has been prepared so that we will never
forget a happy occasion of great significance to Xerox -
the introduction of the 813.

On September 16 to 17, field managers of the Marketing
Division from all over the country were called to
Rochester for their first glimpse of the 813. The meeting centered around a musical production with the theme,
"Take It From Here." We believe the music, especially
written for this important event, tells the Xerox story,
and we believe that you, our co-workers at Xerox, will
be delighted with this tribute to the history and growth of
the company.

Really, it is a tribute to you because you have taken a
"dream of destiny" and helped make it a reality. We
hope you enjoy this album and will "Take It From Here."

Cordially,

JCWilson
gjc

ROCHESTER 3, NEW YORK

XEROX PRESENTS

"TAKE IT FROM HERE"

MUSIC AND LYRICS—WILSON STONE
MUSICAL DIRECTION—MAURICE LEVINE
ORCHESTRATIONS—ARTHUR HARRIS

Produced for the Marketing Division by
The JAM HANDY ORGANIZATION

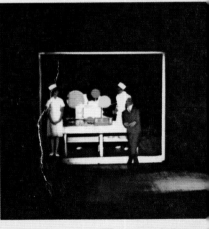

"MONROE ⊞ OPPORTUNITY"

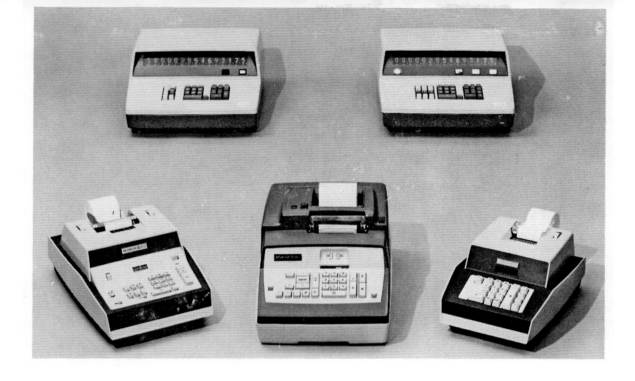

MONROE OPPORTUNITY

This 1967 Monroe Calculator show has a well-honed orchestra and that arrestingly weird cover, but it's almost all rewrites, with lyrics by Joe LeRoy. According to bandleader Sonny Kippe, the overture was the only original music on the record.

A song title like "580-150-570" promises unusual delights, and the song doesn't disappoint. To the tune of "Everything's Coming Up Roses":

Monroe put so much in,
We don't know just where we can begin!
Will it sell? Just you wait! We'll be swell,
*   we'll be great!*
It adds, subtracts, divides, and multiplies!
Here's the 570 from Monroe, it's for you
*   lucky guys!*

Among the show personnel profiled on the back cover is actor-singer Joe Lautner, whose photo belongs in the Headshot Hall of Fame.

RARITY: 2

DOUBLE SHOT: IT'S A BRAND NEW BALL GAME *AND* TELL IT LIKE IT IS

These fraternal twin shows for the Monroe Calculator Company and the Royal Typewriter Company date from within a month or two of each other in late 1969 and were done by the same crew. With an ultra-tight horn-based band led by maestro-composer Sonny Kippe, and some amazing vocal performances, they rank among the best-sounding industrials. And the lyrics by Joe Lapidos and Glenn Moore pack a deranged punch.

The 150! The 116! The 570! The 820!
* The 920!*
The 950! The 990! The 1650 and the 55!
The 1660 and the 65! The 1260 and
* the 1265!*
Yes, here they are, the best team of all!
Because there are no sidelines in our
* game of ball!*

The Monroe Calculator show's theme may have been inspired by the triumph of the '69 "Miracle Mets," who get a mention in the title track. But there isn't time for many baseball references, because there's so much calculator information to impart. In the exhausting "1265 & 1260," operatic baritone Paul Ukena battles through more than six and a half minutes of specs and cheerleading.

With this business machine they can't
* compete!*

There's value here they cannot beat!
With Monroe exclusives through and
* through,*
It will build up tremendous sales for you!
So small, so light, and compact, you see,
With MOS-LSI circuitry!
A constant multiplier and divisor for you
With automatic rounding on both of
* them too!*

In the history of the electronic age,
We start a new chapter and we write
* every page.*
When the history of calculators is read,
Folks will know Monroe is generations
* ahead!*
Yes, our business machine sales will
* surely thrive*
With the new Monroe 1265!

Just so it's not all work and no play, there's the astonishing "Monroe Man." As crooned, growled, and belted by Diane Findlay, it's the best ever, and probably only ever, fusion of sex and calculators.

There's something about a Monroe man,
The way he tries to explain his selling plan.
Although his roots may be square,
He's something right outta Hair.
There's something about a Monroe man.
I dig his scientific floating notations,
His factorials and reciprocals are such a
*   stimulation!*

Meanwhile, things were not as rosy at Royal Typewriter, which like Monroe was a division of Litton Industries. *Tell It Like It Is* attempted to boost the morale of a company that had been through a rough patch. On the back cover and on the record, President

Bob Stewart confesses: "We told the straight story…tempered with humor…we didn't hide the problems…it hurt to laugh because you've been there. You've sold in a tough market place…you've sold in spite of product problems…you sold what you had…because you had to."

If you've ever experienced the heartbreak of bale spring breakage, you're a hot prospect for the new 565.

The 565, the one you're waiting for.
No bale spring breakage, who could ask
*   for more.*
New carbon ribbon, it loads from the top
You ain't seen nothin' yet, just how clever
*   can we get?*
The new carbon ribbon never touches
*   hands*
It's got the price that your customer
*   demands.*

81

STAGE BUSINESS

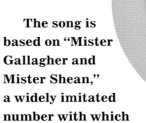

ROYAL KREST CLUB
Las Vegas 1969
Royal Typewriter Co.

Side 2

33⅓ Stereo
MSP 101

1. Secretary's Dilemma
2. Dilemma Dance
3. Mr. Royal - Mr. Royfax
4. This Is Royal's Year
5. We Told It Like It Is

Music by Sonny Kippe
Lyrics by Joe Lapidos & Glenn Moore
Arrangements by Lew Gluckin & Rusty Dedrick
Produced by Sonny Kippe
Directed by Hal LeRoy

It seems, from a close examination of the lyric for "Mr. Royal—Mr. Royfax," that Royal Typewriter Co. had identified within its organization a glaring procedural or philosophical weak spot or something, which demanded better coordination between divisions and departments or whatever, in turn prompting the urgent need for a sort of "rallying cry" for greater bipartisanship amidst sales and service personnel and what have you. Bottom line: the competition had to be prevented from further whipping Royal's corporate ass in the copier market, and the team had better get it together PRONTO.

What better way to shoo away *Glengarry Glen Ross* anxieties pervading whatever the hell I just wrote about—while still getting the dire point across—than a big steaming heap of vaudeville gaiety? The opening, lifted from the "walking theme" of Gershwin's *An American in Paris*, sets the stage for our straw-hatted duo to saunter out from the wings and ham it up, employee chastisement–wise.

The song is based on "Mister Gallagher and Mister Shean," a widely imitated number with which vaudeville legends Edward Gallagher and Al Shean (the latter performer was the Marx Brothers' uncle) slayed 'em at 1922's *Ziegfeld Follies*. This razzle dazzle readymade, invoking what must have been a fading memory even in 1969, does little to clarify the firm's dilemma for us but does offer the pleasure of groaning over deliberately strained rhymes like "When I'm calling on a client/with a contract almost sigh-ent."

At the song's conclusion one can easily picture the pair engaging in a flurry of exaggerated "Me!" "No, ME!" curtain call hogging over the distracted applause of an audience stupefied by the lyric's reference to a "new administration/who'll correct this situation" and all dreadful implications thereof.

—SM

Typewriter ribbons used to be a messy problem. In the unusual "Secretary's Dilemma," the orchestra is accompanied by a carriage return bell as the ladies sing

> *Though our boss never beats us, for that*
> *he'd never do,*
> *It always looks as though he does, 'cause*
> *we are black and blue*
> *With ribbons! Ribbons! Ribbons! Ribbons!*

Royal had a line of copy machines called Royfax. "Mr. Royal—Mr. Royfax" is a vaudevillian complaint about the two lines being unable to work together efficiently, or something. It's another one that must have made sense to the audience.

> *Oh, Mr. Royfax, oh, Mr. Royfax,*
> *On referral fees from you I can't get rich.*
> *And my checkbook's in a rut, I could use*
> *a bigger cut,*
> *I could sell a lot for Royfax but it's hardly*
> *worth the pitch.*

> *Oh, Mr. Royal, oh, Mr. Royal,*
> *It's a situation that could make you flip!*
> *'Cause it happens every day, those*
> *commissions get away*
> *If I had a pill right now, I'd take a trip!*

For the modern listener, no pill is required. These records are trip enough.

RARITY: 3 (Monroe), 2 (Royal)

DOLLS ALIVE!

This 1969 International Paper Company A-lister is rarer than some of the other top industrials such as *Diesel Dazzle* or *The Bathrooms Are Coming!*. With a cover that visually and physically stands out, you'd think more would be in circulation, but perhaps the recipients hated the hexagon points protruding from their neat record library shelves and tossed them.

According to the graphic designer Ernie Cefalu, who went on to create the famous *Jesus Christ Superstar* album design and many other classic album covers, the show had just one performance, in the ballroom of New York's Hotel Roosevelt. Five hundred copies of the record were pressed. *Dolls Alive!* apparently refers to the Rockettes-like cast of dancing girls. Composer Skip Redwine, who also wrote J. C. Penney and York air conditioner shows, is in top form here. The cast is terrific, the wide-ranging music beautifully arranged and performed, and the recording has a wonderful depth and clarity. The opening number, "The Paper Song," careens vigorously through various musical references as the singer proclaims his love.

> *I'm just wild about cardboard, oh, carbon*
> *drives me insane,*
> *Plus my devotion has emotion even for*
> *cellophane.*
> *So, I'm just mad about glossing,*
> *And cheers I add for embossing,*
> *To business grades I do respond,*

You might say we've a beautiful bond.
Well, then my passion continues
For display cards and for menus...
Oh, it's my love for paper, that never
*   seems to taper,*
'Cause it's paper, paper, paper that I adore!

"Let's Get Down to Business" features a burlesque singer explaining that business-grade papers, just like her scarves and feather boas, have to be able to stand up to the daily grind. Of course IP is the answer.

Who's smooth and bright, whose contrast
*   is right,*
A trim that is built for business traffic?
All set to perform, like Tempest Storm,
Here's durable, dependable, my sister
*   Miss Xerographic!*

"How Come You Never Told Me" finds a woman complaining that her husband, for all his marvelous qualities, has kept her in the dark about IP products.

How come you never told me
Uncoated board had such class?
With textures rich and stiffness which
Nobody could surpass?
Your sweet little neck I could throttle!
You didn't hint I could have less mottle!
You could've whispered on a Thursday
*   date,*
"Did you know index doesn't fibrillate?"

Other songs include "Versatility," a mysterious number with comical trombone and tuba passages, occasional chicken and horse noises, and a brief appearance by Donald Duck. It must have made sense to the live audience. There's also "The Finish Is the End" and the extra-catchy "One Big Happy Family," which sounds like the offspring of "Anything Goes" and "Puttin' on the Ritz."

Dolls Alive! appears to have been the only IP show. Between the wild cover with six folding flaps ("Printed in USA by offset on International Paper Company's Feedcote, 18 pt."), one of the world's first nonstandard record album cover shapes, and the excellent music, maybe IP figured it'd quit while it was ahead. And if that mouth on the record label looks familiar, it's because a few years later Ernie remembered it when he was working for the Rolling Stones. He dusted it off, added a tongue, and a rock icon was born.

RARITY: 2

THIS IS TONI

New products keep coming
New promotions keep humming
And there's even new plumbing
Here at Toni today...

New plumbing? What?

That puzzling lyric is one of the few highlights of this 1968 Toni Home Permanents live recording, loaded with forgettable uncredited rewrites of the usual showtune suspects. Executives get musical intros, and Miss America, Debra Barnes, assures the sales force they're doing "a terrific job" and notes that Toni gave the pageant contestants much-appreciated clothing allowances. She even claims that sales meetings are more fun than the formal banquets she gets dragged to. Wow, she must have gone to some pretty dismal formal banquets. Though in the Toni show's defense, it does rhyme *excitement* with *outta-sight-ment*.

RARITY: 1

TEAM ON THE BEAM

A 1962 Colgate-Palmolive Household Products Division show with three songs by Olive O'Neil and Karl B. Norton Jr. on a full-size record. Hand claps and a surprising splash of electric guitar add interest to "Team on the Beam," an otherwise undistinguished meeting kickoff song. "Think Big Mr. Colgate" has an encouraging message with a just-barely rhyme.

Think big, Mr. Colgate, think big!
Think the biggest oak and not the twig!
Think big, Mr. Colgate, think big!

You know you're on the team, you can't renege!

"Go Go Colgate" is a fight song that had cast members in football uniforms with C-P product names such as Ajax, Fab, and Palmolive. We know this because of the photos on the back cover. Industrial show album tip: if your songs aren't that great, be sure to include photos of guys at podiums, dancing girls, and choreography involving shopping carts!

RARITY: 3

OPPORTUNITY UNLIMITED

Another Colgate-Palmolive Household Products Division show, this time from 1965. This one's a good-sounding, energetic production with songs by Robert Haymes that mostly skim along the surface of industrial fun rather than plunging into detail. The title track is akin to dozens of other morale boosters, and two tracks, "Coffee Break" and "Lunch," are okay but take the focus off the business at hand. "Suds and Bubbles" is a slick, noirish tribute to the various C-P brands of laundry detergent. Two songs are rewrites: "Wouldn't It Be Loverly," from *My Fair Lady*, becomes a field rep's meditation on how great it would be to work at the home office, enjoying luxurious perks and not traveling all the time. "King of the Road" reworks the Roger Miller classic.

Here comes our salesman, Dan
Handsome, tall, and tan.
There's nothing finer than
A real live Colgate man!

Not much else going on here, though "When Opportunity Comes A-Knockin' " does

COLGATE-PALMOLIVE HOUSEHOLD PRODUCTS DIVISION

PRESENTS

OPPORTUNITY UNLIMITED

PRODUCED BY GORDON CROWE PRODUCTIONS, INC.

LYRICS AND ORIGINAL MUSIC BY ROBERT HAYMES

include a few faux Beatles *yeah yeah yeah*s and a reference to a salesman from archrival Procter & Gamble coming out of a toupee store. Opportunity unlimited—accomplishment limited.

RARITY: 2

THE NAME OF THE GAME

A 1964 show for Listerine, with music by Julian Stein and lyrics by Ed Nayor. In the opening, the cast chats about the absurdity of putting on a show about Listerine. Having thus tapped into the audience's presumed skepticism, they then insist that "the Listerine story's gonna take you by surprise" and toss off statistics such as Listerine grabbing six out of ten mouthwash sales and growing five times faster than all other health and beauty aids. Okay, I'm convinced!

   "Theme and Variations" tells the history of the product, while "Out for the Money" presents four racetrack denizens who praise Listerine as the only sure bet in the health and beauty aids race. Loretta Swit, years before her *M*A*S*H* fame, has two nice solo numbers. "Gotta Get Your Message Across" is another

entry in the "women-showing-off-their-bodies-as-metaphor-for-advertising" genre. In "I Hate Listerine," she plays a beleaguered store employee.

> *You've made my life a hell and torture*
> *Always having to transport'cha*
> *From the stockroom to your tiny shelf.*
> *Then half my day is spent space chasing*
> *And replacing every facing*
> *I don't have a moment to myself.*

FINALE

Because the Listerine story
   is success that never fails
And you can see it increasing
   both in profits and in sales
If you'll just look you'll discover
   how much more this product earns
Just by discerning volume turning
   and comparing the returns.

We're not standing still
But moving on with skill
We have taken pains
For health and beauty gains
As our story spins
And as you learn the ins
You'll see why we say
There is no better way
Than to grow, grow, grow, grow, grow
With Listerine—Listerine, Listerine . . .
   Oh yeah!

LISTERINE ANTISEPTIC PRESENTS

The Name of The Game

AN INSIGHTS IV PRODUCTION

PRODUCED AND DIRECTED BY EDWARD NAYOR

BOOK AND LYRICS BY EDWARD NAYOR

MUSIC BY JULIAN STEIN

Musical Direction...JULIAN STEIN
Musical Numbers Staged by...EDWARD ROLL
Musical Arrangements...TED SIMONS
Production Stage Manager...MARTIN GOLD
Assistant Stage Manager...EDWARD JULIEN
Scenery Constructed by GARY ZELLER SCENERY
Assistant to the Producer...MARILYN H. RUBIN/JOEY WAIT
Production Assistants...ANDY RASBERRY/BRIAN LEIBOW
Business Manager...ELLIOT ROSE
Company Physician...DR. CHUCK SOLOMON
Production Consultant...J. W. CURRAN

STARRING: JOE CORBY · DAVID HARTMAN · ROBERT KAYE · GLORIA LAMBERT · WILLIAM LINTON · TAMARA LONG · LORETTA SWIT · CAROLE WOODRUFF · BERNARD F. WURGER

Presented by Listerine® Antiseptic, a product of Warner-Lambert Pharmaceutical Co.

store distributors who could be persuaded to drop the loser mouthwash brands and commit to the Listerine juggernaut. It's a fine-sounding show, but you have to wonder if the audience filed out muttering the very first lines: "Can you believe this? A show about Listerine antiseptic?"

RARITY: 3

THE SAGA OF THE DINGBAT

A 1965 show for the *New York Herald Tribune*, with a vibe similar to the previous year's Listerine show. Producer-lyricist Ed Nayor says the Listerine show prompted the *Herald Tribune* to request a similar production. Some of the creative team from 1963's *All About Life* are back for another publication show aimed at advertisers, with the same broad outlines: satirical songs about current events and odes to high-quality journalism and the demographic desirability of the readers.

> *The Trib's more entertaining, there's*
> *appeal for everyone,*
> *A potpourri containing what's important*
> *and what's fun.*
> *Men on the go who have to know*
> *About leading reading things,*
> *All shout, The Herald Tribune Swings!*

"Mr. Herald and Mr. Tribune" employs that reliable motif the vaudeville duo.

> *Say, Mr. Herald — Yes, Mr. Tribune —*
> *Have you noticed how they're eyeing us*
> *much more?*
> *That's 'cause on the local scene,*
> *We've been fighting the machine,*
> *Speaking out about the horrors we deplore.*

Future ABC newsman David Hartman performs "It's Really Simple," an overview of Listerine's television advertising. "The Turnover Tale" asserts Listerine's market dominance.

> *See every shelf, time and again*
> *Check for yourself, we get six out of ten*
> *Turnover tells the tale!*
> *We sell 'em and we rock 'em,*
> *But it's up to you to stock 'em*
> *We're saleable — but you gotta make us*
> *available!*

This song is a clue that the audience wasn't Listerine personnel but rather grocery and drug-

"Every Morning" is a rousing account of the daily battle to get the paper out on time, while "The Saga of the Dingbat" presents a musical history of the newspaper. "Dingbat" refers to the masthead logo, with its allegorical depiction of time, antiquity, and modernity.

The Saga of the Dingbat has decent music by Julian Stein, dense, often clever lyrics, and even the future Barney Miller himself, Hal Linden, all of which served to double ad revenues, according to Ed Nayor. Even then the *Trib* couldn't last in a *New York Times*–dominated market. The *New York Herald Tribune* ceased publication in 1966, though its overseas descendant the *International Herald Tribune* is still published by the *New York Times*. Sadly, the dingbat, after surviving 142 years of mergers and brushes with death, disappeared from the *International Herald*

Tribune's front page in 2008. As of fall 2013, the last vestige of the old *Trib* disappeared when the paper was renamed the *International New York Times*.

RARITY: 3

LIFE presents

ALL ABOUT LIFE
A NEW REVUE

ALL ABOUT LIFE

Magazine and newspaper industrials such as *The Saga of the Dingbat* and this 1963 *Life* magazine show are a little different from other industrials. Rather than motivating and educating their own employees, these shows reached out to advertisers. The songs by Jerry Powell and Michael McWhinney are full of references to demographics and market reach as well as to the greatness of the journalism. *All About Life* played in ten cities, with the lyrics modified at each location to reflect local news stories and personalities.

In "Which Did You Say Was Number One?," *Life*'s three main competitors have a musical argument.

—My net reach is 40 percent of the nation!
—But mine is 42.1!
—I'll treat that figure lightly, you're only a fortnightly,
Besides, my gross impression's more
When all is said and done!

Life's character keeps interrupting with its superior statistics, leaving the competition to splutter:

I'm on the fence!—I'm intense!—I condense!

"On the fence" must have referred to the *Saturday Evening Post*, "Intense" must have meant *Look* magazine, and "condense" could only be *Reader's Digest*. Pretty clever, if a bit obscure fifty years later.

All About Life was intimate in scale, with a small musical combo and a cast of six, led by emcee and narrator Michael Allinson, a British actor who'd taken over for Rex Harrison in *My Fair Lady*. The music is sprightly and the lyrics hold their own. In "As Advertised in *Life*," a young couple sings in a hiccuping, faux rock and roll style.

The records that I loan ya,
Each hairdo that I've shown ya,
The phone I used to phone ya
That time that you had pneumonia
As long as I have known ya,
I've known ya were my guy,
'Cause everything we buy
Is as advertised in **Life***.*

Other songs boast of *Life*'s ability to reach average married Americans and of the magazine's personal touch when dealing with advertisers at the dawn of the computer age.

WHICH DID YOU SAY WAS NUMBER ONE?

GIRL: Which did you say is number one?
 Which did you say is the first?
 After all is said and done,
 LIFE is number one

ALL: Number one in the cigarettes,
 Number one in the shoes,
 Number one in the soft drinks,
 Number one in the booze,
 Number one in the radio,
 Phonograph and TV,
 Number one in the furniture
 Look who's number three.
 Number one in the clothes you wear
 And the gum you have chewed,
 Number one in insurance ads,
 Number one in the food.
 And in major appliances
 Candy bars and new cars,
 Nothing's higher than number one
 Except, perhaps, the stars.

MEN: How do you do it? How do you do it?
 How in the world do you do it?

GIRL: There's nothing to it, there's nothing to it,
 When you've got what LIFE has got . . .

ALL: Quality, versatility,
 And such great flexibility,
 Result stories that spell success,
 26 markets to impress,
 Weekly issues that hit the peaks,
 28 million ev'ry four weeks,
 They reach many people beneath the sun
 And that is why LIFE's number one -

MEN: Yes, indeed it's agreed—we concede—

ALL: That LIFE is number one!

In a nod to *Life*'s mastery of hard news, there's also a humorous song about the aftermath of the Bay of Pigs fiasco and a dizzying high-speed tongue twister about New York governor Nelson Rockefeller's attempt to raise liquor taxes and car registration fees.

That's right, I said a dizzying high-speed tongue twister about New York governor Nelson Rockefeller's attempt to raise liquor taxes and car registration fees. There's always a new surprise lurking in the world of industrial shows.

RARITY: 4

American Society of Magazine Editors & Magazine Publishers Association Present

FLUSH LEFT STAGGER RIGHT
An Intimate Review

Produced and Directed by Nathaniel Greenblatt in association with Edward Nayor, Insights IV Productions

FLUSH LEFT
STAGGER RIGHT
An Intimate Review
Produced and Directed by
Nathaniel Greenblatt
in association with
Edward Nayor,
Insights IV Productions

SIDE 1   MONAURAL LP

1. OVERTURE (Robert Ryan) OPENER
2. FLUSH LEFT STAGGER RIGHT
3. STEP RIGHT UP PART I
    You Are The One Who Wins
4. TWO SHILLINGS, SIXPENCE
5. RICH 6. MUCKRAKING
7. WICHITA
8. STEP RIGHT UP PART II
    Entertainment

Copyright 1966 Insights IV Productions
Playing of this record for
commercial use strictly prohibited.

FLUSH LEFT STAGGER RIGHT

A 1966 show for the American Society of Magazine Editors & Magazine Publishers Association, this production's unusual in that it's about a whole industry rather than a particular company. The subject was magazines—any and all magazines. *All About Life* writers Jerry Powell and Mike McWhinney turned out another show that often feels by-the-numbers but still has flashes of inspiration. The rollicking "Everyone Has a Magazine" is performed by future Tony winner Marilyn Cooper.

Television shows have a magazine,
People without clothes have a magazine,
Midgets, I suppose, have a magazine,
For the folks with jokes there's a gag-azine.

Frenchmen with "La Plume" have a
*   magazine,*
Statesmen, I assume, have a magazine,
Gardens in full bloom have a magazine,
For each hot-rod mod there's a drag-azine.

There are intermittently interesting songs about the history of the magazine business from colonial times to 1966, culminating in the tango-flavored "Optical Scanner," an ode to the miracle revolutionizing the mailing of periodicals. The title track employs a by now familiar whitebread Calypso sound for a riff on fonts.

Cooper Black, Baskerville, maybe Bembo
*   will fill the bill.*
Just look, man, here is Bookman, find a
*   column for it to fill.*
Garamond, Cheltenham, we got typeface
*   ad nauseam.*

In a fake rock and roll number, a pre–*Laugh-In* Arte Johnson represents the youth crowd in the unconvincing "Don't Forget About Us."

We want you, we need you, you're our
*   magazine.*
You're something to believe in that really
*   makes the scene.*

According to cast member Hal Linden, with President Lyndon Johnson in office, he and Arte talked about performing together as "Linden & Johnson," but nothing came of it.

RARITY: 2

PEOPLE TO PEOPLE

This 1965 ABC Radio show is one of the best-sounding live industrial show recordings; apparently ABC Radio had some decent audio

people. Much of the record consists of comedy bits and speeches, but composer William Roy furnishes a few respectable musical moments.

The show played in the six cities with ABC-owned radio stations, attempting to impress local advertisers. "Objectives of Presentation" has a narrator delivering dry talking points about what the show should accomplish, with singers interrupting to mock management and its endless memos and to deliver barbs about insipid pop music and call-in show idiots. A couple tracks trace the history of radio and advertising; there's a lovely a cappella Wheaties jingle before the cast ends up in that mid-'60s *yeah yeah yeah* ersatz rock, rattling off current advertisers such as Coke, Household Finance, and Standard Oil. Other tracks include "The Facts of the Matter," about current radio advertising statistics, and the still-applicable "Phone It In":

Be in the know with radio,
Those telephone debates are really hot!
You get a chance to speak your mind
Whether you have got a mind or not!

People to People has another selling point: people. In addition to color photos of the cast on the front and back, the gatefold contains a mesmerizing array of 1965 suit-wearing guys schmoozing. You can almost taste the scotch.

RARITY: 3

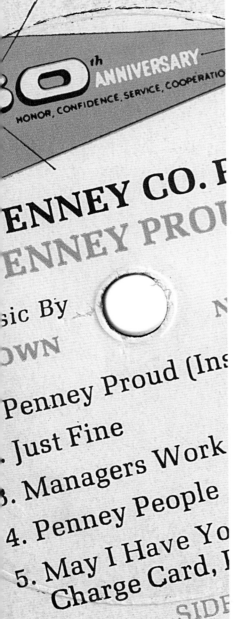

DEPARTMENT SCORE!

In these capsule analyses of industrial show songs and album covers, I've made it a rule to eschew the personal and the wantonly digressive, concentrating instead on proposing a critical framework within which scholars might examine the history and aesthetic evolution of the genre. I will try to maintain that discipline in this essay, but it will be through tears of sentiment and gratitude that I write these words about the very album cover that, for me, "started it all."

Scavengers who peruse today's thrift store LP shelves regularly encounter such titles as *Get Nervous* by Pat Benatar, *Raise!* by Earth Wind & Fire, and *Dream Babies Go Hollywood*, John Stewart's disappointing follow-up to *Bombs Away Dream Babies*. What people forget is that, back when I first came across *Penney Proud*, these were new albums, shrink-wrapped and stickered with the purple $6.99 tag on Sam Goody shelves. In those days, thrift store four-for-a-buck shoppers were likelier to thumb through such overfamiliar covers as comedy blockbuster *The First Family*, Herb Alpert's *Whipped Cream and Other Delights*, and *Trini Lopez at PJ's*. It's crucial to consider this context when evaluating *Penney Proud*.

One's first impression, of course, is the Mondrian-influenced partitioning of the album cover. Varied associations flit across the mind: airport mosaics…"You are here" charts at shopping malls…stained-glass windows on those yucky modern churches where "folk masses" ring forth with insipid sincerity. All these things represent, in their own ways, the idea of transition. And it is transition to which this cover speaks, through an exquisite combination of symbolic abstraction and architecturally precise line drawings.

Right there's the Golden Rule, circa 1902: a humble general mercantile, established in a small Wyoming mining town by a twenty-six-year-old dreamer named James Cash Penney. Probably a thousand stores just like it, but there was only one J. C. Penney, and there, as the eye passes over a gleaming diamond kite that represents the transition of sixty years, we see the fruit of his toil: a grand modern superstore, one of nearly two thousand by then serving the nation. And it's a real beaut. Nice colors too.

But talk about a transition. As soon as that cover entices you to take your first listen to Michael Brown's tour de force, all your Benatars and your Vaughn Meaders become invisible…mere way stations of mainstream boredom, whizzing by unnoticed as we charge forward on an express train to the next industrial, the next "cool find." Of such stuff are the dreams of a lifetime made, and this very book is such a dream, one built on the principles expressed in the *Penney Proud* motto: "Honor, Confidence, Service, Cooperation."

—SM

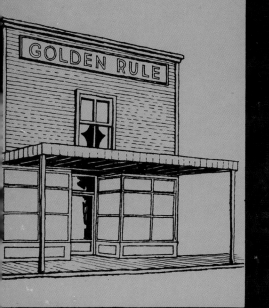

The J. C. Penney Company

presents

PENNEY PROUD

PENNEY'S **60**th ANNIVERSARY

HONOR, CONFIDENCE, SERVICE, COOPERATION

Born in Mexia, Texas, in 1920, Michael Brown left home at fifteen to attend the University of Texas. He initially intended to follow in his father's footsteps and become a doctor but found himself gravitating toward songwriting despite only a brief exposure to piano lessons as a child. During further studies at the University of Virginia, Michael became involved in writing campus musicals, and while serving as a cryptographer in World War II he continued to compose and sing, impressing commanding officers with songs about their wives. Ed Sullivan and opera star Leonard Warren heard him and encouraged him to pursue a songwriting career.

After the war Michael moved to New York, where he established himself at top clubs such as Le Ruban Bleu and the Blue Angel, gaining prominence with songs like "Lizzie Borden" and "The John Birch Society." Fashion world connections led to his first foray into industrials with a fiftieth anniversary show for J. C. Penney in 1952. From there followed a nearly twenty-year run of industrials, during which Michael continued to write and perform other songs and shows as well as authoring the popular children's series of *Santa*

The cast in costumes of 1962. The Sunday School Committee.

Betty Ann Busch as landlady and Arthur Arney as laundryman.

The cast in costumes of 1902. The Weatherby Sisters: Cynthia Wayne. and Beth Oughton.

People of Kemmerer head for the Golden Rule.

Ellen Martin as Evangeline and Tom Mixon as John.

Michael Brown as Mr. Penney in 1902.

PENNEY PROUD

Michael Brown met James Cash Penney in the early '50s and was writing songs for the company as early as 1952. Michael was the go-to showman for J. C. Penney entertainments for nearly twenty years, including this 1962 sixtieth anniversary show. An adept nightclub performer, Michael typically wrote, directed, and starred in his productions. He touts the modern era of consumer credit in "May I Have Your Penney Charge Card, Please."

May I have your Penney Charge Card?
Though it's small, it's such a large card,
For a hat, a zipper, or chemise,
May I have your Penney Charge Card,
*   please?*

"Penney Proud" is a peppy march with large cast.

Proud to be a part of my community,
Proud to own a part of opportunity,
Penney proud, I'm Penney proud, as
anyone can see.

There's also a lengthy musical playlet called "Opening Day at the Golden Rule," about Mr. Penney launching his first store in 1902 in Kemmerer, Wyoming, and dealing with skeptical townspeople. The hardcore industrial number is "The Penney Manager's Work Song." With music lifted from Franz Liszt's *Hungarian Rhapsody No. 2* (the only time Michael borrowed music, he says), Michael delivers a rapid-fire catalog of store manager woes:

Don't buy too much, but buy enough,
And when you buy it, sell the stuff,
Watch the stock and cut expense,
And always use your common sense,
The buyers told you what was new,
And so you ordered quite a few,
Your total sales were only two?
Don't blame the buyers—it was you!
...But Penney! It's all for Penney!
PCC and FMG and A-cup, B-cup, C-cup, D!

Balance, don't lose your balance,
Or someday you'll end up crazy, just
like me!

Dating to 1952, the "Manager's Work Song" was always a hit, especially when accompanied by the humorous pantomime of Michael's favorite performer, Ellen Martin. The song was recycled several times over the years, both for Penney and for other retailers such as Grant's, Woolworth, and Belk.

For extra fun, try to find a copy with sheet music for two songs tucked inside. The whole family can gather 'round the piano and harmonize on "Penney Proud" and "Penney People."

RARITY: 3

MR. WOOLWORTH HAD A NOTION

By 1965 Michael Brown had his shows for retail chains pretty well figured out. His "Manager's Work Song," written originally for J. C. Penney, is here with minor lyric tweaks. "Opening Day at the Five-and-Ten" is a reworking of his Penney song "Opening Day at the Golden Rule." There's some new material, such as the title track, which presents Frank Woolworth's five-and-ten as a breakthrough idea on par with other great historical advances like the wheel. "Shopping at a Woolworth Store" has satisfied Woolworth customers listing their purchases before evoking the space race.

For buying a rack, a rake, or a weeder,
Pillows, candy, or twine,
We're staying true to the logical leader,
Ours since 1879.
We can see the day is coming soon there,

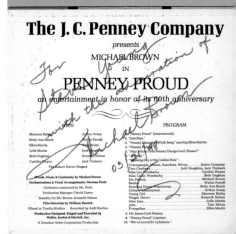

Mouse books. A 1970 J. C. Penney show called *Marvelous Times* was adapted into a Broadway musical *Different Times*, which had a brief run in 1971.

Michael and his wife, Joy, a former Balanchine ballet dancer, have the distinction of making possible one of the enduring works of American literature. In 1956 they gave a substantial sum of money to their friend, the aspiring writer Harper Lee, with a note stating that she was to take a year off from work to write whatever she wanted. The result was *To Kill a Mockingbird*.

Like other composers I've contacted, Michael has been surprised and pleased by the attention now being paid to industrials. I've enjoyed visiting Michael and Joy at their Manhattan home, where I've been privileged to look through their archives and hear their stories.

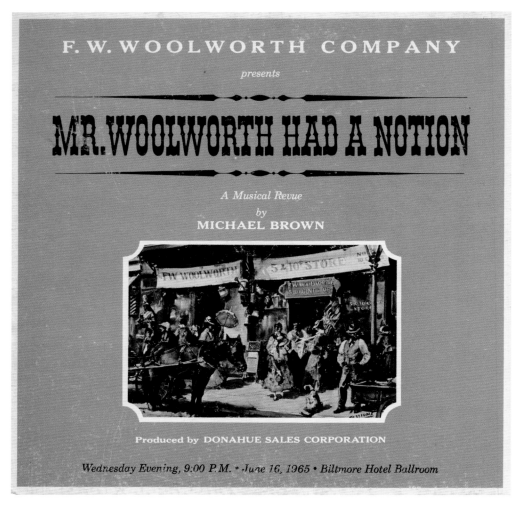

F. W. WOOLWORTH COMPANY

presents

MR. WOOLWORTH HAD A NOTION

A Musical Revue
by
MICHAEL BROWN

Produced by DONAHUE SALES CORPORATION

Wednesday Evening, 9:00 P.M. • June 16, 1965 • Biltmore Hotel Ballroom

And we'd just die if the Beatles got haircuts,
Or we heard any word that they sing!

It must have gotten a chuckle in '65, but people are still listening to those ridiculous moptops today. The Woolworth company, meanwhile, went belly-up in 1997.

RARITY: 3

spirit of 66

SPIRIT OF 66

A 1966 Michael Brown show for J. C. Penney in the mold of his other department store shows, alternating between company boosterism and off-topic fashion show songs. The solid hit is "He's a Penney Man," a satisfying semi-rock number with tight horns and a touch of twangy guitar. Michael and two other singers swap verses about the tribulations of a Penney manager.

If he gets to the store before the light of dawn,
And he stays till the sun has come around and gone,

They'll be selling travel to the moon there,
When they do we'll take a journey through the stars,
Up to Venus and to Mars
Where we'll find red fronts by the score
And we'll do what we did before,
Planet-hopping, shopping at a Woolworth store!

"We'd Just Die," previously used in the 1960 Singer show, mocks teenagers and their fads, with an updated 1965 detail.

And we'd just die if we couldn't have Ringo
For you know he's a wonderful thing,

the spirit of '66

"......there's so much yet to do"

Mr. J. C. PENNEY

Merchandise Clinics, Films and Exhibits
produced by
MULLER, JORDAN and HERRICK
New York City

*Oh man, he's a Penney man, in the great
  tradition of a Penney man.
If he wishes that he could be a simple clerk
When he looks at his office and the
  paperwork,
Oh man, he's a Penney man.*

"He's a Penney Man" concludes with a hint of a change coming to corporate culture: "But we're not through, because that all applies to every Penney woman too!" It feels tacked on, but give Michael and J. C. Penney credit for bothering at all.

Donahue Sales Corporation, longtime producer of Michael's shows for various retailers, sold Talon zippers and other sewing notions. Donahue gets a special nod in the boisterous, Sousa-esque "How Would We Look without Zippers?"

*How would we look without zippers? Awful!
Where would we be without thread? Dead!*

*How could we live with no scissors?
What would we do with no pins?
Without some snaps, it all would collapse,
For that's where fashion begins!*

The obligatory "Opening Day at the Golden Rule" is back, and though "The Penney Manager's Work Song" is in a medley of old Penney convention hits listed in the program, it doesn't appear on the record. Oh, well. Guess I'll have to content myself with only four different versions.

RARITY: 4

THE DONAHUE SALES CORPORATION
presents

SING A SONG
OF SEWING

Words, Music and Script by MICHAEL BROWN

Dorothy Loudon   Ellen Martin   Betty Ann Busch   Emmaline Henry   Marge Redmond
David Carter   Walter Farrell   Gerry Green   Joanne Hill   Patty Ann Jackson
Joe Lautner   Betty Linton   Beth Schackman   Constance Tredwell   Cynthia Wayne
Karen Burkey   Pati Curran   Maria Newell   Anne Newman   Merette Stroyberg

sets and costumes by Tom Lee   musical direction by Norman Paris   staged by Mr. Brown   ballet choreography by Betty Linton

Let's make those Singers sing a sewing,
Keep those belts and bobbins going,
Make those Singers sing a sewing song!

The six-minute "We Don't Sew" is an industrial precursor to side 2 of the Beatles' *Abbey Road*: a suite of short, linked songs in which women give excuses for not sewing.

We don't sew, there's a reason, though,
*   for each:*
—My machine's in the closet out of reach.
*   —I need bobbins!*
*   —I am frightened!*
*   —My machine goes screech!*

The piece becomes a waltz with lyrics about the woman who needs a bobbin, then a woman who never learned to sew who hopes her daughter will acquire the skill.

Because if she can do so, maybe someday
*   on her trousseau*
She may sew, so that is true, so you see,
Sewing's very important to me.

Then it's on to the better-than-average imitation rock and roll "If I Had a Whatchamacallit," bemoaning a missing machine part.

Oh won't somebody help this poor soul in
*   distress!*
Or I will diminish 'til I'm much too thinnish
To fit in my unfinished dress!

Future Tony winner Dorothy Loudon sings the mini-song "Sewing Frightens Me," which careens from frenetic to languorous and back. Dorothy then turns her vocal and comedic talents loose on the melodramatic "All for Lack of a Bobbin," complete with sobs.

SING A SONG
OF SEWING

Much of Michael Brown's work was concerned with fashion, thanks to his relationship with the Donahue Sales Corporation, a zipper and sewing notions manufacturer with ties to J. C.Penney, Woolworth, and other stores. Donahue also had a relationship with Singer Sewing Machines and turned to Michael to create this show introducing Singer's sewing aids and sewing library for National Notion Week in early 1960. The swinging title track sets out the goal.

Out of the closet, off of the shelf, in use
*   where they belong,*

All for lack of a bobbin, the needle went
    hungry for thread,
No thread was sold, so the needle grew
    cold,
And rust soon appeared on his head.
He was never too fat, he grew thinner
    than that,
And his eye from much weeping was red,
All for lack of a bobbin, for thread to a
    needle is bread.

"A Thing of Beauty," accompanying a fashion show segment, and "Great Big Beautiful Morning" are nice but have no Singer angle. "I'd Just Die" is a snarky look at teens who crave their ridiculous fads, such as Elvis, but also, curiously, their sewing machines. In the end, the sewing problems from earlier in the show are resolved.

We're so, so, so, so, so happy
To be sew, sew, sewing at home,
We're so, so, so, so, so happy
To say we sewed it at home!
We know, know, know there's no pleasure
That we more, more, more, more, more
    treasure
Than to say we sew, sew, sewed it at
    home, sweet home!

With several catchy melodies, intricate lyrics, a light, frothy sound, and some great performances, this cheerfully goofy show ranks at the top of Michael Brown's industrial output. Even rarer than the full show is the 7-inch invitation record, which features Michael playing a sample of the title track and inviting recipients to send in the attached postcard to reserve tickets for either the 5 p.m. or 11 p.m. show.

RARITY: 2 (full show), 1 (invitation record)

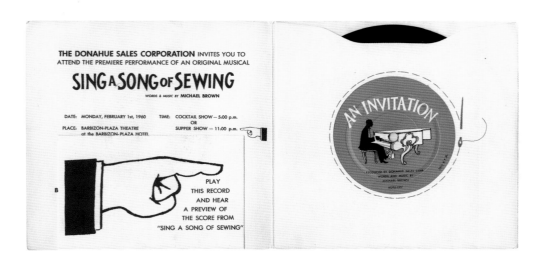

THE FURTHER ADVENTURES OF CHARLIE ABERNATHY

Du Pont was another of Michael Brown's long-standing clients, and he created a few of these small-scale shows touting the latest

Du Pont Textile Fibers Department innovations. This 7-inch 1962 disc has just two songs, and although we learn nothing about Charlie Abernathy or his adventures, we do get Michael singing about Du Pont's fibers in "Put a Lot of Du Pont in Your Line."

You'll make clothes they can't resist,
If you'll use a modern twist,
And put a lot of Orlon in your line.

Other fibers you might enjoy adding to your line include Antron and Dacron.

Michael mentioned to me that MAGIC-BAGIC, referenced on the cover and in the lyrics, was an acronym for Men's Apparel Guild In California and Boys' Apparel Guild In California. Oh, right, I knew that.

RARITY: 2

SEVEN SONS ON A SEESAW

Another Michael Brown mini-show touting Du Pont's miracle fibers, this time from 1963. From "65/35 Bossa Nova":

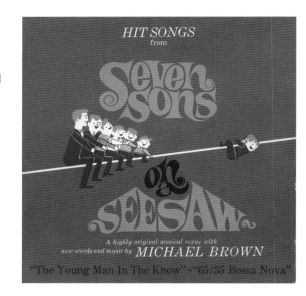

65/35 Dacron and cotton,
That's the blend that can't be forgotten!
65/35 Dacron and cotton
Rings those bells! [CASH REGISTER
SOUND EFFECT]

The liner notes mention that this was Michael's ninth show for Du Pont. He went on to create Du Pont's elaborate "Wonderful World of Chemistry" show for the 1964–65 New York World's Fair, which was a sort of public industrial show seen by more than five million people. *Seven Sons on a Seesaw* was seen by, well, closer to seven people.

RARITY: 2

GO FLY A KITE

This 1966 General Electric Utility Executives Conference show album is the first industrial I ever saw. Even though I didn't understand what I was encountering with *Kite* (as we few i-show geeks call it), I knew it was something very strange and interesting. I knew nothing of Broadway, and it wasn't until years later that I learned that John Kander and Fred Ebb

were the superstar team who wrote *Cabaret* and *Chicago* and "Theme from New York, New York," among many others. They'd already had a show on Broadway the previous year, *Flora the Red Menace*, in which Liza Minnelli made her Broadway debut. Even as *Cabaret* prepared for a November '66 opening in New York, Kander and Ebb found time to knock out an industrial. And *Kite* wasn't their last: they wrote a Ford introduction show the following year, although it doesn't seem to have been recorded. Collaborator Walter Marks, meanwhile, wrote the scores for the Broadway musicals *Bajour* and *Golden Rainbow*, and his song "I've Gotta Be Me" was famously covered by Sammy Davis Jr.

The plot involves a leprechaun who takes utility executive George and his wife, Martha, back in time to get advice from Ben Franklin on the problems facing the industry. Other characters appear, such as misguided hillbillies who, in the wake of the previous year's big Northeast blackout, naively think they can get off the grid and start "Makin' Our Own."

That utility's our nemesis!
Let's make it on the premises!
When their lights grow dim and twinkly,
We'll be watching **Huntley-Brinkley!**

The utilities were on the defensive on several other fronts. Sign-wielding protesters perform "Atom and Evil," an imitation rock number "good-naturedly spoofing unreasonable and misinformed views of nuclear power."

Don't jar our genes! Don't boil our fish!
Don't put our landscape in a terrible
  condish!
You want to build some new atomic plant?
Well if you do, you're gonna boil our fish!
So let me tell you, mister, that you can't!
We wouldn't give permish!

GENERAL ELECTRIC PRESENTS

GO FLY A KITE

FIFTH ELECTRIC UTILITY EXECUTIVES CONFERENCE
WILLIAMSBURG, VIRGINIA
SEPTEMBER 19-21, 1966

"No, No, Not That!" finds a utility executive on a shrink's couch, venting about his wife, daughter, and mother, who want him to be cheaper, more efficient, more reliable, safer, and less disruptive to the landscape—but don't have any suggestions as to how to meet those goals. Fortunately there's some good news. In "PDM Can Do," George learns about the wonders of Power Distribution Management from three well-informed PDM dames.

Can you spot and forecast trouble,
Switch equipment in and out?—Can do!
  Can do!
Can you sense things well enough

"Go Fly a Kite"

"Big Fat Wife"

"Through the Magic Door"

"We're Makin' Our Own"

"No, No, Not That"

To make reports about?—Can do! Can do!
We can read folks' meters and make out
   the bills they get!
What can't we do?—The waltz, I bet.

The music takes a brief left turn into "The Tennessee Waltz."

PDM will help your system with reliability,
As steady and sure as a waltz!
By predicting every failure in equipment
   in your system,
They give advance warning of faults!

The possibility of the industry moving toward high-voltage direct current inspired "Be Direct with Me," a love song in electrical terminology, or perhaps an electrical song in love terminology. Carole Woodruff teases, croons, and belts it out.

Play it straight as Hoyle, and our love
   won't spoil,
But please don't get bored and flow back
   toward
Some other coil.
I require lots of watts, so you see
You must be direct with me.
Two straight parallel wires
Bearing current in the same direction
Attract each other, if you know what
   I mean.

"Manpower" describes the industry's great need for smart young men. We learn that George and Martha have a son who scorns stodgy jobs like those in the power industry: he's a talentless but popular singer named Dingo, one of several mid-'60s industrial digs at youth culture. "Dingo's Protest," peppered with screaming girls, is an odd little gem of absurdity.

I protest Miss Mary Poppins, Howard
   Johnson's,
And Lawrence Welk too!
I protest every one of the St. Louis
   Cardinals!
And baby, I protest you!

Martha, played by future Tony winner Mary Louise Wilson, has a duet with none other than the Devil (Ted Thurston) in the bouncy, delightful "Heaven out of Hell." Martha has tricked him into switching hell over to electric power, and to the Devil's horror it's now clean and efficient.

M: *You've got a rapid transit that crosses*
   the River Styx! Isn't that heaven?
D: *Isn't that...*
M: *Uh-uh, please, sir, watch your*
   language!
D: *No more, those fiery furnaces I used to*
   love to fix!
M: *Isn't it heaven?*
D: *I think it's...*
M: *Uh uh, please, sir, watch your*
   language!
D: *I feel just like the devil, why did we*
   have to meet?
M: *I'll tell you on the level, my joy is*
   shameless, your heat is flameless!

There are lots of other songs with various charms (including the same rhyme that Herb Kanzell came upon in 1957, *utilities* and *ill-at-ease*), and a gatefold cover that includes show photos as well as song descriptions and a listing of the twenty-six speakers appearing over the three days of the meeting in Williamsburg, Virginia. It's a relatively common show, as it was widely distributed within GE and within the power industry, but many of the pressings are low-quality and noisy. Try to find

AND DINGO WAS HIS NAME-O

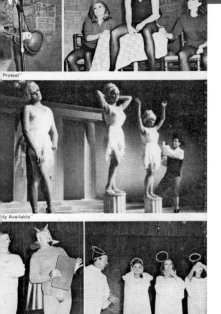

"Protest"

"...ly Available"

"...Out of Hell"

"...Woman Out of Your Wife"

Seldom does one get as complete a sense of what a production was like in person as with the deluxe, dialogue-and-all *Go Fly a Kite*. This isn't always ideal; sometimes the main delight of an industrial cut is its out-of-context unfathomability (an attribute that musicologists refer to as *potrzebie*). But Kander and Ebb's excellence survives even the stark light of coherence, making the album a fascinating study.

For example, let us look at a most unusual section of the show: three short, snide songs I'll call "The Dingo Trilogy." The character Dingo (his name perhaps a portmanteau of Dylan and Ringo, two teen idols whose unconventional looks and voices puzzled and amused grown-ups of the era) is a protest singer. What could be more ridiculous? The fact that kids can't get enough of the stuff, that's what. Dingo's mother, heartbroken that the lad prefers life as a superstar protest singer to level-headed business pursuits, complains, "They're always giving him testimonial dinners after every millionth record he sells."

Dubious reactions to the protest music scene were rife at the time, from Jan and Dean's savage, dissonant "Folk City" and "Universal Coward" to one-offs by clean-cut types like Johnny Sea and the Spokesmen, whose "Day for Decision" and "Dawn of Correction," respectively, were uptight answer records to P. F. Sloan's "Eve of Destruction," a smash hit for Barry McGuire.

The first number in our trilogy, "Dingo's Protest," is the closest to this kind of thing, a down-with-everything travesty that plays like Conrad Birdie gone mock-relevant, replete with Dingo's fatuous introductions and the screaming response of his female fans. Next up is "We're 21," a one-joke bonbon in which a couple demands respect for at last reaching the age of twenty-one...after all, "she's eleven and I'm ten." Hold the guffaws, though, because finally Dingo "gets serious" with "That Great Big a-Go-Go in the Sky"—a clear precursor to "Rock and Roll Heaven" that eerily anticipates the death of Elvis Presley by a decade, and even name checks the Righteous Brothers...*who would crack the Top 5 in 1974 with their comeback recording "Rock and Roll Heaven"!!!*

By the way, the composer of "Rock and Roll Heaven" was Alan O'Day, destined for big chart success with his own recording of "Undercover Angel" in 1977. Interestingly, eleven years earlier, just as *Go Fly a Kite* was wowin' the gathered GE executives at Colonial Williamsburg, O'Day was busy recording his earliest sides for Dunhill records, working alongside—are you ready for this—P. F. Sloan and Barry McGuire!

Given that *Go Fly a Kite*'s plot touched upon the theme of time travel, these "coincidences" begin to transcend the merely baffling and suggest enough heady metaphysical hoo-hah to damn near make you swallow your gum.

—SM

BIOCHEMICALS INTERNATIONAL SALES MEETING • SEPTEMBER 26-27-1966

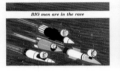  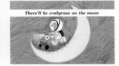

a clean, good-sounding example rather than a "Crackle Kite." Yes, we few i-show geeks have lots of secret lingo.

RARITY: 4

GO GO BIO

I don't know how much Du Pont Biochemicals had to pay him, but the company got NBC newsman Chet Huntley to record a cameo for this space-themed 1966 convention. He briefly anchors a fake newscast about a "Bio 1" rocket launch, followed by woodenly acted chatter between the Du Pont executive "astronaut" and his colleagues at "mission control," until the space capsule is wheeled onstage. Then the Du Pont bigwig crawls out and begins the meeting, with presentations such as "Future Missions" and "Marketing—in Orbit."

Go Go Bio isn't much of an industrial show. Most of it is speech excerpts, and despite a photo of two young women dancing onstage in white-fringed outfits, there's really only one brief, underwhelming song, "Go Go Bio," performed by men in a barbershop quartet style.

We kill the weeds and feed the crops,
Bio men will never stop—go, go, bio!
We predict it will be soon
There'll be crabgrass on the moon—
    go, go, bio!
So get us to the launching pad,
We will make the Moon Men glad—
    go, go, bio!

Taking place in September 1966 just days after the top-tier *Go Fly a Kite*, *Go Go Bio* is the other extreme of business meeting entertainment. But with a lavish ten-page

108

ARRIVAL—SUNDAY SEPT. 25TH

MONDAY A.M. SEPT. 26TH

RECREATION

booklet crammed with lyrics, event schedules, and a jaw-dropping array of mediocre snapshots, it's a great window into what it was like to attend a convention in the 1960s.

RARITY: 1

PERSPECTIVE FOR THE 70s

Many of the themes of *Go Fly a Kite* are touched on in this 1969 Westinghouse Power Systems show performed at the Sixth Future Power Forum: the public's worries about nuclear power, the expectation that electricity must be reliable and clean, and the challenges of supplying a growing appetite for energy. The team of Fred Tobias and Stan Lebowsky, who also wrote the remarkable '71 Keds show, turn in some memorably odd work. "Power Flower"

inverts the countercultural slogan for a hippie tribute to the electric power industry.

Make the power flower! Make the wattage bud!

Keep the power flowering, it's America's lifeblood!

You're the ones we're counting on to take us all away

Come on, sock it to our sockets with your energy bouquet!

Make the power flower! Blossom of the juice!

Make the power flower, there'll be no end to all its use!

Plug in those guitars now with those psychedelic lights

And you'll turn us on forever with electric sounds and sights!

"The Nuclear Kid" portrays nuclear power as a western gunslinger who at first scares the townsfolk.

> *He said he'd like to stay a while and*
> *   maybe settle down,*
> *He said he thought that he could offer*
> *   something to the town.*
> *His manners sure were perfect, his*
> *   appearance clean and neat,*
> *But still there were his shootin' irons, with*
> *   all their blazing heat,*
> *Real waste management heat.*

When the disruptive "Brothers Peaking" come to town and the sheriff ("an old fossil") proves useless, the Nuclear Kid saves the day. Adding to the flavor is the live recording on this track, with audience laughter and several prominent coughs.

Other songs include "Dream City," a utopian vision of a clean, slum-free all-electric city; "Garbage," a tongue-in-cheek song sung by a man from the future who misses the pollution eliminated by the power companies; and "Urbanopolstein," an extended musical parable. Urbanopolstein is a town famous for its wine until the little old winemaker is overwhelmed by the demand. But don't worry: Westinghouse is working hard to ensure adequate future supplies of "wine."

"Urbanopolis, 'Oratorio'" is unlike anything else in the industrial show genre. A back cover photo shows about thirty people onstage singing with books in their hands, and the overall effect is that of a poor man's Handel's *Messiah*. The lyrics deal with the three classic power utility problems: what kind of plant to build, where it should be located, and how big it should be. I'm willing to bet it's the only oratorio that mentions load peaks, rights-of-ways, kilowatts, water supplies, and public hostility.

A unique detail: it's the only known industrial show album to have a retail price. Printed on the back is "$4.98," maybe so recipients might think it was too valuable to throw away.

RARITY: 4

BIG SELL BIG WORLD

You probably haven't heard of IMC (International Mineral and Chemical), which peaked decades ago and then slid into decline and dissolution. But the once powerful fertilizer company left behind a fine bit of corporate entertainment.

With two speeches and some James Bond skit material taking up significant space on the 1965 record, you might not have high hopes. Luckily the songs, with music by Bob WeDyck and uncredited lyric contributions by Arnold Midlash, have a strong batting average. And

BIG SELL / BIG WORLD

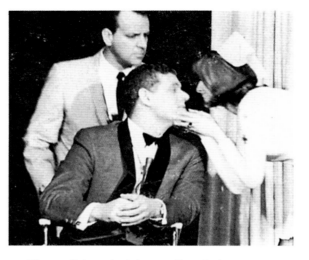

even the Cold War plot is amusing: Soviet spy organization PIE-SKIE (Peaceful International Expansion of Soviet Knowledge, Industry, and Egriculture) sends Anna Potashoff (get it, fertilizer buffs?) to the U.S. to disrupt IMC, which threatens to bring prosperity to the world. Meanwhile, James Bond is dispatched to counter Anna, and they both encounter IMC salesman Charlie. Anna and Charlie express their opposing philosophies in dueling songs. Anna has the authoritarian, minor key "Forcemanship."

> *No need to be resourceful, providing you*
> *   are forceful*
> *With a farmer who is failing in his yield.*
> *Just remind him men have wound up*
> *Being accidentally ground up*
> *By the guys who come to fertilize the field!*

Charlie responds with the sunny "Salesmanship."

> *You gotta follow every lead, and serve*
> *   your customer's need,*
> *Use your sales tools as intended,*
> *When you do, you're using splendid*
> *Salesmanship! That IMC salesmanship!*
> *Wide-awake-always-looking-for-ideas*
> *   salesmanship!*

The well-traveled James Bond gives a globalization seminar in the weirdly hypnotic, swirling "Distribution."

> *Distribution! That's the thing that counts*
> *   today!*
> *Distribution! That's the way to make*
> *   things pay!*
> *Assuming things are equal when the*
> *   game begins,*
> *The one who gets there fastest is the man*
> *   who wins!*
> *When the product must be shipped in bulk*
> *   amounts,*
> *People will pay you tribute, if you can*
> *   distribute,*
> *Distribution is the thing that counts!*

The big surprise is the wannabe renaissance-style "The Ballad of the Plant Food Man." Backed by quiet guitar, bass, and a distant, reverb-y chorus, Charlie sings:

> *And then to battle he did go,*
> *Across the land, where farmers grow.*
> *Behold his image new and bright,*
> *This plant food salesman is a knight!*
> *(Sing ho the salesman! Sing ho the*
> *   salesman!)*

Sing ho the salesman, he travels far and wide.
He brings new plans and programs to be tested, to be tried...

Like many outstanding industrial show tunes, it's both ridiculous and beautiful.

In the end, Charlie and James Bond win Anna over to the glories of the capitalist system, and together they sing "This Is Our Time." The three-person cast is uncredited, although Bob WeDyck identified two of them as Bonnie Herman and Dick Noel. Plus, there's a cameo by a big name at the beginning: NBC newsman Chet Huntley welcomes the IMC men to the meeting and stresses the worldwide nature of their work. For those of you keeping

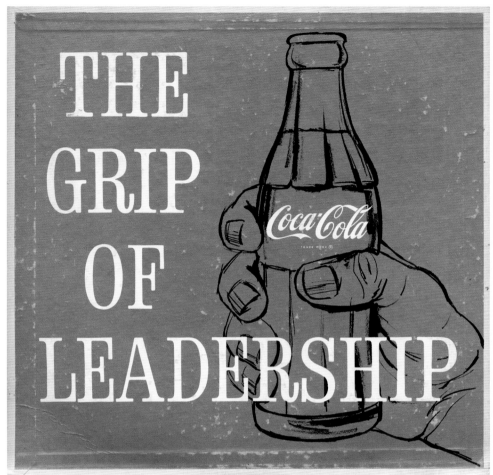

score, Chet Huntley's also in *Go Go Bio* and mentioned in *Go Fly a Kite*. If you're not keeping score, don't worry: I am.

RARITY: 2

THE GRIP OF LEADERSHIP

Good for all America, for our economy...

One of the most bombastic, jingoistic industrials ever, Coca-Cola's 1961 seventy-fifth anniversary show *The Grip of Leadership* implied that Coke was America in liquid form.

BOTTLED EMOTION

"Hot Seat"...and how. This baby comes on strong with a swing intro so legit, so authentically Copa-cetic that you expect Sammy Davis Jr. at any moment. Instead you get a trio of Coca-Cola bigwigs, each one introducing himself with drum roll and fanfare, like a contestant on *To Tell the Truth*. Their "I've got it the roughest," "No, I've got it the roughest" kvetch kompetition reveals this as an example of the whining executive genre of industrial number, designed to elicit knowing chuckles from the bottling plant crowd.

Likely, such numbers served a few purposes apart from mere entertainment. Bottlers and plant managers, finally surrounded by others who understood their job pressures, could share a pressure-valve laugh over all the clueless idiots with whom they had to deal every day. Also, the shared plight of the chaps onstage promoted intra-company empathy and unity. Obviously, these messages were important enough that show composers—in this case the outstanding Wilson Stone—were expected to deliver them with style and humor while making sure to include company jargon and key sloganeering at every possible opportunity.

It's often easy to overlook the skills necessary to pull this off, but not with work as excellent as *The Grip of Leadership*. The performers and band are all first class, with arrangements that navigate a range of styles from soft-shoe to mambo with seamless skill. Coke's extensive reuse of Stone's material attests to his brilliance and, as he told Steve, he takes deserved pride in this show and the many others he created: "I never hacked it... I didn't feel that just because it was 'less than Broadway' that I could get away with doing it on the cheap. I did it as well as I could and I enjoyed it."

—SM

Coca-Cola
TRADE-MARK®

THE GRIP OF LEADERSHIP

SIDE 1

LP-33 ⅓

1—Overture
2—American Heritage
3—Here and Now
4—Hot Seat
5—Packaging and Pricing
6—Keep Things Jumping
Orchestra and Chorus
under the direction of
MAURICE LEVINE
(NOT FOR BROADCAST PURPOSES)
MO7P—3545

Produced by The JAM HANDY Organization—Manufactured by RCA Victor Custom Records

Copyright 1961, The Coca-Cola Company

Two of the songs have "America" or "American" in the titles, and other tracks hit the theme as well. It was as much orchestra and cast as big soda money could buy, and Wilson Stone's Jam Handy–produced songs still sound impressive, if sometimes hokey, to modern ears.

Beyond the caramel-colored flag-waving, there are some great songs about selling and business. In the smokin' "Hot Seat," a bottler, a plant manager, and a territory sales executive bemoan their problems.

We call it the hot seat, it's always the
hot seat,
Where all of the big red hot decisions got
to be made!
Should we make a killing today, and throw
the future away,
Or look for the long view of the trade?

"Packaging and Pricing," featuring Jam Handy stalwart Wayne Sherwood (uncredited again), is a cheery blueprint for metaphorical business violence.

Now I take these pliers, packaging, and
pricing,
Working together like so.
(Oh? How you gonna work it with a pair
of pliers? Tell us so we'll know!)
I'll take 'em in a grip of iron and squeeze,
mister, squeeze,
(You're gonna take 'em in a grip of iron
and squeeze, squeeze, squeeze!)
Gonna squeeze the starch out of
competition with my great big pair
of pliers,
Squeeze so hard he'll have nothing left
but his unrequited buyers.

Promotions and campaigns are the way to "Keep Things Jumping at the Point of Sale."

There'll be no stoppin' at the point of sale
If you keep things hoppin' at the point
of sale.
You've got the know-how, get set to
go now,
Keep 'em jumping at the point of sale!
Build up the interest, break down the
boredom,
Keep 'em jumping at the point of sale!

Other numbers include "The Same in Any Language," about Coke's worldwide presence, and "Look to the Leader," in which a shopkeeper advises confused female customers that to avoid disappointment they should always buy the leading brands.

This was Wilson Stone's first industrial show, and he proved he had a knack for catchy songs about sales strategy as well as the big lump-in-the-throat anthems. Wilson was off and running. Over the next twenty years he wrote shows for Xerox, Ford Tractor, Chevrolet, VW, and Cessna, as well as one more blowout Coke extravaganza. But first, his '61 Coke show would travel the world. Circa 1962 souvenir records exist with the songs (minus the rah-rah American ones) translated into Dutch and German, and in 1976 Coca-Cola of Mexico translated the show into Spanish for its fiftieth anniversary. Wilson was astonished to learn that songs such as "The Same in Any Language" had in fact been translated into several other languages.

RARITY: 3

A native of Webster Groves, Missouri, born in 1927, Wilson Stone showed an interest in the piano by age five. His mother arranged for lessons and he rapidly progressed. He attended Northwestern University, where, like fellow alums Lloyd Norlin and Sheldon Harnick, he wrote songs for the annual Waa-Mu show. One Waa-Mu song, "Back in the Old Routine," was later recorded by Bing Crosby and Donald O'Connor.

Like many young creative hopefuls, Wilson came to New York City after graduation. He began writing songs for films such as *Shane* and *War and Peace*. Eventually he was asked by Jam Handy musical director Maurice Levine if he'd like to try an industrial, which led to his '61 Coke show *The Grip of Leadership*. Over the next decade, he did many other Jam Handy shows, for Xerox, Chevrolet, Cadillac, and Ford Tractor, though most weren't recorded. Throughout, Wilson continued to work on nonindustrial projects, including a 1969 musical starring Martha Raye titled *Hello, Sucker*.

As the 80s dawned, he noticed that the calls to write industrials stopped coming. But during the golden age, Wilson found industrials to be an enjoyable way to practice his songwriting craft, make money, and work with great people. Like other composers I've contacted, he's amazed and delighted that his long-ago industrial show work is receiving attention in a new century.

HOW MANY COOLERS DID YOU SELL TODAY, JOE?

The attraction here is the packaging. As a follow-up to a 1962 convention in Miami, Coca-Cola bottlers were encouraged to run a contest at their plants. The folder for the 7-inch record included a contest entry form. Meanwhile, the record, which included two Wilson Stone songs from *The Grip of Leadership* as well as one new song, was to be drummed into the sales force's heads. The inside of the folder contains great period graphics showing the record in use at warehouses and meetings, with the suggestion that bottlers use the record to "increase

the spizz in your campaign kick-off." The definitions of "spizz" at urbandictionary.com suggest the meaning was different in 1962.

The new, uncredited song "How Many Coolers Did You Sell Today, Joe?" hectors the salesmen into action.

> *Be the king pin in your line; make success*
> *be yours to stay,*
> *Build up a future through the cooler*
> *campaign—*
> *Sell coolers every day!*

Great prizes were at stake, like no longer having to listen to the record all day at the plant.

RARITY: 2

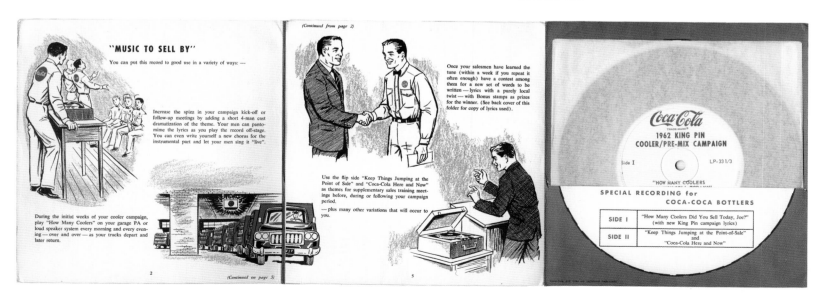

COOLER HEADS WILL PREVAIL

As Steve points out, *How Many Coolers* is notable mainly for its booklet sleeve, a pleasantly ridiculous primer on how to bring the sales convention's motivational themes back home and hammer them, on a daily basis, into the skulls of the sales force. Collectors of vinyl and paper ephemera are familiar with similarly conceived campaigns, such as Campbell Soup's *Club 15* album, which attempted to foster a nationwide network of teenage girls banding together in informal exercise clubs, groovin' away the pounds to a series of instro-pop variations on the "Mmm Mmm Good" jingle, each one tied to a specific dance move, as described in the album's gatefold sleeve.

With its *My Weekly Reader* line art and suggestions to play the record "over and over," this lovably dorky booklet describing Coca-Cola's employee incentive program is strikingly similar to the style and stance of *Club 15* or, for that matter, to kid-targeted brochures on how to run a backyard fund-raiser "carnival" for MDA. The importance of the mission is implicit, the tone somewhat paternal: you know you're part of a vital team effort...we'll provide some some fun tips on how to achieve results, and now it's up to you to apply some initiative.

Whatever the message may be, this piece typifies the tactile kick of ink on paper and grooves on vinyl: two increasingly quaint

HERE IS YOUR PERSONAL COPY OF A SPECIAL RECORDING — WITH NEW "KING PIN" LYRICS — OF THE MIAMI CONVENTION'S COOLER CAMPAIGN HIT TUNE

SELL COOLERS Every Day

"HOW MANY COOLERS DID YOU SELL TODAY JOE?"

BOTTLER SALES PROMOTION • BOTTLER SALES DEVELOPMENT DEPT.   THE COCA-COLA COMPANY • ATLANTA, GA

media that go great together. You don't get none of that from the zeroes and ones that everything is made of these days, consarn it. Pulled out of a flea market box full of old *Look* magazines and recipe pamphlets, an object like this demonstrates a large part of the charm of industrial musical recordings, little archaeological treasures from a lost age as chronologically recent as it is culturally remote.

—SM

WALKING ON SUNSHINE

Whenever someone stops me to ask how one might best summon the essential spirit of industrials, I glance with conspicuous impatience at my watch, reply "Minute Maid sales meeting brochure, '63. Now, if you'll excuse me...," and stride off purposefully, seemingly oblivious to their beaming admiration. Hubris? Not really; just a little trick o' the trade I copped from this handsome pamphlet's key photo. It's a citrus-fresh, Florida-bright image of a go get 'em salesman with a certain resemblance to Gary Crosby, whose father, Bing, not only was Minute Maid's longtime pitchman, but also helped create the product itself. By investing early in the company's "flash freezing" technology, Der Bingle snagged the lucrative position of sole West Coast distributor and, ultimately, chairman of the board, all the while remaining America's most beloved entertainer and, according to Gary's allegations, one lousy dad.

But enough palaver about the Crosbys. Note how this photo's confusion of hard angles and sinuous tropical vegetation lends a somewhat woozy effect, as if Mr. Go Get 'Em has gone and gotten a little something "extra" mixed into his juice glass. Why?

Now that you think about it, he doesn't look too happy. Could he be like one of those weary Bible peddlers in the Maysles brothers' cinéma vérité milestone *Salesman*, resolutely trudging from refusal to crushing refusal? Is this man an avatar of the American Dream being squeezed to a pulp?

Aw, just pulling your leg. Look at the guy; he's brimming with vitamin C, and that stands for Confidence. Wouldn't do you nor me any harm to start each day with a tall, cool glass of that, I'll tell ya what.

—SM

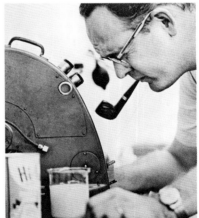

THE LOOK OF THE LEADER

Minute Maid was, and still is, a division of Coca-Cola. Guess what songs were used for the 1963 Minute Maid convention? Yes, the songs from Wilson Stone's endlessly adaptable '61 Coke show, *The Grip of Leadership*.

A few tweaks were required. "Coca-Cola Here and Now" became "Minute Maid Is on the Move." In "Cooperation," the word "Coca-Cola" was changed to "Minute Maid." "Hot Seat," "Keep Things Jumping," and "Look to the Leader" are the same recordings from two years before. Why not? The orange juice guys hadn't been to the Coke convention. And to my mind, the fantastic visuals make up for any lack of originality on the disc.

Like the foreign Coke shows, the existence of the Minute Maid show was a surprise to

Wilson Stone. Production company Jam Handy not only saved money by reusing songs, it economized by not bringing in the big-time creative talent to change half a dozen words.

Side 2 has songs by a vocal group, the Four Saints. They had been scheduled to perform on the last night of the convention, but nobody was in the mood on the evening of November 22, 1963.

RARITY: 2

SELL COCA-COLA HERE AND NOW

Two years after 1961's *The Grip of Leadership*, there were apparently still some parts of the Coke empire that hadn't gotten the message. The '61 show was aimed at the elite, the bottlers; in 1963 the songs were targeted to the route salesmen. Again, Wilson Stone's lyrics underwent cosmetic surgery. "Hot Seat" became "Hot Spot," with a troubled housewife and a storekeeper needing guidance from a wise route salesman; "Packaging and Pricing" became "Product and Confidence," still with the motif of the two concepts forming a pair of pliers with which to crush the competition. Grim? They didn't call it the Cola Wars for nothin'!

RARITY: 2

A STEP AHEAD

Coca-Cola's 1966 show *A Step Ahead* was aimed at the route salesman rather than the bottlers and executives targeted by *The Grip*

a Step Ahead

This album recaptures the dramatic moments and musical highlights of the national tour of "A Step Ahead" that was presented for salesmen and plant personnel of Coca-Cola Bottling plants throughout the country.

This rousing, humorous show was directed by Michael Stanley with choreography by Doug Rogers and book by David Blomquist.

Featured in the cast:

Mace Barrett (Henry Baxter) recently played a feature role in the Broadway hit musical "What Makes Sammy Run?" where he also doubled as understudy for Robert Alda. Mace had the honor of being chosen to sing our National Anthem at the 1964 Democratic Convention. He is one of the most sought after leading men in music tents throughout the country. He has played the leading role in such shows as "Music Man" and "Kismet."

Nancy Dussualt (Mary Baxter) recently co-starred on Broadway in the musical comedy "Bajour". Nancy made her Broadway debut as a leading player in "Do-Re-Mi" which starred Phil Silvers. She was starred on Broadway in "Sound of Music" in the Mary Martin role. Nancy has also handled starring roles in the New York City Civic Opera Company in "Street Scenes" and "The Mikado."

Patti Karr (Auntie Olsen) appeared on Broadway in featured roles in the hit review "New Faces of 1962" and in the dramatic play "Come on Strong." Also has appeared in various national stock company productions of "Bye Bye Birdie" with Van Johnson.

Bill Shirley (Bill) is the voice you hear singing "On the Street Where You Live" in the motion picture version of "My Fair Lady." Before moving to New York, Bill appeared in dozens of films and has sung leading roles in summer theaters throughout the country.

Joe Ross (Delbert) was featured on Broadway in "Body Beautiful" and "She Loves Me." He also has an extensive background in stock and on television. His own act, in which he plays five characters, has scored with supper club audiences from coast to coast.

Original Music and Lyrics
by
Wilson Stone

Overall Artistic Supervision
and Music Direction
by
Maurice Levine

Orchestration
by
Arthur Harris

a Step Ahead

Produced by The Jam Handy Organization, Inc.
Copyright 1966, The Coca-Cola Company
Not for broadcast purposes — High Fidelity 33⅓ R.P.M.
Manufactured by Columbia Record Productions

SIDE 1

Overture—Orchestra (3:17)
A Step Ahead—Henry and Ensemble (4:04)
I'm A Tiger—Henry and Mary (3:33)
Close Harmony—People at the Plant (2:40)
I Couldn't Do It Without You—Henry and People
         at the Plant (2:10)

SIDE 2

Understanding—Henry, Bill and Other Salesmen (3:48)
He Helps Me Every Way He Can—Auntie Olsen and Delbert (4:03)
Man of the World—Henry, Bill and Salesmen (3:35)
The Personal Touch—Henry, Bill and Ensemble (4:08)
Finale: I Couldn't Do It Without You—Henry, Mary and Ensemble (4:22)

of *Leadership*. A contemporary account claims three touring companies put on the show in forty-one cities in two months, reaching 20,000 people. It's a deluxe-with-all-the-trimmings industrial experience, as you'd expect from something billed as the biggest and most costly ever. Jam Handy's favorite songwriter, Wilson Stone, penned another batch of slick tunes punched out by a big orchestra. The plot concerns a route salesman, Henry Baxter, who juggles a changing marketplace, as well as his wife, Mary, who only sees him being tired and useless around the house. Henry insists that, at work, "I'm a Tiger."

> *On my own route, you should see me,*
> *Ready to pounce like that!*
> *On any angle I can wrangle to knock the*
> *   others flat!*
> *Check the coolers, check the facings,*
> *Fill up the shelves with more...*

Henry takes Mary along on his route so she can see what he's up against. She learns about "Understanding."

> *Take a subdivision district, everybody's*
> *   new,*
> *All of them have different tastes, and*
> *   what are you supposed to do?*
> *To appear as kind as Santa, simply stack*
> *   your sleigh*
> *With Tab, and Sprite, and lots of Fanta!*
> *Watch 'em come your way!*

In the end, Henry wins a sales contest and Mary realizes that he truly is a powerful tiger-Santa hybrid.

RARITY: 3

COKE '68 GREAT

A 7-inch souvenir record of a 1968 Coca-Cola Bottling Company of Los Angeles show. There's a Beach Boys–esque group called the Lively Five who perform at least a couple rewrites, such as a version of "Up, Up and Away," but other songs might be original. "Most Unusual Guy," about a master salesman, contains a fun period detail.

> *Most unusual gent, a guy you could never*
> *   invent,*
> *He could sell soap, they say, to the*
> *   hippies today,*
> *He's a most unusual gent.*

Take a bath, cut your hair, get a job, and drink a Coke, you damn hippies!

RARITY: 1

1962 7-UP INTERNATIONAL DEVELOPERS MEETING

Launched in 1929, 7-Up contained lithium citrate, a mood-stabilizing drug, until 1950. As I listened to this show by Alan Fishburn and Gerald Myrow, I found myself wishing that I had some of that original 7-Up. The music is listless and meandering, often losing any sense of melodic forward motion, and the lyrics sometimes throw in the towel and quit rhyming. From "There Is a Market Place That's Ours":

> *We must develop it right now*
> *Placing all of the 7-Up we can*
> *It's simply got to be really available*
> *In this market place that's ours*

Odd little musical asides try to create the illusion of excitement in "A.P.A. — The 7-Up Way."

> *So let's not carp, let's play it sharp*
> *Let's place 7-Up on the market (doo doo*
> *   doo doo doo)*
> *Each package size will harmonize*
> *With needs that are shown in each outlet*
> *   (doo-wah, doo-wah)*

The song never does mention what "A.P.A." stands for. Luckily, the next track on the record is a speech about All Package Availability. In fact, twelve of the seventeen tracks are speeches. It's like the old joke: "The food was terrible!" "And such small portions!" "And no lithium citrate!"

RARITY: 2

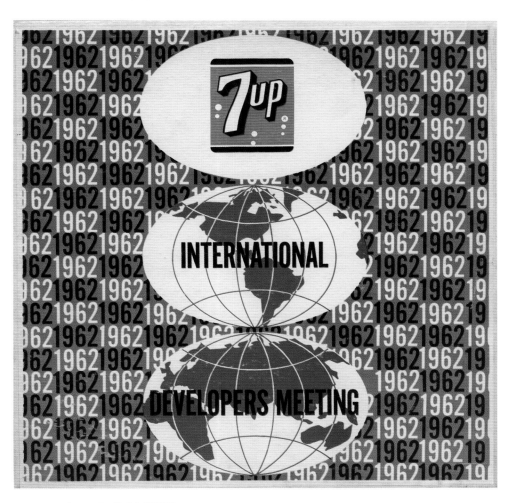

PEPSI POWER PHASE TWO

The only Lloyd Norlin show to credit Lloyd, 1960's *Pepsi Power Phase Two* served as a Rosetta stone. When I tracked him down, Lloyd identified himself as the composer of several mystery shows such as '57 Ford car and truck, '57 Standard Oil, and Hamm's. His Pepsi show fills only one side of a record but has several solid entries, such as "Pepsi Power," an unusual musical preview of the meeting

DO IT ALL -- DO IT RIGHT -- DO IT NOW!

PRIVILEGE

Most cover art of the *Logo-au-Go-Go* variety is fairly static and two-dimensional, presumably adhering to principles of tone and proportion set forth by Moholy-Nagy or someone of that ilk. Not so this feisty entry from Pepsi, in which a pair of symbols seem locked in...what? A primal struggle for market dominance? Is this some thermonuclear sea urchin attacking a cousin of the Newport cigarettes symbol, itself all pointy with rage at the fore 'n' aft pincer grasp of its opponent? Unlikely, as this would make no conceptual sense whatsoever.

What, then? An erotic pas de deux, saucily insinuating a very special "merger" in which the blazing sun rays of innovation penetrate the arrowhead of competitive drive? Do we bear witness to the very zygote of a burgeoning Pepsi Generation, as this Carolina-born soda pop—ever the bridesmaid—sought to "hit the spot" (brand dominance–wise) so complacently occupied by its Georgia rival?

Perhaps only a mind benumbed by overexposure to all things industrial could entertain such fever dreams and errant fancies, but surely something explosive occurred during those four days at the Waldorf-Astoria. Come to think of it, Joan Crawford had only just sat down among the board of directors at this time...is our mysterious pictogram merely a representation of a fit of pique touched off by a wire hanger?

—SM

PEPSI POWER
PHASE TWO

1 - "BE SOCIABLE"   1:02
2 - "PEPSI POWER"   4:14
3 - "STAKE YOUR CLAIM"   1:44
4 - "PEPSI ALL AROUND"   2:47
5 - "LIGHT UP AMERICA"   3:04
6 - "YOU GOTTA SHOW THE
        MERCHANDISE"   2:08
7 - "FINALE"   3:36

A Wilding Production

L7OP-0693

PEPSI-POWER
PHASE TWO

PEPSI-COLA COMPANY

presents

PEPSI POWER

PHASE TWO

Produced by
WILDING INC.

Music and Lyrics
LLOYD NORLIN

Orchestra Under the Direction of
AL EVANS

WHO'S WHO IN YOUR PEPSI POWER CAST

NOT FOR SALE / NOT FOR COMMERCIAL USE / 33⅓ Long Playing

Stake your claim in the new mobile
markets,
The parking lot and every service station!
Stake your claim on the space in the
stands,
On the highways across the nation!
You've got the tools and the weapons to
fight for the space,
To sell more Pepsi by the carton and
especially by the case!

The title track serves as a mission statement:

What we'll try to do in the next three days
Is entertain and inform.
So when you get back home again
You'll feel like selling up a storm!

There it is: the whole theory of industrial shows in four lines.

RARITY: 2

MUSIC TO DISPENSE WITH

This 1966 album from the Container Division of the Scott Paper Company stretches the definition of "industrial show" to the breaking point. There was no show associated with this one-sided promotional album given to vending industry VIPs to promote Scott cups, but it's so charming that I had to include it.

Allan Sherman was a television writer and producer in the 1950s who had a knack for humorous song parodies. His 1962 album *My Son, the Folk Singer* became a surprise hit, and for a few years he was a star thanks to songs like "Hello Muddah, Hello Faddah." Sherman's endearingly schlubby

topics, and "Light Up America," a push for illuminated signage with a carefully rhymed recitation of the fifty states. "You Gotta Show the Merchandise" (also in the Hamm's show) is one of many songs that compare a woman's charms to effective product displays. "Pepsi All Around" finds the cast dismissing a long series of inferior beverages. "Stake Your Claim" urges salesmen to establish Pepsi in new developing markets.

There's a greater share of the market
to tap,
There's a way for you to raise that per-
cap...

Created by Allan Sherman for the Container Division of Scott Paper Company

COLD DRINKS with ICE

Music to
dispense with
by
Allan Sherman

SCOTT MAKES IT BETTER FOR YOU

MUSIC TO DISPENSE WITH

Created by
Allan Sherman
for the
Container Division of
SCOTT PAPER COMPANY

LONG 33⅓ RPM PLAY
CUSTOM PRESSED BY
COLUMBIA RECORD
PRODUCTIONS

SCOTT Ⓢ MAKES IT BETTER FOR YOU

1. Makin' Whoopee . . . . . . Kahn-Donaldson
(Makin' Coffee) B.V.C. Music (ASCAP)
2. Vending Machines . . . Sherman (Curtain Call Music, ASCAP)
3. There Are Cups . . . Sherman (Curtain Call Music, ASCAP)
4. There'll Be Some Changes Made . . . Higgins-Overstreet
(That's How the Change Is Made) E. B. Marks (B.M.I.)
5. The Wonderful Tree in the Forest . . . Sherman
(Curtain Call Music, ASCAP)
6. Scott Cups . . . . . Sherman (Curtain Call Music, ASCAP)

SP-12

voice is the perfect match for songs like "Vending Machines."

Vending machines sell you apples and combs,
Stockings and sandwiches, split-level homes.
And last week I read in three news magazines
They've got vending machines that sell vending machines!

At least two of the songs are parodies: "Makin' Coffee," a takeoff of "Makin' Whoopee," and "That's How the Change Is Made," a parody of "There'll Be Some Changes Made." The other four are allegedly by Sherman, though presumably an uncredited composer wrote the spiffy music. "The Wonderful Tree in the Forest" tells the story of a magnificent tree that's cut down and pulped, but "you'll thank them for chopping you up, when you find you're a nice paper cup." And what a cup, as we learn in "Scott Cups."

Ice is colder in Scott cups,
Scotch tastes older in Scott cups.
Any cola tastes so much colier,
Holy Water is somewhat holier.
You can't lose when you use
Cups manufactured by the people at Scott.
Bees make honey in Scott cups,
Scott makes money from Scott cups.
So keep ordering, and eventually
Scott will come out okay financially.

The jazzy, clarinet-laced "There Are Cups" has scathing words for the competition.

There are cups that bend when vending,
There are cups that tip and tilt,
There are cups so clumsy when descending
That their contents frequently get spilt.
There are cups whose seams are slightly fractured
So they break or bulge or bend or warp,
We deny those cups were manufactured
By the good ol' Scott Paper Corp!

This record makes a convincing claim for Allan Sherman's talent, narrow as it may have been. And if the songs leave you wanting more, the back cover has cup photos and talking points such as "Complete Lip Roll" and "Improved Waxing." A delight all around.

RARITY: 3

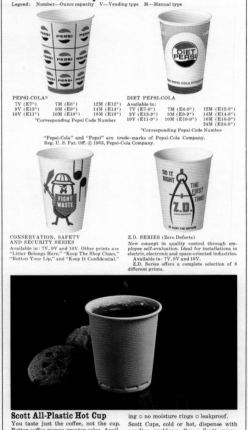

Music to dispense with

A limited-edition recording for a few select people in the refreshment industry. Created by Allan Sherman for the Container Division of Scott Paper Company.

We think you'll find this recording enjoyable because it pokes friendly fun at an industry we're all close to . . . the refreshment industry. We make cups, you fill them, so we felt you'd enjoy some good-natured joshing about both ends of the business. We're convinced everybody has a "funny bone" no matter what his cup brand allegiance. To tickle that bone, we called on Allan Sherman. Allan takes ordinary things and makes them extraordinary. He smoothes wrinkled brows. He relaxes people. He makes you laugh at yourself. He is a laughable guy to promote a laudable product. The photos and information will tell you more about this product. The name is Scott® Cup, and you can't buy a better brand. Its quality is tops, and its price is rock bottom.

Container Division
Scott Paper Company

Music to dispense with

Created by Allan Sherman for the Container Division of Scott Paper Company.

No use may be made of these arrangements or parody lyrics without the express written permission of the copyright owner.

1. Makin' Whoopee   Kahn-Donaldson
B.V.C. Music (ASCAP)
Makin' Coffee—Special lyrics by permission of B.V.C. Music. Not licensed for public performance.
2. Vending Machines   Sherman
Curtain Call Music (ASCAP)
3. There Are Cups   Sherman
Curtain Call Music (ASCAP)
4. There'll Be Some Changes Made
Higgins-Overstreet
E. B. Marks (B.M.I.)
That's How the Change Is Made—Special lyrics by permission of E. B. Marks Music. Not licensed for public performance.
5. The Wonderful Tree in the Forest   Sherman
Curtain Call Music (ASCAP)
6. Scott Cups   Sherman
Curtain Call Music (ASCAP)

Art Direction: Lester Fried.
Cover Photography by Cal Bernstein.
Vending machine courtesy of
The Vendo Company.
Made in U.S.A. 4/66

What makes Scott Cups valued partners in your operation:

Heavy Sidewall Board
In the popular 9V and 10V sizes, heavier board gives better "wet" strength. The stiffness of a Scott Cup outlasts the drink, iced or not.

Complete Lip Roll
A full, 360-degree lip roll gives added cup strength and improved vending reliability. Scott Cups for vending even have special lip waxing.

Improved Waxing
Scott Cups are protected by a special wax that impregnates and coats the paperboard fibers. All-new facilities at Scott provide a superior waxing job on both manual and vending cups. Put simply . . . the drink doesn't "get to" the cup.

Extraordinary Seam Strength
Scott Cup seams offer you the assurance of a leak-free joint. Ask a Scott salesman to show you the "Boiler" test. You'll be convinced.

Controlled Quality
Scott Cups are prevented after waxing. They even pass an electronic "leak" inspection that eliminates human error in checking cup bottoms.

Excellent Printing
Modern new presses with special Scott refinements give clean results. Your identification shows up bright and sharp on each cup.

Quick Service
Seventy-two-hour delivery anywhere. There are 14 regional warehouses around the country. Scott isn't limited by only a few shipping points.

Plus
All this Scott quality and service sells at unbeatable prices. In 1960, Scott began a marketing program that's resulted in a 9 to 14 percent drop in paper cold cup prices. Over the past four years, every paper cold cup price reduction was initiated by Scott. Your industry's support has made this possible.

Here's the Scott® Cup line

Legend: Number—Ounce capacity V—Vending type M—Manual type

PEPSI-COLA®
7V (E7°)   7M (E6°)   12M (E12°)
9V (E13°)   9M (E9°)   14M (E14°)
10V (E11°)   10M (E10°)   16M (E16°)
*Corresponding Pepsi Code Number

DIET PEPSI-COLA
Available in:
7V (E7-9°)   7M (E6-9°)   12M (E12-9°)
9V (E13-9°)   9M (E9-9°)   14M (E14-9°)
10V (E11-9°) 10M (E10-9°) 16M (E16-9°)
24M (E24-9°)
*Corresponding Pepsi Code Number

"Pepsi-Cola" and "Pepsi" are trade-marks of Pepsi-Cola Company. Reg. U. S. Pat. Off. © 1963, Pepsi-Cola Company.

CONSERVATION, SAFETY AND SECURITY SERIES
Available in: 7V, 9V and 10V. Other prints are "Litter Belongs Here," "Keep The Shop Clean," "Button Your Lip," and "Keep It Confidential."

Z.D. SERIES (Zero Defects)
New concept in quality control through employee self-evaluation. Ideal for installations in electric, electronic and space-oriented industries. Available in: 7V, 9V and 10V. Z.D. Series offers a complete selection of 8 different prints.

Scott All-Plastic Hot Cup
You taste just the coffee, not the cup. Better coffee means greater sales. Available in: 7- and 9-ounce.
Toast brown color □ 100 percent plastic—no paper taste □ seamless □ fully-rolled, flag-free lip □ platform nesting—no sticking □ no moisture rings □ leakproof.
Scott Cups, cold or hot, dispense with vending problems. See a Scott representative. He'll get free samples for you. Then all your worries will be over, and you can sit back, relax and listen to Allan Sherman.

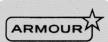

NATIONAL SALES MEETING
DECEMBER 1966
GRAND BAHAMA ISLAND

S-4991   33 1/3 RPM

1. "THE EDDIE MÄCK CALYPSO"
By The Adderly Johnson
Bahama Scorpions
DEDICATED TO "THE MRS. MÄCK"
2. "WE'RE FACING THE FACTS, BOYS"
By "The Armour Oinkers"

ARMOUR NATIONAL SALES MEETING

An insidiously entertaining, thoroughly absurd specimen from 1966. This Armour show has just two songs, on a one-sided 10-inch disc, and the one known copy turned up without a cover. But "The Eddie Mäck Calypso" appears to have been performed by Bahamian locals and has an air of authenticity beneath the bizarre lyrics.

> *But I'm sure you find he have you all in mind*
> *When those money checks he sign.*
> *He always pay you off in time,*
> *And will pay you better when profit climb.*

"We're Facing the Facts, Boys" borrows the music of the then current hit "Winchester Cathedral" for a pork-selling pep rally performed by the Armour Oinkers.

> *So get the standing orders, and we'll think it's just fine,*
> *With a standing order, you get delivery on time.*

> *Say, sell the whole hog — oh no! Not only some cuts!*
> *Loins, hams, ribs, and trimmings, bellies, picnics, and butts!*
> *That's what we're singin' singin' singin'!*

It's bad enough to get "Winchester Cathedral" stuck in your head, but it's worse when you can't stop singing the pork version.

RARITY: 1

THOUGHT FOR FOOD—FOOD FOR THOUGHT

This 1969 Durkee record might not count as a show in the usual sense. The notes on the back mention that it was an audiovisual presentation with screens; apparently there was no live music or cast. Much of the single-sided disc is a spoken retrospective of the preceding decades along with observations about the food service industry. But the one song is so good and the cover is so freaky, it deserves mention.

Marshall Barer and Charles Lind are credited as writers, though it's unclear whether they wrote the audiovisual portion, the song "Things Are Changin', Changin'," or both. The song starts with a worried-sounding piano riff that gives way to hectic horns and driving chord changes, with a vocalist warning against complacency.

> *The guy who thinks he's still just peddlin' groceries*
> *Is gonna get an awful lot of no-sirrees.*
> *You're not just sellin' barbecue sauce, the concept is the thing,*
> *That gets customers to come around and registers to ring!*

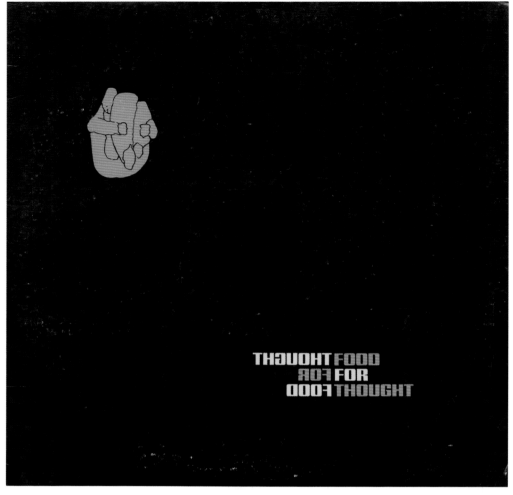

THAT'S SHOW BIZ!

Clear plastic wrap for food wasn't new, with Dow's Saran Wrap on the market since the late '40s. But Goodyear's Film Products Division kicked off the 1965 introduction of its own Prime-Wrap with much fanfare, claiming "this precision-made cast film has everything you'd want in a meat packaging product," such as "clarity, strength, elasticity, puncture resistance, and high bloom-retention." Yes, that's definitely show biz!

This is a small-scale show with a cast of five, a handful of musicians, and five songs on a 7-inch disc. But a couple of the melodies are reasonably catchy, as you'd expect from composer Lee Pockriss ("Johnny Angel," "Itsy Bitsy Teenie Weenie Yellow Polka Dot Bikini"), and the meat-related lyrics by Sid Brooks are certainly odd enough to please. From "What's New":

I know a former winner who is now an
  also-ran,
I hope I'll never say that of a Glidden-
  Durkee man.

Yes, "Things Are Changin', Changin'." Except, oddly enough, Durkee had another meeting in 1972 and put out the *exact same record about how everything's changing.* At least the cover was different, though I prefer the '69 version with the pink man in a fetal position falling through endless blackness. Must have been a fun company to work for.

RARITY: 2

Your meat looks delightfully real
When it's Prime-Wrap making the seal!
New York pork, Chicago veal,
Now at last all meat'll look real!

In "Welcome to Schultz's Market," the cast members personify different cuts of meat in various musical styles and accents. It quickly gets tedious, although there is a startling couplet:

I told my heart that someday, some cook
  would come along
And take me in his arms and sing a crazy
  pork chop song.

The inside of the jacket is sprinkled with dubious, anonymous reviews such as "Brilliant Show!" "Sensational!" "A Stunning Success!" I wouldn't go that far, but it's good to know that, finally, there was a way for meat to look real.

RARITY: 2

MUSIC FROM WHERE THE ACTION IS!

The Bastian-Blessing Company made cafeteria equipment such as steam tables. The photo of a hundred or so guys outside the Grand Haven, Michigan, Community Center hints at a very limited pressing of this murky 1967 live recording. Speeches are interspersed with skits and song parodies written, produced, and directed by Don Logay, who for twenty years had a successful career as the low-budget alternative to the big production companies such as Jam Handy and Wilding.

MUSIC FROM
WHERE THE ACTION IS!

The 1961 hit "Big Bad John" gets retooled as "Big Len," introducing plant manager Len Janke. Other rewrites include "Hey, Look Me Over," "Georgy Girl," and the *Beverly Hillbillies* theme song. There's a Jack Benny sketch and a visit from "President Lyndon Johnson," both starring impressionist Simon Wilder. Don Logay must have been an expert at tapping into the sales force's hopes and fears, because much of the material is met with howls of laughter. A noteworthy moment comes at the very end, when an executive announces that the show has been recorded.

The more I hear it, the more I think memories of this first meeting here would be really great if we could take and cut out the parts where we talk so damn much — [laughter and applause] — and let you hear some of these songs — wouldn't you like to have a recording like this to have for the rest of your life, of all these darn songs? [smattering of applause] We'll get 'em made up — I think we can put it on one record and do a real great job of it.

Not sure about the real great job, but they did manage to put all the darn songs on one record, along with a fair amount of the executives talking so damn much.

RARITY: 1

THE HBP GO SHOW

A circa late 1967 show for Owens-Corning Home Building Products Division, *The HBP Go Show* makes a great first impression with its super-groovy cover. Unfortunately the audio quality of the live recording isn't great: uncredited writer-producer-director Don Logay

says that the low budgets of his shows, plus the necessity of hurrying on to the next project, meant that he never did studio albums. A small cast with piano accompaniment performs song parodies on topics such as insulation, fiberglass screens and tub and shower units, and sales-crimping production bottlenecks, to the delight of the audience. Several numbers are based on familiar Broadway tunes, but the audience also got new versions of the Beatles' "When I'm Sixty-Four" and "(Theme from) The Monkees."

Hey hey, it's the Go Show!
Gonna get it off the ground!
Gotta get the sales year going,
We're gonna count it down!

IT'S A FIBER-GAS!

The cover art for this Owens-Corning Home Building Products Division show is so perfectly mod in every detail that it almost seems like a too-ideal current-day retro design. In fact, it's the McCoy, albeit—as is common among cover designs for industrials—just a wee bit behind the curve: the *Shindig!* teenybopper, hot pink 'n' black color scheme and construction-paper-cut-out lettering have more of a '65 or '66 feel than '67–'68. Sure, man, nitpicking's a drag...but this is, like, serious history.

If it hasn't happened already, some indie label that reissues rare garage-psych singles ought to steal this design for yet another cd compilation of infra-obscure tunes from that fecund moment when the British Invasion yielded to the first fuchsia blush of the Lysergic Pop Revolution. The music of bands like Edgar Allan Pomengranate and the Fairie Tayle are crying out to be paired with a cover image like that of *The HBP Go Show*.

—SM

SIDE 1

BAND 1 Opening-Count Down
BAND 2 Fiberglas 6&3
BAND 3 Mr. Snookums
BAND 4 Thoroughly Modern Screening

MONAURAL 33 1/3 RPM

THE HBP **GO** SHOW   THE **ORIGINAL CAST**

HOME BUILDING PRODUCTS DIV.
OWENS-CORNING FIBERGLAS CORP.
TOLEDO, OHIO

8-8654A

THE HBP

GO

SHOW

ORIGINAL CAST ALBUM

HOME BUILDING PRODUCTS DIVISION · OWENS-CORNING FIBERGLAS CORP. · TOLEDO, OHIO

The songs are interspersed with skits, including a NASA mission control guy who can't stop turning every conversation into a countdown. While not a top-tier show with original tunes, the *HBP Go Show* (along with the previous year's *Go Go Bio*) did fulfill President Kennedy's grand 1961 vision: "I believe that this nation should commit itself to achieving the goal, before this decade is out, of creating sales meeting shows with the twin motifs of go-go dancing and the race to put a man on the moon."

RARITY: 2

HANG-UPS OF '69

This small-scale 1968 PPG Industries revue put on at a New York City hotel is a blizzard of uncredited song parodies and wisecracking asides in silly accents. Wholesale buyers were bombarded with sales propaganda about the company's fiberglass drapes.

> *Girls do it, guys do it, seven people in Van Nuys do it,*
> *Let's do it — let's sell PPG.*

> *Let us come and train you, let us help you sell...*

The real eye-opening moment, in the middle of a "Gee, Officer Krupke" parody about the new advertising campaigns, is a woman cooing:

> *If the drape is inevitable, relax and enjoy it!*

Maybe it shouldn't be a surprise, considering the soft-porn cover.

RARITY: 2

1961 DISTRIBUTOR ROAD SHOW

A souvenir of a presentation about Westinghouse fluorescent lights, this sleeveless 7-inch disc is a smaller capacity 45 rpm, just one-sided, *and* one of the three songs is an instrumental—and it's *still* a humdinger.

A jazzy combo and a handful of vocalists swing through two jargony songs about the sales-building features of the improved light fixtures. The lyrics prove that the show was not intended for the layperson. From "Mainliner":

THE GOLDEN VALUE LINE OF THE '60's

This 1960 GE Major Appliance Division show, by Phyllis Williams and Ray Jaimes, covers a lot of ground in twenty-two tracks. Every kind of appliance gets its moment in the spotlight, with vocalists performing in character as china praising a dishwasher (in a dubious Chinese accent), a Disposall boasting about its sound shield and cushion mounting, or a woman who claims "I'm the new G-E Icemaker":

> *And if you think Greta Garbo is cold, hold it please,*

Now. take the housing mighty strong,
*   much stronger than before (oh, yes)*
New two-way ribs across the top are what
*   you've waited for.*
And there are no U-brackets (notice that,
*   mmm-mmm)*
No clumsy piece to seat!
Built-in supports that swing in place,
Makes mounting fast and neat!
All ballast will be fused (Yes, sir!)
In every fixture you...
Remove reflector, check the fuse, and
*   check that ballast too!*

The odd interjections, the sudden flashes of striking harmony, the burbling piano and noodling electric guitar, the "inside baseball" lyrics all make for an extremely tasty little slab of translucent yellow vinyl. Plus, if you're like me, you've been aching to get rid of those maddening U-brackets.

RARITY: 1

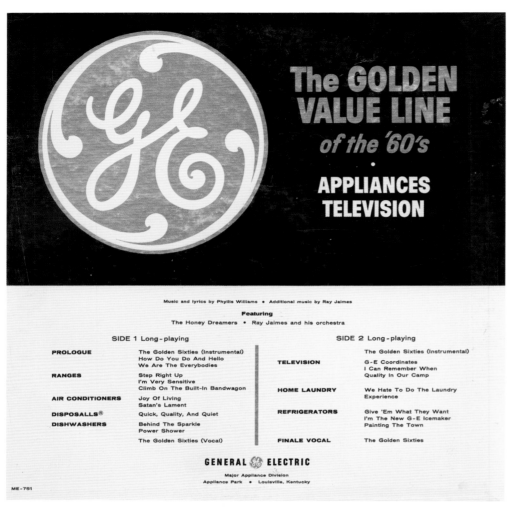

Look like chicken fricassee—ha ha ha!
*I can take all the bloom off, if you don't
cool the room off*
With air conditioners by GE!

With solid if unexciting music, better-than-average lyrics, and some amusing vocal performances, *The Golden Value Line of the '60's* makes me break out with a mild case of prickly heat.

RARITY: 1

ON THE GO WITH WESTCLOX

A triumphantly giddy corporate artifact, this 1963 Westclox show has a great period sound with lots of xylophone and shimmering vibes, fantastic vocals, and plenty of lyrics about clock features and marketing. Plus, the remarkable cover that blurs the line between sexy and creepy.

The show, with music by Jerry Abbott and lyrics by Alice Westbrook, kicks off with "Hi There," a meeting opener that quickly morphs into that problematic genre: greeting dozens of salesmen by name. "Let's Get Going" moves into product-specific wackiness.

We've got travel clocks that travel lighter!
Wind-up clocks that wind up tighter!
Batteries that never fail!
Even our electric alarm has charm!

"How Far Can You Travel" praises the line of travel clocks.

We've got the most complete selection,
Designed with tender loving affection,
Merchandised with typical Westclox
perfection!

*'Cause I can outdo Miss Garbo by twenty
degrees.*
*Yes I'm afraid to start cryin', my teardrops
might freeze.*

The most entertaining number is the gleefully evil "Satan's Lament."

*I chuckle when old biddies collapse with
swollen feet,*
*I love to see the kiddies break out with
prickly heat.*
*When it gets hot as Hades, and lovely
ladies*

ON THE GO
WITH
WESTCLOX

WESTCLOX MARKETING CONFERENCE — DRAKE OAKBROOK... MAY 12th, 1963

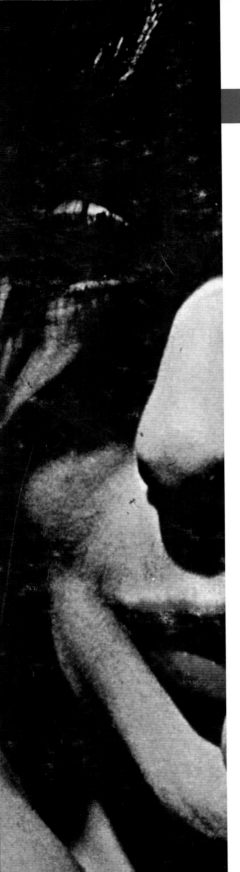

LES CHIMES DU MATIN

On the record label:

COLUMBIA RECORD PRODUCTIONS

33⅓ R.P.M. LONG PLAYING MICROGROOVE

LP · A DIVISION OF COLUMBIA BROADCASTING SYSTEM, INC. NEW YORK-BRIDGEPORT-HOLLYWOOD-CHICAGO-TERRE HAUTE

"COLUMBIA," LP TRADE MARKS. REG. U.S. PAT. OFF. MARCAS REGISTRADAS. ⚙ TRADE MARK - MADE IN U.S.A.

PRESSED AND RECORDED IN U.S.A. BY COLUMBIA RECORDS

"Westclox On The Go"
1963 Sales Meeting
Produced by Grant Jacoby and Frank J. Westbrook
Original Music by Jerry Abbott
Lyrics by Alice Westbrook
Musical Arrangements by Paul Severson

XCTV-90196
Side 2.

33⅓ R.P.M.

MUSICAL NUMBERS
7. Pull The Plug
8. The Battery Blues
9. Sing-Along
10. Madison Avenue Tango
11. A Big Push
12. Goodbye Now

Copyright 1963

How much can one honestly expect from a song that barely tops the half-minute mark? Well, plenty…if the song is "Sing-Along" from the 1963 Westclox marketing conference show, *On the Go with Westclox*.

Drop the needle and a big, juicy show band kicks in with alarming abruptness; a coed vocal combo as cheerful as an Easter basket full of Dinah Shores wastes no time belting: "Battery clocks! Yes, we've got battery clocks!" If ever assurance was needed that "we" do, no bout adoubt it, have battery clocks "that nobody's got" this sunburst assault of high-grade WTF provides it con brio.

Here is a number that—especially when savored out of context—exemplifies the disarming pleasures to be found in the industrial oeuvre: direct and slick as a vintage AM radio station ID jingle, but serving some weird, specific purpose we can barely begin to fathom before we're ordered, "Now everybody sing it!" by the sort of midcentury varsity coach voice you just don't hear no more.

In its moment, in its intended setting, surely this small, brassy gem inspired packed tables of regional managers and their dates to keep the glee going, reprise after reprise, swaying arm in arm all down the line. One can easily imagine its glad strains still ringing in the mind of each newly inspired participant later that night, as ice buckets were refilled at the convenient and reliable hallway dispenser of some Best Western motel, so that highballs might be lifted in giddy midnight toasts to the record third-quarter earnings certain to result from aggressive promotion of battery clocks.

But *tempus fugit*, and at this later date, baffled though we may be about exactly how and in what way those celebrated battery clocks were "hotter than hot," our ears know that here, at least, in the kickline sublimity of this precious recording, brevity is the soul of "hit."

—SM

"Big Ben Blues," about the Big Ben alarm clock, is a smoldering big band blues with a risqué moment.

His movement is beyond improvement,
He even glows in the dark.
He's got a key in his back, he's not much
*   of a swinger,*
But when he goes off he's a ring-ding-
*   dinger.*
He's got a little tick and a great big...tock
If I didn't know better, I'd swear he was a
*   clock.*

Other fun clock-specific songs include "Pull the Plug" and "Battery Blues," promoting the modern battery clocks. "Madison Avenue Tango" trumpets the power of Westclox's advertising, and "A Big Push," introducing a sales incentive plan with prizes such as vacations and sporting goods, includes the line "shoot a duck." "Sing-Along" was an attempt to get the audience to join the cast in proclaiming

Battery clocks, yes, we've got battery
*   clocks*
That nobody's got
Our battery clocks are hotter than hot!

We'll never know how much audience participation they actually got. But I can report that in the late '90s, when this song was on the *Late Show* as part of "Dave's Record Collection," the audience dutifully sang along. My heart swelled with pride.

RARITY: 2

SPIRIT OF '78

Make way, household names Ford, GE, and Coke! Convertors Division of American Hospital Supply Corporation coming through! Convertors had introduced Surg-O-Pak, its disposable paper surgical gowns, drapes, and sheets, in the late '50s, and by 1967 the line was well established as well as song worthy.

The uncredited 1967 show is a modest production, with a small cast and a handful of musicians performing five songs. The main attraction is the bizarre lyrics inspired by the subject matter. From "I Never Enjoyed My Operation More":

I really enjoyed my appendectomy,
Loved my hysterectomy,
Love those drapes and caps and those
  towels by Convertors.

If the patient gets bloody, real bloody
Surg-O-Pak is the way.
If I mess up the cover, we'll get another
And throw the old ones away.

The title is confusing: the show did not take place in 1978 or evoke the spirit of 1878. "78" was a sales formula whereby once a hospital ordered Surg-O-Pak, it'd presumably reorder every month, and if a salesman added just one new hospital to his roster each month, after a year he'd have sold 78 orders. Now that it's been explained, doesn't it make beautiful sense?

Side 2 consists of a lecture, "Asepsis in the OR," delivered by Miss Frances Ginsberg, R.N. As you might imagine, it's quite a hoot.

RARITY: 1

TO KNOW ONE IS TO KNOW THEM ALL

Considering all the big corporations that I know did shows that never made it onto vinyl (Kodak, John Deere, Frito-Lay, and Whirlpool, to name just a few), it's a little odd that Convertors Division of American Hospital Supply Corporation managed *two* souvenir records. The industrial show gods are fickle, and we must accept their whims. Sid Siegel, the songwriter for the landmark *The Bathrooms Are Coming!*, has less to work with here, in terms of both budget and inspiring source material, but he lands a couple of punches in this 1968 show. From the sarcastic "We Hate You, Convertors":

Bring back the days of infection,
When surgery had some romance.
Now life is just rotten—let's bring back
  the cotton,
When a poor little germ had a chance.

A couple melodies sound promising, but the level of production is feeble compared to *Bathrooms*. Again, the fun is mainly in the lyrics' glimpses into an arcane world.

It's cheaper...cloth just can't compare.
Better...wicking action there.
Convenience...dispose it anywhere.

Nowadays there are countless pop songs and show tunes that mention the superior wicking action of paper surgical products, but it was revolutionary in 1968.

RARITY: 1

EVERYTHING'S COMING UP PROFITS

This 1968 GAF Floor Products Division show has a hypnotically grim cover, which unfortunately the record can't live up to. The five-member "GAF Salesmakers" cast and a pianist plow through a one-sided disc's worth of turgid Broadway rewrites, all about sales aids, boosting sales figures, and how the hot new advertising will grab a bigger share of the sheet vinyl and floor tile market in 1969. One odd detail is the narrator who introduces songs with patter like "It's not just new products that will mean a bright new sales year! Let's get the latest on point-of-sale promotions from the GAF Salesmakers!" The anonymous lyricist did snatch one piece of low-hanging fruit: an obvious rhyme for *tile*.

Surg-O-Pak
Surg-O-Pak
LEADERSHIP THROUGH IMAGINATION
CONVERTORS
To Know One
Is
To Know Them All
SHIELD
Surg-O-Pak
SHIELD
SHIELD
TO HELL WITH EVERYTHING

LET'S TAKE TO THE FLOOR

In one adroit phrase, GAF sums up the entire industrials mystique by giving a tangy corporate twist to a familiar Broadway lyric reference: *Everything's Coming Up Profits*, a great title that should really be used more often. The cover of this "original cast recording" (beware inferior revivals and regional theater or high school productions) of the "World's Greatest Floor Show" serves, in and of itself, as a tantalizing View-Master glimpse into those heady days when the form was at its arguable peak.

A backdrop of stock market listings represents the metaphorical "floor" and "walls" of our enterprise. Notice I didn't say "ceiling" because, pal, the sky's the limit. Over this, the designer has cleverly "tiled" a selection of pertinent b/w photos, like those two shots of GAF honchos standing at the lectern, yammering about who-

the-hell-knows. We instinctively glance at our wristwatches and *know* how it felt to endure their carefully crafted speeches, one after the other, on and on, through each salient point and every last corny aside.

We might, for a numb moment or two, stare at shots of the performers givin' it their all, "concert-style," but, inexorably, the eye is drawn to a haunting essay in shadow and light we can only call The Strange, Ominous Corridor Up Top Right. Here, like sacred statuary in cathedral alcoves, examples of the product line are displayed in arched grottoes that inspire hushed reverence, particularly now that the company concentrates on roofing materials, leaving behind *L'Age d'Or* when Academy Award laureate Henry Fonda extolled GAF's sheet vinyl flooring, color print film, and 8mm movie gear.

—SM

"EVERYTHING'S COMING UP PROFITS"

**ORIGINAL CAST RECORDING FROM
THE WORLD'S GREATEST FLOOR SHOW**

GAF 1969 National Sales Meeting and
Southern Region Distributor Conference
December 16-17, 1968

Central Region Distributor Conference
January 5, 1969

Eastern Region Distributor Conference
January 12, 1969

Western Region Distributor Conference
January 17, 1969

gaf GAF Corporation, Floor Products Division, 140 West 51 Street, New York, N.Y. 10020

Sell our floor tile, it's the blue chip of tile
Sell our sheet vinyl, with all its beauty
and style.

Industrial meta-connection: "Salesmaker—Salesmaker" is a parody of the *Fiddler on the Roof* classic "Matchmaker," by our '59 Ford Tractor show heroes Harnick and Bock. So far no parodies of their '59 Ford Tractor songs have come to light.

RARITY: 1

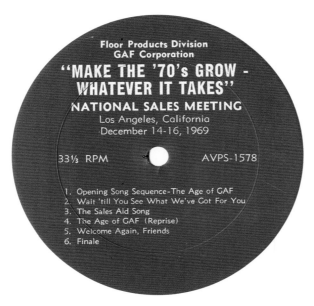

MAKE THE '70's GROW—WHATEVER IT TAKES

Was the sad little 1968 GAF show really such a boost that everyone demanded another one in 1969? Maybe GAF had money to burn, because it boasted

It was a very good year, you sold a lot of
sheet vinyl,
You sold a lot of sheet vinyl, Alhambra,
Palais,

To name just a few, of patterns so new,
With rainbow colors so clear,
They made your sheet vinyl year.

It's another one-sided disc with labored song parodies, one piano, and a small cast. The uncredited lyrics give off an air of having been scribbled down in a panic fifteen minutes before the show: "The Age of Aquarius" becomes "The Age of GAF" and "I'll Never Fall in Love Again" becomes "You'll Always Sell More GAF."

The company, once also known for cameras and film as well as the View-Master line, apparently couldn't follow through on the show's title. The Floor Products Division is long gone, and today GAF makes mostly roofing products.

RARITY: 1

MY INSURANCE MAN

Ooh, a musical titled *My Insurance Man*! This 1968 Continental Assurance Company show was one of the first industrials I found, and it seemed to beg for mockery. But Bob WeDyck and Arnold Midlash, the creative team behind the fine '65 IMC fertilizer show, turned out some memorable work, nicely executed by a strong three-person cast and a tight band.

The key word in the show's title is "My." Much of the material on side 1 is about professionalism and how people become possessive of the professionals they rely on: "my doctor" or "my insurance man."

My insurance man! (Is that what they call
you?)
My insurance man! (Is that what they say?)
Are you sure you're recognized as the
man who's organized,
Who makes the most of every single day?

There are concrete things to do!
There's incentive here! It's invented here!
Each day brings something new!

Complaints about taxes are eternal, but in "Taxes and Money," a surprisingly kick-ass chunk of corporate funkiness, the details are especially colorful.

I questioned my insurance man, though I
*   didn't need to ask it,*
Besides the tax on my estate, they've got
*   one on my casket!*
They run the whole economy on balances
*   and checks,*

My insurance man, the man we rely on!
My insurance man, the best of them all!
He serves all coverage needs, that's why
*   he succeeds,*
My insurance man — is that what they call
*   YOU?*

"Dear Miss Smith" is an unusual spoken piece with a soft jazzy background. Agency owner Irv Deal muses to himself about how much he depends on his secretary.

Do I ask too much? Make you work
*   too hard?*
Load you down each working day?
And what was I before? Doing so
*   much more,*
In my inefficient way.
My days are free of trouble! Output more
*   than double!*
Thank you, Miss Smith.

Miss Smith is also grateful.

How the hours fly by! And there are
*   reasons why!*

And when their goal is birth control,
—They'll slap a tax on sex!

Musical theater, insurance, and sex: thank *you*, Miss Smith.

RARITY: 3

LIZ AND FRED SING OF '64

Folk music meets a Dow Jones Industrial Average component in this unusual 1963 Alcoa presentation. Music and lyrics are by Fred Albitz and Liz Seneff, who also play guitar and sing. The single-sided disc was clearly recorded well after the National Association of Aluminum Distributors convention, with Ms. Seneff telling the listener that they introduced a great program last fall in Arizona, and "if you missed the meeting, here it is again."

We bring you art that has the body of
a glass of vintage port,
And copy with the punch of German beer!
'Cause Alcoa's very big on distributor
support,
That's the plain unvarnished reason why
we're here!

Ms. Seneff narrates highlights of the '64 Alcoa marketing campaign, doing a believable job of sounding enthusiastic about how "we're making it easy for Mr. Aluminum Buyer to get in touch with you." Sprinkled throughout are micro-songs, such as

If a useful little giveaway should happen
just to be your dish,

We've got advertising premiums, you can
use them any way you wish!

The talented duo also performs a couple off-topic songs, including "Ragtime Cowboy Joe," as a nod to the Arizona convention site, and "They Call the Wind Maria" from *Paint Your Wagon*. Liz Seneff, who'd released a 1963 solo album titled *Now Listen to Liz*, was later in a short-lived semi-psychedelic band, the Split Level. But first she had at least one more aluminum-related industrial to get through.

RARITY: 1

A FAIRY TALE/ BRIGHT IDEA

Cole National Corporation used to be a major player in keys. Today a descendant survives as a vision care company, but in 1965 the company's big news was car key blanks made of colored aluminum rather than the usual brass. In the golden age of industrials, that was sufficient excuse for a show.

The first hint of trouble: the front cover is titled *A Fairy Tale*, while the label claims it's *Bright Idea*. The back cover, which insists it's both, describes a strained plot involving characters Colonel Constantine Colenat, Dick Deficit, Pussy Katz, and Madame Roselda Rifkin, but for better or worse none of this folderol made it onto the record. A three-person cast and a pianist grind through a one-sided disc's worth of lukewarm uncredited material, much of which feels like industrial show trunk songs with no Cole National content. "Y'Gotta Display It!," with a plea for effective advertising and merchandising, gets a little better.

The plant at National stamps those blanks
out with care,

Memorable music from the stage play • Cole National Annual Sales Meeting, July 30, 1965

Cole National Corporation
in association with
Wilding / Dramaturgy, Inc.
presents

**BRIGHT IDEA
A FAIRY TALE**

. . . the musical numbers from Cole National's stage show introducing Car Keys in Color, July 30, 1965.

THE STORY . . .

Colonel Constantine Colenat, super-titan of the key industry, is unhappy. No new worlds are left for him to conquer . . . until he decides to create a super-salesman who will serve as an inspiration to the entire sales force. Unfortunately the sole salesman available is his feckless nephew, Dick Deficit. Glamorous Pussy Katz, Colenat's blonde secretary, joins the Colonel in a devious plot to turn Dick into a leader of men . . . a fearless, confident dynamo of sales energy and skill. Colenat and Pussy initiate Dick into the ancient mysteries of selling as they sing The History of Salesmanship. Inspired by the example of "Lightning Lester Ruf", Dick charges off to sell his first account. Little does he know that Ma and Pa Proctor are actually Pussy and the Colonel in disguise. Although he fails to sell them, they teach him how to Fight Fair. Much later in a dismal day, Dick encounters Pussy again, in the guise of Madame Roselda Rifkin . . . and learns that, in order to sell the merchandise, Y' Gotta Display It! Depressed by his failures, Dick again meets Pussy . . . on Skid Row . . . and determines to sell Super Amalgamated Federated Woolgrants International. A happy accident colors his key samples red, blue, green and orange . . . and he sells them! Color is the Thing!, proclaims Dick on his return. All are so happy they join in The Latest twist. Dick becomes a Vice-President, and Colenat hits the road . . . to become a super-salesman. National Hooray forecasts a bright future for all.

*Makes 'em look real fine, but if they're
  not sold
Then the cupboard is bare!*

"Color Is the Thing!" is obliquely on-topic but doesn't mention the new colored keys. The most pertinent, yet also most awkward, song is "The Latest," which has a halfhearted rock *yeah yeah* feel and vocalists that get half a beat ahead of the piano.

*The latest twist! Who can resist?
Car keys in color made of aluminum!
To make 'em smile, it's got the style,
It's gonna make all our sales reports hum!*

Cast member Liz Seneff, from the charming Alcoa show, is largely wasted here. I hope Cole National at least gave her a heap of free car keys.

RARITY: 2

DEAL ME IN

U.S. Steel's very entertaining presentation at the 1961 convention of NADA (the National Automobile Dealers Association), promoted the benefits of modern steel in cars. The hilariously corny plot is studded with snappy songs by Bernie Wayne, cowriter of "Blue Velvet," who also wrote the familiar "Miss America" theme song and the "Chock Full o' Nuts" coffee jingle.

Auto dealer Mr. Rutt arrives at work, singing an insanely cheerful "Good Morning" song. Rutt explains to his cynical salesmen that something wonderful happened the night before. At home, tired and grumpy as usual, he'd sung about his depressing mail in "Bills and Magazines." His wife was also in a bad mood, dissatisfied with her husband, who should be

"DEAL ME IN"
a presentation of
UNITED STATES STEEL

33 1/3 RPM
LB-108

Not For
Broadcast

a feature of the
N.A.D.A. CONVENTION
San Francisco, California
January 28 - February 1, 1961

providing "Thrills and Limousines." But upon opening the mail, Rutt was intrigued to find a sales kit from U.S. Steel. Its mention of an automotive design research center sends Rutt into a reverie about what it would be like to run such a facility.

We need a new light steel for this new
*   model!*
The steel we have is older than King Tut!
— Let's change it! A pinch of this, a pinch
*   of that,*
There, that ought to do it! — You've done it
*   again, Mr. Rutt!*
— With two ts!

His wife, Martha, sings of her fantasy of being elected Woman of the Year at her club on the strength of Mr. Rutt's newfound success, noting "A vote for me is a vote for modern steel." As the Rutts compare their steel-themed fantasies, who should knock at the door but U.S. Steel representative Mr. Steelman, inquiring how Rutt liked the new sales kit. They invite him in and he sings about how men with dreams have built our country, using steel to create railroads, planes, and cars. Then he launches into a frenetic, upward-building musical description of steel production, from the mining of ore and the smelting of ingots,

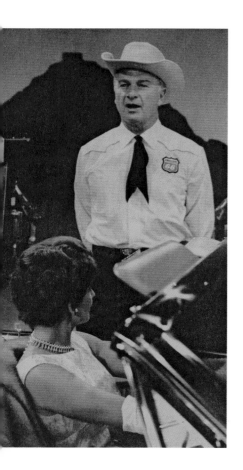

...up to the sheet mills! The pipe mills!
*   The plate mills!*
The rolling mills, the merchant mills, and
*   shape mills!*
The furnace making steel with that
*   modern slant!*
Then by train from the mill to the auto
*   plant!*
That's when the work on the auto starts!
Forging crankshafts, camshafts, steering
*   gear parts!*

Mr. Steelman explains U.S. Steel's new ad campaign, complete with pocket-size selling guides for all Rutt's salesmen. Upon hearing this thrilling tale from Rutt, the burned-out salesmen become fired up again.

It's simple arithmetic, your sales'll click,
You'll watch 'em zoom right up to the
*   blue,*
Sell steel — it sells for you!
You've got the pitch, start sellin'!
You've got the pitch, start sellin'!
You'll strike it rich, just leave it to steel!

A minor classic, with no cover, but with an engagingly ridiculous story and a handful of implausible songs that are better than they have any right to be.

RARITY: 1

MUSIC FROM "THE SPIRIT OF 66"

This obscure 1966 Phillips Petroleum flexi-disc contains just a few short uncredited dealer meeting songs, but there are a couple high-octane moments. In the borderline creepy title track, film and TV star Eddie Albert encourages dealers to make friends in the community.

We'll say, How do you do there?
How's your family? How are tricks?
I'm your friendly dealer down at
*   Phillips 66!*
I'd like to have your business,
Oh you lovely, lovely chicks!
I want to share the spirit, oh the Spirit
*   of 66!*

An anonymous lyricist turned out some memorable lines in "Friendliness Will Always Get You More."

When you're showing her the dipstick,
And she's making with the lipstick,
And all your fervent pleas she doth
*   ignore,*
Don't raise a hullabaloo, Bob,
Or you may not get her lube job!
And friendliness will always get you more!

If you'd like to find a copy, the disc was bound into the spring 1966 edition of the Phillips 66 employee magazine. Happy hunting!

RARITY: 1

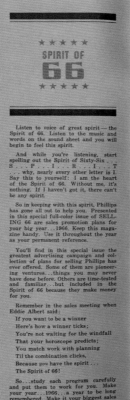

★★★★★
SPIRIT OF
66
★★★★★

Listen to voice of great spirit — the Spirit of 66. Listen to the music and words on the sound sheet and you will begin to feel this spirit.

And while you're listening, start spelling out the Spirit of Sixty-Six . . . S . . P . . I . . R . . I . . T . . . why, nearly every other letter is I. Say this to yourself: I am the heart of the Spirit of 66. Without me, it's nothing. If I haven't got it, there can't be any spirit.

So in keeping with this spirit, Phillips has gone all out to help you. Presented in this special full-color issue of SELLING 66 are sales promotion plans for your big year...1966. Keep this magazine handy. Use it throughout the year as your permanent reference.

You'll find in this special issue the greatest advertising campaign and collection of plans for selling Phillips has ever offered. Some of them are pioneering ventures...things you may never have done before. Others are time-tested and familiar...but included in the Spirit of 66 because they make money for you.

Remember in the sales meeting when Eddie Albert said:
If you want to be a winner
Here's how a winner ticks;
You're not waiting for the windfall
That your horoscope predicts;
You match work with planning
Til the combination clicks,
Because *you* have the spirit . . .
The Spirit of 66!

So...study each program carefully and put them to work for you. Make your year...1966...a year to be long remembered. Make it your biggest sales year with The Spirit of 66!

Spirit of 66

★★★★★★
DEALER
SALES
MEETING
★★★★★★

Everyone was stampeded with the spirit of 66 as Phillips marketing men conducted hundreds of dealer meetings in past weeks. The air was electrified with wholehearted enthusiasm as they unfolded Phillips big advertising campaign and sales promotion plans for 1966.

★ ★ ★ ★ ★ ★ ★ ★ ★ ★ ★

The sales meeting was the kind you'd expect Phillips 66 to have in '66 — the biggest and best year ever. Television stars Eddie Albert and Susan Barrett along with Minne Um-Hum and Phillips top management team played important roles in presenting this year's money-making marketing programs.

★ ★ ★ ★ ★ ★ ★ ★ ★ ★ ★

Heading this year's events is the week-long celebration beginning April 4. The special "Spirit of 66 Week" starts "The Gasoline That Won The West" advertising campaign across the nation. This is the week Phillips jobbers and dealers go calling on the general public so they will know it's 66 in '66.

★ ★ ★ ★ ★ ★ ★ ★ ★ ★ ★

At the meeting, a Show Program was distributed to all those in attendance. Each program was numbered. An April issue of the SALES-MAKER will contain a listing of numbers pulled out of a Stetson. If your program number jibes with one of them, you've won a new style "Gasoline That Won The West" service station uniform. And, since it's 66 in '66, one of the lucky numbers has already been pre-determined a winner. It's 6666. Do you have it?

★ ★ ★ ★ ★ ★ ★ ★ ★ ★ ★

The phonograph record attached contains the music and songs from the Spirit of 66. When you hear the music again . . . the songs were especially written for this show . . . it will bring to mind many of the production numbers. Remember how it went . . .

YOU'RE THE TOP

Oldsmobile's dealer announcement show for the '61 line was built around a selection of Cole Porter songs. In a rare move, Olds actually obtained Mr. Porter's permission, which is noted on the record label. Bill Hayes, costar of the '58 through '60 shows, had moved on, but Florence Henderson was back, knocking out swell versions of "Night and Day," "Blow, Gabriel, Blow," and "You're the Top." The songs are mostly unaltered, though the opening trumpet notes on "Blow, Gabriel, Blow" evoke "In My Merry Oldsmobile," and in "You're the Top" we're told that "TOP" is short for "Typical Olds Perfection." "Beauty Queen Medley" introduces

the latest 98 model, with exhortations to "Swing down, sweet 98," and encourages the salesmen to drink the Kool-Aid.

There's many more live rubber mountings
Between you and the bumps in the road!
The Skyrocket engine is standard,
   brother!
Olds can carry a load!
You'll fall in love with the new Olds
When you get behind the wheel,
If you really want to sell that car,
That's the way you gotta feel!

The plot seems to have involved a political campaign, which would have resonated in the late summer of 1960, but so far no program or Playbill has turned up to fill in the blanks. Also, all the Olds shows from '59 to '61 are invariably found without covers. They may have been part of training material boxed sets, in which the records just came in paper sleeves. Oldsmobile experts? Conspiracy theorists? Anyone?

RARITY: 2

THE MOST FABULOUS YEAR

This Cadillac ultra rarity doesn't look auspicious: the crude cover is put together with black tape, and a test pressing label adorns the one-sided disc. But when I dropped the needle onto the vinyl, I was in for a surprise: the four '62 introduction show songs by James Fagas and Edward Reveaux are delightful. And rather than the big bombastic orchestra, Cadillac plays it cool with a small combo and a cast of three, recorded with sparkling clarity.

The opening number, "The Most Fabulous Year," sounds like a standard-issue shot of industrial optimism, until the twist: it's 1902,

and the cast has been praising the very first Cadillac. "Meet the Man" is a reminder that salesmen need to be proactive:

> *Get out and meet the man! Tip your hat to*
> *   people!*
> *Cover ground, don't sit around*
> *Like an unwanted parcel in the lost-and-*
> *   found!*
> *Make it part of your Cadillac plan to meet*
> *   the man!*

Top honors go to the brilliantly swingy and catchy "We're Thinking of You."

> *Service! Service! Man your stations!*
> *It's the answer to better customer relations!*
> *They've been having work done*
> *   somewhere, take it from me.*
> *But that somewhere's really nowhere, in*
> *   quality.*
> *Get those owners coming through,*
> *Get 'em all, not just a few,*
> *And we'll even take those Lincolns too!*

Sadly, this appears to be the only Cadillac show ever to make it onto a record. More material like this, with a nicer cover, could have made Cadillac the industrial show "Standard of the World."

RARITY: 1

GOT IT MADE

For the '62 model year, Ford issued a unique presentation of a forgettable show. Three small flexi-discs are bound into the souvenir program and booklet. The hole in the eye of the gentleman on the cover goes straight through, allowing the whole booklet to be placed on a record player. The program pictures stars

such as Harpo Marx and Mickey Rooney; however, those big names were apparently in separate film portions and weren't involved with the music. The songs are rewrites of familiar hits: "Everything's Coming Up Roses," now "Everything's Coming Up Money," and "My Heart Belongs to Daddy," now "My Heart Belongs to Fairlane." The lyrics are by Edward Eliscu, who'd written songs for movies such as *Flying Down to Rio*. Eliscu was at this point still unable to find work in Hollywood after being blacklisted in the early 1950s. Industrial shows: a lifeline for victims of political oppression!

RARITY: 2

Hank Beebe, c. 1975

Pitman, New Jersey, native Harold "Hank" Beebe was born in 1926 and showed musical talent at an early age. During his World War II navy stint, he spent his off hours organizing and playing in musical groups, and after the war he earned a master's degree in music composition from the University of North Carolina. By the mid-1950s, Hank was in New York City, playing his own songs at nightclubs and looking for a break. An agent encouraged him to try out for "the Chevy show"—the first Hank had ever heard of industrials. After beating out several established Broadway composers, Hank wrote the '57 show music, Chevy's first introduction show with original music and lyrics. Hank recalls a cast of thirty-six and a $3 million budget—far higher than the budget for a Broadway show of the time.

During an industrial lull in 1961, Hank met Bill Heyer on an off-Broadway revue, and they wound up working together for nearly twenty years until Bill's death in 1980. Newark, New Jersey, native Bill was a trumpet player, comedian, and actor, and he performed in many of their industrials as well as writing the lyrics and comedy material.

Hank was straitlaced; Bill was a loose cannon. Hank recalls the dress rehearsal of their first American Motors show, attended by the top

RAMBLER '64

GOING GREAT!

...WITH THAT RAMBLER SPIRIT!

THE HIT SONGS FROM THE '64 ANNOUNCEMENT SHOW
BY THE ORIGINAL CAST

Directed by: Julian Stein
Lyrics: Bill Heyer
Music: Harold Beebe

TO BE USED BY RAMBLER DEALERS AND SALESMEN IN SHOWROOMS DURING PUBLIC ANNOUNCEMENT OF THE '64 RAMBLERS

THE CAST

John C. Becher	E. J. Peaker	Jack Manning
Hal Linden	Kelli Scott	Eric Barnes
Gina Penn	Bob Brooks	Dick Hermany
Marilyne Mason	Bruce Kirby	Ray Hyson

As performed in MIAMI BEACH · DALLAS · NEW YORK · LOS ANGELES · SAN FRANCISCO · CHICAGO

This recording is not to be used for radio or television broadcasts or other commercial usage.

GOING GREAT!

Going Great!, the '64 Rambler announcement show, was the first Hank Beebe–Bill Heyer collaboration to be recorded, and the first of four shows they wrote for AMC/Rambler. Two disappeared without a trace, but we have the fine *AM Route 66* show as well as this one. *Going Great!* has less material, and a lesser cover, compared to the later show, but the songs are big, tuneful, and fun. "That Rambler Spirit" has a euphoric brassy strut.

That Rambler spirit, it doesn't disappear, it
Gets you from the minute you hear it,
That makes Rambler unique!
Management—(they've got the spirit!)
Dealers and salesmen—(they've got
*   the spirit!)*
Rambler people are a special kind,
They all have a one-car mind!

"1964-Ward March" is a high-steppin' tribute to the upscale Ambassador, with a hall-of-fame rhyme.

> *Your word for '64 is luxury,*
> *In the greatest Ambassador of all!*
> *I must admit she's brought some luck*
>   *to me,*
> *How could anyone pass a door*
> *Where they sell an Ambassador?*

The Ambassador rates an additional song, the super-suave "Easy on the Eyes," performed by Hal Linden. The restyled compact American is introduced as the "Star of the Show." The mid-range Classic is touted in "Comin' around Every Corner," sung by Bob Brooks.

> *You'll recognize it a mile away,*
> *It'll take your smiling rival's smile away,*
> *Comin' around every corner in '64.*
> *Now, I've been selling Ramblers for years,*
> *Must be eight now,*
> *And every year I get a little bit prouder,*
> *I was proud of the Classic Six,*
> *And proud we've got the eight now,*
> *Which somehow makes me want to shout*
>   *it all the louder!*

Two of the songs are repeated several times on the flip side, an unusual move apparently tied to the cover's suggestion that the record be played in Rambler showrooms. "No thanks, I'm not in the market for a new car. I just like the music!"

RARITY: 3

MUSIC FROM "AM ROUTE 66 (FOR FRIENDLY GIANT-KILLERS)"

Under George Romney (Mitt's dad), American Motors' Rambler brand became a strong contender in the late '50s as America developed an appetite for smaller cars. By the mid-'60s, the company had de-emphasized the Rambler name and was trying to compete with the Big Three on luxury as well as economy. Even if the cars themselves didn't prove to be "giant-killers," the '66 model year show is top notch, a typically rollicking Hank Beebe–Bill Heyer tour de force. The jolly "Friendly Giant-Killers" threatens rivals with a flurry of rhymes and wordplay.

> *We're courteous, nice, but Mustang*
>   *beware!*
> *Easy-going swell, 'til we smell a Corvair!*
> *Our favorite food is Barracuda—*
> *Include a Chevy II too!*
> *From now on, Friendly Giant-Killers,*
> *Friendly Giant-Killers is our role!*
> *Unless your name is GM, Ford, or Chrysler,*
> *We're kind as Old King Cole!*
> *A dirge for Dodge we're all gonna sing,*
> *The Dart'll come apart when we start*
>   *to swing.*
> *We'll make the Fairlane their loss, our gain*
> *Outsell Chevelle as well!*

The station wagons rate a stirring western-themed anthem, "Classic Wagon Train." We learn "A Woman Has a Right to Change Her Mind" when confronted with the sporty Marlin fastback. The larger, more luxurious Ambassador is the subject of an amazing love

brass. Just before the show started, Bill, in a panama hat, loud floral-print shirt, shorts, and sandals, strode up the aisle, pointed at the CEO, and barked, "Don't screw with me, I can buy and sell you," and kept on walking. Everyone gasped in horror, except for the CEO, who was shaking with laughter. Soon all the other guys in suits were roaring along with the boss. Hank: "Bill took that chance, and we got three more shows."

In addition to their long string of first-rank industrials, most of which were not recorded, Hank and Bill wrote commercials and an off-Broadway revue, *Tuscaloosa's Calling Me...But I'm Not Going!* This award-winning 1975 show, which grew out of an earlier industrial show, was "successful every way but financially." The pair then worked on the Broadway musical *Hellzapoppin'*, but the show closed out of town during previews.

After Bill's death, Hank continued writing industrials for a couple more years until the work dried up. He moved to Portland, Maine, where he remains active, with a library of more than four hundred published sacred choral works and many other songs and productions to his credit.

Hank: "We all gave these projects our best shot, not only because we were well paid for it, but because we took pride in our professionalism."

I'VE GOT A SILVER MACHINE

If the names Beebe and Heyer come up a lot in these pages, it's for the same reason that Andersson and Ulvaeus figure so prominently in histories of Swedish pop music, and the same goes for Gilbert and Sullivan in operetta, Buchanan and Goodman in comedy "drop-in" records, et al: they're the masters, second to none in the art and craft of this form's particular, deceptively tricky requirements.

"Doing the Ambassador" is the duo's take on rock 'n' roll, and as such it's strictly L-7. But in one of those conventional-wisdom-shattering perspective shifts with which this book has repeatedly blown your mind (admit it), this is some very hip squareness, indeed. Dig: on one hand, take something like the Sherman Brothers' "Let's Get Together" from *The Parent Trap*; on the other take "It's a Gas" by Alfred E. Neuman. The former, a nostalgic recording for many who enjoyed the Disney movie as tots, certainly has its charms, but "rock" it most certainly don't. Now, the Neuman side (composed by Norman Blagman and Sam Bobrick, the Beebe and Heyer of "free in this issue of *MAD* magazine" novelty records) employs a comparably lumpen faux-rock beat, but it has certain "extras" going for it: the record itself is cardboard square, for one thing, a conceptual masterstroke. King Curtis on sax takes it a long distance further and, decisively, the music's actual *hook* is some guy *belching*. I mean, c'mon, right?

So back to Hank and Bill. Sure, "Doing the Ambassador" is nerdy: it's a dance number about a luxury automobile, and even if, as *Motor Trend* magazine observed, the '66 DPL model with a 327 engine "definitely has snap we hadn't felt before," it's still a dance number about a luxury automobile, doomed to dickdom along with similar promo-dance attempts like Gary Lewis's dire "Doin' the Flake" for Kellogg's. But hold the phone: check those strangely emphatic rhythmic disruptions on the pickups (where the singers go "Wiiiith a..." and "Wheeeen they..."), which probably establish some wild and weird time signature that I promise to elaborate upon in future, expanded editions of this book. Remind me.

As the tune goes along, one becomes aware of the ceaseless, as-one attack of every performer, from the singers screaming bloody murder to the pumping pianist and lip-splitting reedmen. It never lets up, eventually placing it alongside Deep Purple's "Highway Star" and Judas Priest's "Heading Out to the Highway" as high-intensity car rock of the first rank. Finally, if you can listen to lyrics like "When you're doin' the Ambassador, the Ambassador is doing you proud" without imagining smutty rewrites concerning Shirley Temple Black, then maybe you just don't *get* rock 'n' roll.

—SM

c from _AM_ Route 66
(friendly Giant-Killers)

American Motors dealer announcement show

AM ROUTE 66

Ambassador Marlin Classic American

song, the lush "Big and Beautiful," sung by Chuck Green.

> *Once in a while, we get to see a great car,*
> *That's what you've come to be, a great car.*
> *You're big and beautiful, bold and*
> *   beautiful,*
> *We're sold on you, beautiful Ambassador.*
> *And did you stay satisfied with all the*
> *   public said?*
> *No, you went out and got more beautiful*
> *   instead!*
> *How great you are, is what we want to*
> *   tell you,*
> *And boy, it's such a joy to sell you!*

The Ambassador also gets a rip-roarin' dance craze number, "Doing the Ambassador." "Demonstrate" employs a pungent metaphor.

> *I know a girl who was almost engaged,*
> *But her fiancé she enraged, by saying*
> *"When we're married you can kiss me, not*
> *   till then."*
> *He never came back again!*
> *Everybody got to demonstrate,*
> *   demonstrate,*
> *Gotta let them get the feel!*
> *Everybody got to demonstrate,*
> *   demonstrate,*
> *You're ahead, when they're behind the*
> *   wheel!*

The economical American is serenaded by three lonely gas pumps in "Hello American."

> *Do we like the new American? We love it!*
> *But we don't see enough of it!*
> *Waitin' for Americans, we could rust,*
> *Covered in cobwebs, knee-deep in dust!*
> *We're glad their business isn't all we've got,*
> *'Cause their tanks—just a memory...*

For just that line, the melody shifts to "Thanks for the Memory."

This show is the first known instance of African-American cast members in an industrial, prompted by American Motors starting to employ African-American salesmen. Hank Beebe says they got some hard looks at a hotel in the South.

The Big Three giants finally killed American Motors in the 1980s, but it put up a brave musical fight.

RARITY: 3

1965 CHEVROLET SHOW MUSIC

Although this uncredited show on a 10-inch disc was for a blue-chip company during the heart of the industrial show golden age, producer Jam Handy doesn't seem to have been trying very hard. "Whatever America Wants in a Car, It Gets in a Chevrolet" is decent, but it sounds as if various Jam Handy songs from earlier Coke and Ford Tractor shows have been run through a blender and poured into a new title. "Adaptability," about the truck line, is also okay but may already have been a Jam Handy trunk song, since a version turns up in 1972 for Timken bearings. The best of the bunch is "The Corvair Song," a slinky, pseudo-beatnik ode to Chevy's rear-engined compact, which would soon be doomed by Ralph Nader's book *Unsafe at Any Speed.*

> *If you're ever going to swing, mister, swing,*
> *The car is the thing,*
> *That's gotta prove you're in the groove*
> *And not out in outer space!*
> *This baby's got class! We're sure to make*
> *   Joysville,*

158

GREAT GOING AHEAD!

● 1965. A new model year of promise and opportunity.

The Chevrolet dealerships that profit most from the opportunity will be those who, through continuous training, have developed a team of knowledgeable and enthusiastic people to mind the store.

To help you strengthen your dealership team during the months ahead, Communication will bring you complete training with fresh approaches and new ideas on important topics for all dealership departments.

1965 CHEVROLET SHOW MUSIC!

On this record, the smash hits — words & music — that set the tempo for 1965 selling action.

NEW CAR DELIVERY

FOLLOW-UP SELLING

BEATING THE COMPETITION

BETTER CLOSING

HOW TO SELL TO WOMEN

BUILDING ENTHUSIASM

NEW CAR CONDITIONING

ACCURATE QUALIFYING

SELLING SERVICE

SUPER CHEVROLET SERVICE

BUILDING OWNER LOYALTY

POSITIVE PROSPECTING

MANAGING TIME

PRODUCT INFORMATION

SELF-DEVELOPMENT

COMMUNICATION '65!

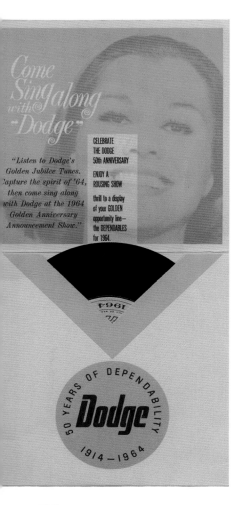

Let's — write! Let's — write! Ratify 'em, gratify 'em, let's write!

The rest of the track is a negotiation between a dealer and a customer who waves off the compact Dart, the standard Dodge, and even the top-of-the-line 880, demanding something bigger.

*It looks like the dealer is out of luck!
What's a little bit bigger?
  — You mean...? — A truck!
Let's write, let's write, write it up right,
Let's write another truck sale, well all
  right!
Write it in the daytime, write it at night,
And you won't get left as long as you
  write!*

The show also included fraternal twins "What a Thrill to Buy an Automobile" and "What a Thrill to Sell an Automobile," as well as "What Have We Got," which provides an overview of the whole line for '64 and includes rhymes for *Polara* such as *tiara* and *Aunt Clara*.

RARITY: 3

THE 1970 DODGE ANNOUNCEMENT SHOW

This late 1969 show boasts a translucent red vinyl 7-inch disc, a hip cartoony cover, and some high-quality material. Like the '64 Dodge show, it's uncredited, but again no match for my amateur sleuthing. I thought it sounded like the work of Hank Beebe and Bill Heyer, and a call to Hank confirmed it. Bill Heyer faced the same challenge that Michael Brown had six years earlier: rhymes for *Polara*. His solution

*While all of the rest are hopelessly square!
So take a tip from the all-time hipster, the
  car with the flair,
It's the all-new '65 Corvair!*

Giant corporations trying to understand what the young people think is hip: that's my kind of Joysville.

RARITY: 2

MUSIC TO SELL DODGES "BUY"

Dodge's 1964 golden anniversary show might have remained anonymous forever had I not seen a copy of the 7-inch record in the archives at Michael Brown's Manhattan home. Listening to it with that knowledge, it immediately sounds Brownian, and his voice is discernible in the unusual "Let's Write." Against a thundering drum background, the cast chants:

*Qualify 'em, classify 'em, satisfy 'em,
  pacify 'em,
Amplify 'em, clarify 'em, multiply 'em,
  verify 'em,*

is one of the loopiest chunks of lyrics in all industrialdom, encompassing both poet John Keats and novelist Margaret Mitchell:

> **Truth is beauty, and beauty is Polara**
> **Scarlett O'Hara**
> **Never has gone with the wind**
> **Like Polara goes on with the wind.**

"Dart" claimed Dodge's compact car would help guys score with chicks.

> **It's the new young thing to do the Dart**
> ** game**
> **When you want to swing, you do the Dart**
> ** game**
> **Gets you to your favorite patch of beach**
> **And the girls who seem so hard to reach**
> **Dig you…in a Dart they dig you.**

Maybe, but a few years later, the creators of *The Dukes of Hazzard* didn't put Bo and Luke in a Dart; they put them in a Dodge Charger. With nimble horns, a stinging guitar solo, and adventurous rhymes, "Charger Charges On" suits the legendary muscle car.

> **Put this Charger up against competitors,**
> **Then call all the nation's leading editors.**
> **Just let 'em choose their own glowin'**
> ** metaphors.**
> **Charger charges on!**

Truth is beauty, and beauty is rhyming *competitors*, *editors*, and *metaphors*.

RARITY: 3

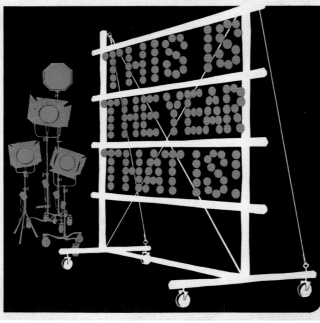

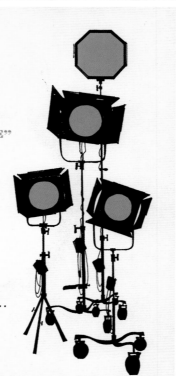

**"THIS IS THE
YEAR THAT IS"**
●●●●●●●●●●●●●●●●●●●●●
SIDE 1

"THIS IS THE YEAR"
The beginning of a great New Year . . .
New Products . . .
New Styling . . .
New Markets . . .
Designed for the Prosperous Mid-Sixties!

"SOMETHING FOR EVERYONE"
The 1965 Plymouth Family . . .
The Roaring '65's . . .
Plymouth Fury . . .
Plymouth Belvedere . . .
Plymouth Valiant . . .
Plymouth Barracuda.

"NEW STAR IN THE SKY"
The Plymouth Belvedere for 1965 . . .
A new way to swing without going out on a limb!

SIDE 2

"STRETCH"
Introducing the big 1965 Plymouth Fury . . .
It's the flame on the torch . . .
The plushiest Plymouth ever built.

"MOVE UP TO CHRYSLER"
Announcing the most beautiful Chrysler ever built . . .
Model 1965!

"FINALE"
This is the Year Your Sales Will Soar
This Is The Year You've Been Waiting For
Truly . . . THIS IS THE YEAR THAT IS!

CHRYSLER-PLYMOUTH DIVISION ⬥ **CHRYSLER** MOTORS CORPORATION

DOUBLE SHOT: THIS IS THE YEAR THAT IS! AND SWING-UP 1966

The music on these '65 and '66 shows by Walter Marks, on 7-inch records, alternates between swingin' and youthful for Plymouth and sedately elegant for Chrysler. Many of the songs mention "bigness," since in '65 Plymouth was reversing an ill-advised 1962 downsizing move. Although most of the songs appear to be originals, the tune for "Something for Everyone" was borrowed from "Comedy Tonight," the opening number from *A Funny Thing Happened on the Way to the Forum*. The Plymouth model names inspired some unusual rhymes:

> *Come judge a Fury, you be the jury,*
> *Something for everyone, the roaring '65s!*
> *Come on and leer at this Belvedere*
> *Some happy family takes it from here.*
> *We're asking you'ta try Barracuda,*
> *Come take a Valiant for a drive.*
> *Sixty different Plymouths born in '65!*

"Swing-Up" is a memorable concoction of economics and smut. A woman tosses in breathy interjections that must have been puns about her large breasts.

> *The growth in industry is gonna be*
> *   outstanding!*
> *The whole economy is gonna be*
> *   (ooh . . . expanding.)*
> *What opportunity there's gonna be to*
> *   sell up!*
> *Your high hopes you can fill because*
> *   business will (ooh . . . develop.)*
> *And Chrysler-Plymouth's in this boom*
> *   that we've discussed,*
> *So join this business boom! (Don't ever*
> *   think about bust!)*

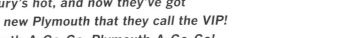

the stars of the show
in their order
of appearance...

IMPERIAL:
*The finest of
the fine cars built by
Chrysler Corporation.*

CHRYSLER:
*If the '65 broke
all sales records,
think what the '66 will do.*

PLYMOUTH:
*Let yourself Go: Plymouth '66
—All New FURYS, BELVEDERES,
VALIANTS, BARRACUDAS . . .
PLUS VIP—A VERY IMPORTANT PLYMOUT*

Entire Presentation produced and directed by KERBAWY-MP.

Big corporations and rock and roll are always an iffy mix, but Chrysler-Plymouth proves that The Man can very nearly get hip with "Plymouth-A-Go-Go," billed as "the latest dance craze." Wailing horns, crashing drums, and tasty guitar licks back up the raucous corporate message.

You wanna step with all those swingers,
You wanna ride the newest rage?

You better latch on to the latest,
Like the lady in the cage!
The Valiant is a winner,
The Barracuda is a fastback with utility!
The Fury's hot, and now they've got
A fine new Plymouth that they call the VIP!
Plymouth-A-Go-Go, Plymouth-A-Go-Go!

Plymouth-a-going-going-gone, as of 2001.

RARITY: 3 (both)

The stage setting for BFG's 12 sales meetings.

Joan Dunham explains The Tire Value Calculator.

"Nice to know a man you can trust..."

THAT'S THE SIGNPOST UP AHEAD

Submitted for your approval: an essay in graphic chaos, in which any expectations of coherence in color, proportion, or perspective...any reliable standards of geometric and typographical consonance are skewed seven ways from Sunday. A nightmarish chimera of incompatible imagery in which Brobdingnagian middle-aged men loom above cerulean-hued simulacra of Frank, Shirley, and Dean, whose very shadows seem to spell the word "HIT." Optimistic promise? Or brutal threat?

Observe Akron-based O. K. Lynn, shown on the very eve of his fortieth year of service to B.F. Goodrich, raising a point of mutual interest to the smiling, nametagged W. B. Flora, then unaware that his son William would, in two decades, take one Susan Kramer as his lawfully wedded wife in Wilmington, Delaware, a long drive from Akron, across the entire state of Pennsylvania...though by then, Flora *père* would be retired to Florida, an even greater distance, not only of miles but of mind-set.

Here, though, long before all that, in the eternal, urgent NOW of an album cover, witness the ominous spectacle of General Managers (Dealer Sales and Retail Sales, respectively) as twin Colossi: mossy overlords of an empire built on bald ambition, sheer guts, and the pursuit of traction. Behind the stolid ambiguity of the men's expressions, sickly green clouds gather, pervading the very air with an acrid tang of utter malevolence. Here is the "Push, push, push" world of American Business made terrifyingly manifest... the insistent drumbeat *pounding*, pounding...was that scream I heard only inside my head?

No, it's not fair to blame the General Managers; they're no different. The Tire Game has them as dead to rights as anyone. We're all just playing the hand we're dealt, and it looks like aces and eights to me. But what, then, shall be our comfort? Yes, of course, bread and circuses. Let's train our wizened gaze upon the entertainers as they gambol and cavort in the spotlight for our "amusement." And for god's sake, let us be "amused" enough to forget that other spotlight: the one that follows any fool impetuous enough to try to escape this veritable prison camp of the soul that some call Big Rubber.

—SM

BFG Retailers at the Atlanta meeting.

B.F. Goodrich

1966 SALES MEETING

O. K. LYNN, BFG'S
GENERAL MANAGER
OF DEALER SALES.

W. B. FLORA, BFG'S
GENERAL MANAGER
OF RETAIL SALES.

The responsive audience at The New York sales meeting.

Dave Shelley, Joan Dunham, and Tom Elrod in ad writing skit.

BFG retailers from Dallas and Houston zones at the Dallas meeting.

"Hey, MATA HARI! I'm leaving . . ."

B.F. GOODRICH 1966 SALES MEETING

Even if the disc inside were blank, that Stalinist cover would be worth seeking out. And while much of the live recording is devoted to speech excerpts, there are a few decent musical moments with uncredited original material performed by a three-person cast.

The theme of the show, and of the 1966 advertising campaign, was "Straight Talk," an admission that tire dealers had a reputation on par with that of used car dealers. In the "Straight Talk" song, all tire dealers, even the BFG guys in the audience, are said to be guilty of "playing games." BFG insists that company leadership will set a better example.

> *From this moment on, we're gonna talk*
> *   straight,*
> *It's the way to make profits congregate!*
> *In the tire trade, it's something that's*
> *   really new,*
> *We're gonna talk straight talk to you.*

The most interesting song from a thematic point of view is "A Girl Who's Making It Big." A lazy truck and industrial tire salesman is shocked to find that he's been replaced by a woman, who sings:

> *When I'm sellin' tires, I know what to say,*
> *My sales will climb higher and higher*
> *   each day.*
> *My selling has turned out great, chum*
> *They like hearing talk that's straight, from*
> *A girl who's making it big in this great big*
> *   man's world!*

It's a scenario that was played for laughs, as all the speeches by BFG executives are addressed to men. As in, "Gentlemen, we need sales and profits in 1966 — will you help us do the job?" The response: moderately enthusiastic applause!

Despite the fact that the show played in twelve cities to more than 3,500 company personnel, only a couple copies have ever turned up. Maybe the recipients threw the records away because the cover gave them nightmares.

RARITY: 1

THE ESSO '68 EXTRA

Like the International Harvester show *Hitting a New High*, this is a British 7-incher with songs by the team of Michael Sammes and American ex-pat Herb Kanzell. Esso gas station owners received a mixture of flattery and pressure.

> *All the campaigns and all the plans, how*
> *Well they succeed is in your hands now.*
> *You hold the key to extra impact all*
> *   across the nation.*
> *You are the most important man, sir,*
> *You are the man who's got to answer*
> *When opportunity knocks at your own*
> *   Esso station.*

Esso still exists as a brand in the UK and elsewhere, but in the U.S., Esso became Exxon on January 1, 1973. The cutting-edge futuristic new name is now over forty years old.

RARITY: 2

RUN FOR THE MONEY

This 1969 Gulf Oil Canada show was allegedly "the funniest, fastest-moving, most star-packed show of its kind ever to hit the stage in Canada." I'm not in a position to disagree.

The comedy team Wayne and Shuster (pictured on the cover) provided the star power, although they're not a major part of the record. Several uncredited songs are crammed onto the 7-inch disc, and they're pleasant enough, with a youthful, "with-it" feel. "You Gotta Look Good" is in the tradition of industrial show tunes about women displaying their assets as a metaphor for product merchandising. "We Hurry" is in the vein of other oil company show songs, encouraging the dealers to provide prompt customer service. "The Most Important Person" is typical dealer flattery.

> *You can have your directors, accountants, and inspectors,*
> *Titles don't mean a thing to me.*
> *'Cause my admiration is for the feller with the station,*
> *The feller who's the seller is the VIP.*

One more observation to ponder:

> *Just like a sexy Swedish movie*
> *Gulf is comin' on real groovy!*

Once it's been pointed out, the similarity is obvious.

RARITY: 2

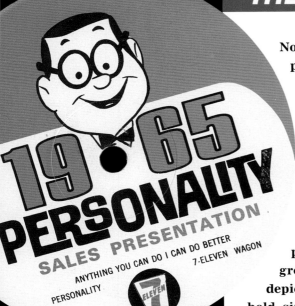

THE CHEER LEADER

Not so very long after 7-Eleven produced the show that produced this album, the convenience store chain made a big national splash with the introduction of the Slurpee, described on a 1967 promotional single "Dance the Slurp" as "The Wildest...The Kookiest...The Grooviest...The Slurpiest," but here in 1965 there's nothing especially wild, particularly kooky, or even vaguely groovy/slurpy about the character depicted on this cover, let alone the bold, simple design he and his inane grin inhabit. (Wouldn't the whole thing look great printed on an inflatable pillow, though?) No, this cheerful little fella symbolized an era rapidly passing, and perhaps a word about another symbol might clarify matters.

J. R. "Bob" Dobbs, the pipe-smoking godhead of the Church of the SubGenius, was a salesman (drilling equipment, as it happens). Dobbs, prophet of Slack and central figure of the twentieth century's most profound and beautiful spiritual movement, is always represented as the sort of half dad–half cad dreamboat who informed the aspirations of midcentury suburban strivers and haunted the fantasies of their wives, whose beehived heads buzzed with new and confusing possibilities courtesy of Helen Gurley Brown and Searle pharmaceuticals.

Of course, the no-nonsense mind of the average American salesman knew that it was not his lot to flaunt the insouciance of that grin-gripped pipe; far be it from him to try and strut about with the ineffable confidence possessed by the drill-gear guru named Dobbs. No, he'd content himself with being a buddy, a sidekick, a kind of Tony Randall to "Bob" Dobbs's Rock Hudson, getting by on—yep—personality.

Which is, of course, the title of 7-Eleven stores' 1965 show album, and our bespectacled pal on the cover is a perfect illustration of the kind of Second Banana Dorketype I mean. A bit Wally Cox nebbishy, a bit William Daniels uptight, but 100 percent eager to convince that he`s 100 percent eager. Perhaps if we're more honest with ourselves, we'll admit that all the gambits and ploys we employ in this crazy race, Life, can't really compete with simple cheerfulness. Maybe a little trust in one's own "personality" really is all it takes to find the grooviness and...heh heh...*slurpiness* within us all.

Let those who would sell drilling equipment sell it, and may Providence supply them all the glamour and all the glitz they can handle; think I'd rather shake the hand of the man whose friendly smile promises twenty-four-hour availability of beer and smokes at a reasonable price.

—SM

PERSONALITY

7-Eleven's 1965 Southwestern Division show has a great cover, but it's a minor item. There are just three uncredited songs, and at least two are rewrites, though they're nicely executed. "7-Eleven Wagon" is an adaptation of "The Wells Fargo Wagon" from *The Music Man*, and "Anything You Can Do (I Can Do Better)" is a version of the *Annie Get Your Gun* classic with two feuding store owners.

> *I can sell a wiener!*
> > *My school supplies are cleaner!*
>
> *I sell candy!*
> > *My cold cuts are dandy!*

The argument escalates to include gunfire and warplane sound effects. It may have been the soundtrack to an animated film; the character on the cover looks like he belongs in a cartoon. "Personality" is a rallying cry to store managers:

> *The store that gleams from floor to*
> > *ceiling,*
>
> *Point of sale that's packed with feeling,*
> *That's what makes the competition cry!*
> *An ice cream chest filled to the top!*
> *The freshest bread, the coldest pop!*
> *That's what makes 'em walk right in*
> > *and buy!*

An inspiration to three-fingered storekeepers everywhere.

RARITY: 1

MATTEL-ZA-POPPIN!

Writing original music and lyrics is the way to earn true industrial glory. But if you're going to do a song parody show, make it as goofy as this 1964 Mattel show. Also helpful is a cool label and a cover that gets your eye-za-poppin'. My copy also happens to be autographed on the back by Mattel founder Elliot Handler and his wife, Ruth, who created Barbie.

The titles of the uncredited parodies tell you most of what you need to know: "There's No Business Like Toy Business," "Everything's Coming Up Barbie," "76 Plastic Molds."

The latter is about the Vac-U-Form toy that allowed kids to mold things out of sheets of styrene plastic. "Chat Chat Chatty" borrows the music from "Toot Toot Tootsie" for the Chatty Cathy doll. "Never on a Sunday" reviews the comprehensive weekly lineup of Mattel television commercials and ends up admitting that in fact some do air on Sunday. The "Baby Pattaburp Song" borrows the tune of "My Favorite Things" to deliver a noteworthy rhyme:

> **When you feed her from her bottle, milk**
> ** will disappear.**
> **The baby accepts this,**
> **But later she crepses,**
> **She belches right in [BELCH] your ear.**

Crepses appears to be a mangling of *crepitus*, meaning the sound produced by the grinding of joints or gas inside the body. Certainly high on anyone's list of favorite things.

The crowning glory of comedy torture is "Twelve Days of Christmas." Various annoying childlike and/or cartoonish voices run through a list of Mattel toys their true loves gave to them, including Barbie, Vac-U-Form, Larry

Lion, Magnatel, and plenty more. It goes on for a long time. I've listened to some lengthy, challenging industrial show tunes, but this is the only one I've never gotten all the way through.

You win, Mattel. *Mattel-za-Poppin!* broke me.

RARITY: 2

BOLD NEW BREED: SOUNDS OF THE SIXTIES

This 1969 Arrow Shirt Company record is a bit of an anomaly. Sure, it's loaded up with sales meeting songs but, as the spoken introduction informs us, they're favorite sales meeting songs from the entire preceding decade! It's the only industrial show greatest hits album!

Some of the uncredited songs may actually be originals. "Mach II (March Meeting)" and "Mach II (August Meeting)" are modern soulful rockers, appropriate for Arrow's excitingly patterned Mach II dress shirts. "Father's Day," "Power of Fashion," and "Decton Practicality" are stodgier numbers about the polyester-cotton no-iron shirt. The real fun is in the over-the-top song rewrites, such as "Impossible Dream."

> **To dream the impossible dream, to**
> ** increase sales by 20 percent,**
> **To check stock, and to fill in the staples,**
> **To make sure sport shirts keep getting**
> ** sold...**

Simon & Garfunkel get industrialized in "Here's to You."

> **Doo doo doo doo doo, do all you can**
> **To capture a larger share!**

SOUNDS OF THE SIXTIES
A PRELUDE TO THE SOARING 70's

"All of us at The Arrow Company wish you and your families a happy Holiday Season and great success in the New Year."

Norbert G Schmidt

Art —Ron Naar

SIDE ONE

WHEREVER YOU GO
ANN VIVIAN AND CHARLES BARLOW

FATHER'S DAY
ANN VIVIAN

HOW TO SELL SHIRTS
ANN VIVIAN AND CHARLES BARLOW

DECTON PRACTICALITY
ANN VIVIAN

POWER OF FASHION
ANN VIVIAN AND CHARLES BARLOW

BOLD NEW BREED
ENSEMBLE

 Produced by
Management Communications, Inc.
270 Madison Ave. New York, N.Y. 10016 MU 5-1477

SIDE TWO

MACH II (MARCH MEETING)

IMPOSSIBLE DREAM
DOYLE NEWBERRY

HERE'S TO YOU
ELLEN KOLE

GONNA' BUILD A MARKET
ELLEN AND DOYLE

MONDAY SHIRT
ELLEN KOLE

DECOY SONG
DOYLE NEWBERRY

PAYDAY SHIRT
ELLEN KOLE

MACH II (AUGUST MEETING)

Music arranged and conducted
by Lee Norris

Get with the youth crowd eighteen to
thirty-four!
'Cause we've got the fashion in fancier
knits,
We're gonna sell them!
Every way we can, we're gonna score!
So here's to you, Arrow salesmen,
Arrow loves you more than you will know,
Whoa whoa whoa.

Distributed to Arrow employees in December 1969, the record concludes with wishes for a Merry Christmas and a Happy New Year and success in "the soaring '70s." Locating any Arrow industrials from the soaring '70s has so far proved to be an impossible dream.

RARITY: 2

BOLD NEW BREED

the no iron shirt.

Dector perma-iron.

Much it

the shirt that went
around the world without a wrinkle.

The Industrial Show Rhyme Hall of Fame

Why does the business of kitchen
utilities
Cause hypertension to make me feel
ill at ease?

> 1958 Westinghouse appliance
> show *the shape of tomorrow*

How could anyone pass a door
Where they sell an Ambassador?

> 1964 Rambler announcement
> show *Going Great!*

Slow speed fan, enclosed compressor
Make the customer say "Yessir"

> 1968 York air conditioner show
> *Up from the Valleys*

To waterproof a parasol
To help the spray from aerosol

> 1973 GE Silicones show
> *Got to Investigate Silicones*

Cups from Scott and not from Lily
Not from Dixie, don't be silly
Not from Sweetheart or Monsanto
Or Conex or the Continental Can Co.

> 1966 Scott Paper Corporation
> album *Music to Dispense With*

Our competitor says in a thin voice,
"We do this, but we don't do that!"
So for one operation, one invoice,
York is where it's at!

> 1969 York air conditioner show
> *Million Dollar Opportunity*

So keep your parchment and papyrus
For just one thing am I desirous

> 1969 International Paper
> Company show *Dolls Alive!*

The guy who thinks he's still just peddlin'
groceries
Is gonna get an awful lot of no-sirree's

> 1969 Durkee Foods show
> *Thought for Food — Food for Thought*

Though a married female's problems may
be myriad,
Thanks to us she can usually expect her
period

> 1971 Ortho Pharmaceuticals show
> *The Challenge of Change*

And from the Industrial Show Rhyme Hall of
Shame:

A round toe last and a wedge heel
The first children's wedge heel

> 1971 Keds National
> Sales Meeting show

HEY, LOOK! ANOTHER... *John Russell* "INDUSTRIALS" ANECDOTE!

HERE IN THE INNOVATIVE NEW MEDIUM OF THE "GRAPHIC ADDENDUM" (START ENGRAVING THAT TROPHY, MR. PULITZER!) WE LEARN ABOUT THE "TEMPTING" SIDE OF SALES MEETINGS! HERE, JUST AS HE LIVED IT, IS JOHN'S ACCOUNT OF **THE CORPULENT CORPORATION!**

I DID A REALLY **TERRIBLE** SHOW FOR THE SALESMEN OF HOSTESS, THE COMPANY THAT MADE TWINKIES AND OTHER **HIGH-CALORIC** ITEMS.

IT WAS DONE IN A MOTEL CONFERENCE ROOM THAT COULD JUST BARELY ACCOMMODATE THE SALES FORCE ... MAINLY BECAUSE THEY ALL WEIGHED AROUND **300 POUNDS.**

ON EITHER SIDE OF THE ROOM WERE TABLES **LOADED** WITH HOSTESS PRODUCTS...

...AND DURING EACH BREAK THEY WOULD ALL **DESCEND** UPON THESE TABLES AND ABSOLUTELY **STUFF** THEMSELVES WITH TWINKIES & SO ON.

THEN THEY WOULD **WADDLE** BACK TO THEIR CHAIRS FOR THE NEXT SPEAKER OR MUSICAL NUMBER.

BECAUSE OF THEIR GIRTH, ONLY **TWO** WERE ABLE TO FIT AT TABLES THAT WERE DESIGNED FOR **THREE.**

YOU COULD TELL THE **NEW HIRES**...

BECAUSE **THEY** WERE THE ONES WHO WEREN'T **FAT** YET...

...BUT THEY SOON **WOULD** BE.

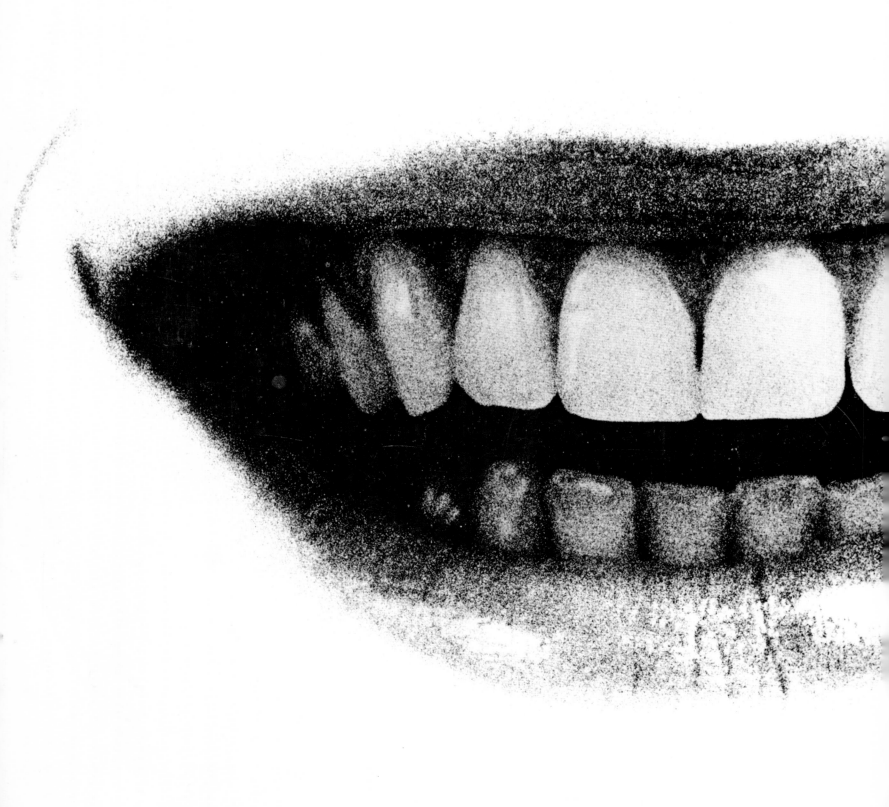

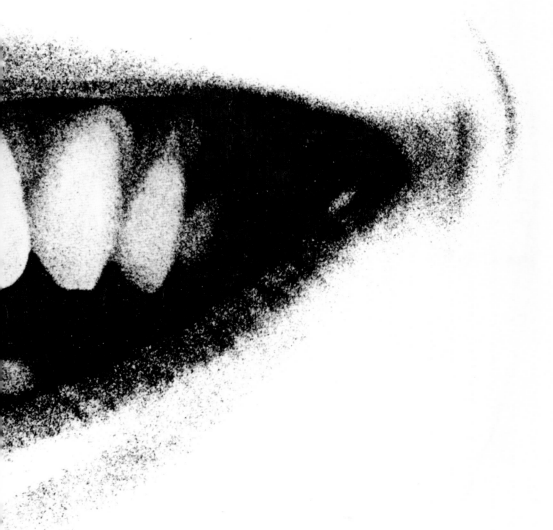

The 1970s
and Beyond

GOT TO INVESTIGATE SILICONES

Got to have this record.

Got to Investigate Silicones, written by Hank Beebe and Bill Heyer in 1973 for General Electric's Silicone Products Department, is one of the genre's pinnacles of wacky genius. Like *The Bathrooms Are Coming!*, *Silicones* has attracted a little notice in the outside world; choice cuts have been celebrated on odd music radio shows and websites for years. I was once privileged to attend a live performance of one of the songs at a New York City club by a group that included Sport.

No vague titles or generic boosterism here: this is a hardcore show about silicone products and their profitable industrial uses. The show, which toured nine cities, kicks off with the three-person cast acknowledging that the subject matter is tricky.

> *Should we talk about silicone*
> *Like they talk about the invention of the*
> *   telephone?*
> *Should we show how releasing a tire*
> *   works?*
> *Or should we just set off some fireworks?*
> *How can we demonstrate silicone's*
> *   powers*
> *Without going on for eight and a half*
> *   hours?*

Unsure of how to proceed, they make tentative stabs at different styles: operetta, tap dance, sitcom, Broadway, and finally settle on a movie. This segues into the film that was part of the show, *Love Is the Answer*. Songs from the film include "Silicones, Silicones."

> *To waterproof a parasol, to help the spray*
> *   from aerosol,*

> *Silicones! Silicones! They*
> *Can wash your product's problems away!*
> *They're very good at saving the day!*

Clearly the audience wasn't GE employees; it was representatives of various other businesses who could benefit from silicone in its various forms: fluids, rubbers, resins, and RTV. That's "room temperature vulcanizing," you hick!

Businesses are warned to avoid that villain "False Economy."

> *He never thinks of how, he only thinks*
> *   of now!*
> *He only mentions pennies that you've lost!*
> *He makes you put on blinders,*
> *Never mentions such reminders*
> *As down time and down-range cost!*
> *He'll never tell you silicones now mean*
> *   savings later on...*

The improbability train keeps a-rollin'. The title track is a skit and song about cops investigating silicones as the force behind a widespread protection racket — protection against cold and heat. It's unique among comedy bits for including the word *dimethylpolysiloxane*. "Sand" is a lovely number about the silicon building blocks of silicone products, with an elegant solo by vocalist Joy Garrett. The pièce de résistance is the nearly six-minute slab of musical information "The Answer." It's an exhaustive cataloguing of the industrial uses of various types of silicones — a binder's worth of data heroically crammed into a six-minute song so challenging that lyricist Bill Heyer has to jump in to help the overtaxed cast.

*Silicones are just a must, they're also
    used on the lunar dust!*
*When man walked on the moon picking up
    stones,*
*The soles of his boots were made of
    silicones!*
*As a construction sealant it's really worth
    noting,*
*For industrial roofs, it's weatherproof
    coating,*
It works on the tops of the big sports domes!
For sealing and for caulking in motor homes!
Insulates the transformer on your TV set,

*Makes custom ski boots the best you
    can get,*
*It's the coating on your waistband to
    make your waistband hold!*
*Environmental coating to protect from hot
    and cold!*

Even if the music were inept, this show would still be noteworthy thanks to the lyrics. But it's a Beebe-Heyer show, so the melodies are genuinely catchy and the production is crisp, with laser-sharp horns and a crackerjack rhythm section. *Got to Investigate Silicones* is a dizzying example of industrial awesomeness: so nutty that it must have been invented by comedy writers, yet it's for real, and better than you could have expected.

RARITY: 3

THE GREAT LIFE

For B.F. Goodrich's 1979 Hawaii convention, writers Elliott Delman, James Tullio, David Kravitz, and Joan Beugen supplied a few pleasant but unremarkable numbers about the joys of off-roading, cruising in a van, or impressing folks with your muscle car, all with the proper BFG tires, of course. The real attraction is the story of BFG dealer R.J., who makes a brash bet. If R.J. can't sell a dauntingly large number of tires within three months, he'll lose his soul—and his franchise—to the Devil!

Why the Devil wants a tire dealership is never explained. Infected by the malaise of the 1970s, the Devil has surprisingly modest plans, as laid out in "His Soul Is Sold."

A full T/A line, with one net pricing,
*The territory's mine, sales training is
    the icing!*

Not to mention the local advertising;
Wait'll they see my in-store merchandising!

T/A, as you know if you Googled it like I did, stands for "traction advantage." Everything comes to a head in "Tires to Sell," with ominous ticking clock music and a chorus chanting overlapping lines.

He's...got...tires to sell...
If he doesn't sell them, he'll land in hell...
Five, ten, fifteen, twenty tires to sell...
Twenty, thirty, forty, fifty tires to sell...

The Devil is sure R.J. is doomed, but our hero draws upon hidden reserves of tire-sellin' pluck. As the scary diminished chords change to confident major chords topped off with heroic horns, R.J. shifts into carnival barker mode, touting the full T/A range of performance, van, pickup truck, and family car tires, and asserting:

I'm on the move now, I'm in the groove now.
A sellin' pro, I'm on the go, I'm gonna
show 'em how.

I've got tires to sell!
[chorus] He's got tires to sell!
[Devil] He'll never sell that many tires!

R.J. prevails and continues to live the BFG "Great Life," while the Devil ends up sadder and wiser. Although not every song is a killer, overall it's an engaging show lyrically, musically, and theologically.

RARITY: 3

RED CARPET TEAM RALLY 1977

A tragic missed opportunity.

Sid Siegel, songwriter for the legendary 1969 American Standard show *The Bathrooms Are Coming!*, provided typically adept music for this 1977 Standard Oil, Western Region show. But it's a low-quality live recording, with singers apparently accompanying prerecorded musical tracks that sound only marginally better than if they were coming through a phone.

At least one song is recycled: "Glorious Years" is a rewrite of one of Sid's *Bathrooms* songs, with lyrics about primitive old-time gas stations rather than primitive plumbing. "Here's to the Losers" is a tribute to the underachieving competition, while "They'll Hear from Us" is a typical riff on the power of advertising.

Got the greatest advertising to sell our
gasoline!
With our brand-new advertising, you'll see
a lot more green!
Great new ads and new promotions, it's
gonna be a plus
And you, you, you'll be the winner—they'll
hear from us!

I've got the tires for every wheel.
I've got tires to sell.
(Devil)
I'll get your soul,
Your franchise, too,
And there's not a single thing
   that you can do.
(Chorus)
He's got tires to sell.
(Devil)
He'll never sell that many tires!!

5. THE GREAT LIFE CLOSE
Oh, we've got The Great Life;
Goodrich means The Great Life.
T/A's the tire for today,
Another generation
   rollin' 'cross the nation.
B . . . F . . . Gee, a new 50 and 60,
B . . . F . . . Gee, now here comes
   the best;
A sellin' sensation,
This new generation's
The tire they'll be racin'
   ahead of the rest.
Oh, I've got The Great Life,
Yeah, I've got The Great Life.
This franchise get's better
   each day.
With certification,
   I'm acceleratin'.
B . . . F . . . Gee,
A full family of tires,
B . . . F . . . Gee,
With a great sellin' look.
When it comes to performance —
The class and the romance,
The specs and the look,
We wrote the book.
Oh, we've got The Great Life.
Goodrich means The Great Life.
T/A's the tire for today . . .
Watch me world, I'm growin';
Cash is really flowin',
B . . . F . . . Gee, it's been tough,
But I've done it;
B . . . F . . . Gee,
Workin' hard day and night.
I'm livin' my dream and the dream
   that I schemed
Seems to me to be
   turnin' out right.
Future's bright . . .
It's a Great Life.
It's been grand, dear.
Hand in hand, dear.
It's been grand, dear.
And the dream that I schemed
Seems to me to be
   turning out right.
Future's bright . . .
Oh, I've got The Great Life,
Yeah, I've got The Great Life . . .
I have my place in the sun . . .
When I'm wheelin' dealing
I get a happy feeling . . .
B . . . F . . . Gee,
I've grown tall and I love it.
B . . . F . . . Gee,
And it's all up from here.
He's sharing his dream
   and it sure seems to me
We've grown nearer and nearer
   this year.
Oh, we've got The Great Life.
Goodrich means The Great Life . . .
My job gets tougher each day
Since I lost that franchise,
I've really opened my eyes.
Vannin' or 'Vettin',
Truckin' or gettin' it on
   or off roadin' . . .
We're number one . . .
And that's why we say
BFG . . .
What a Great Life we're livin'
BFG, What a great way to go.
BFG . . .
What a Great Life we're livin'.
BFG . . . Number one,
          Number one,
          Number one . . .
Way to go!   811075-1249

"Red Carpet Team Rally 1977"

In "What a Pair," two women personify the new grades of unleaded gasoline.

We're your team from Amoco, and we're free of lead
Gonna make you lots more dough, you'll be way ahead
You'll love us, 'cross the nation, a winning combination
Dealers, we're the team for you.

There's an intermittent sports theme with commentary by "Howard Hardsell," a bit of an executive's speech, and a strange moment involving an audience member winning a bingo game. Overall, an interesting hodgepodge, but it could have been so much better.

RARITY: 2

THE SPIRIT OF ACHIEVEMENT

What better way to celebrate the 1976 bicentennial than with a celebration of American freedom as seen through the lens of laissez-faire capitalism?

This ambitious Exxon show by Claibe Richardson has a number of memorably pro-business songs. Government meddling is slammed in "Efficiency."

Efficiency, efficiency, speaking
  governmentally,
Efficiency is in a sorry state.
The government, now it steps in,
And business takes it on the chin.
Who can be efficient and still regulate?
Reasonable government guidelines — now,
  that's okay!
We don't mind the government having its
  fair say.
But too much control now, that just gets
  in the way
Of efficiency!

It's not all political complaining. The spookily cheerful "Dealers' Heaven" envisions an Exxon-specific afterlife.

the SPIRIT of Achievement

1976 EXXON CONVENTION

A thousand tires a month you'll sell,
And "shortage" a word you'll never hear,
The washroom wreckers will be sent
  to hell,
And no employee griping in your ear!

One might think that heaven means no longer having to work at a gas station. Apparently one would be wrong.

Other standout numbers include "Up Came Oil," a rousing history of the petroleum industry, "We Got 'Em," a sprightly encouragement for station owners to provide

1976 EXXON CONVENTION

The 1976 EXXON Convention was developed to speak to issues that are extremely vital to all of us. The story of EXXON is your story; the spirit of achievement is your spirit. What better way to remind us all of our future goals and opportunities than with this album. Here then, are the songs that helped to weave our convention into a living, breathing story. A story about you and EXXON, THE ACHIEVEMENT TEAM!

LET THIS FUEL RUSH IN

Stylistically, Exxon's "Up Came Oil" marks the crossroads of two distinct eras of musical theater: the booming Americana of *Paint Your Wagon* or *Oklahoma!* and the rock influence that Stephen Schwartz brought to the boards in the 1970s with *Godspell* and *Pippin*. Given the historical importance and popular success of these two Broadway styles, it stands to reason that "Up Came Oil" would be at least twice as great as "Oh, What a Beautiful Mornin' " and "Day by Day." But to merely acknowledge this fact is to sorely underestimate its magnificence.

Here, rather than a traditional large band we have a piano-based pop combo, rollicking from the git-go with whammo major sevenths and a tambourine so frantic and merciless it hurts one's wrist just to contemplate the recording session. Over this propulsive pocket, the entire saga of oil and its fast track to energy dominance is limned by alternating solo singers who thrust to the fore in full, manly unison with each breathtaking gush of the chorus.

> *Once that Edwin Drake dude*
> *Struck the bubblin' crude*
> *As his drill cut through the soil,*
> *Up…came…oil!*

The surging, erotic (there, I've said it) power of such passages is enhanced by the most ravishingly ingenious use of concert harp this side of Brian Wilson's "Catch a Wave"; even as we find ourselves flush with sudden carnal yearnings we are reminded of that day in 1859 when "Colonel" Edwin Drake first rammed his newly invented drive pipe into the daunting rock of Titusville, PA, and struck the fossil fuel motherlode. We are lifted…somehow ennobled…and certainly empowered.

So far all's well, but just when the song's message and modulations seem to have taken us to the very summit of possibility, a tympani roll introduces the song's bridge.

> *From the hunches and divining rods,*
> *Goin' against all of the odds,*
> *To the power and the lubrication*
> *For every type of transportation*
> *And equipment you can name…*
> *Since up…came…OIL!*

Each of us may entertain our own private reveries of how all this was performed on stage…perhaps a conga line of gents all tricked out like David "Scar" Hodo's role as the "construction worker" in the Village People? Sure, if you like. But one thing's for certain: since "Up Came Oil"—a piece at once so crude and so refined—nothing in this world has been the same.

—SM

great customer service, and the gospel-tinged "Be an Achiever."

> *Be an achiever, be an achiever,*
> *If you're gonna be in business at all.*
> *Who can love average? Be above average!*
> *Be the top one, run with the ball!*

The talented Claibe Richardson wrote many shows for Ford and Chevy as well as Sony, Sanyo, and Stroh's beer, but sadly *The Spirit of Achievement* was his only recorded industrial. According to cast member John Russell, there were two touring companies, one east, one west. For the album, an all-star team was selected, which led to some hurt feelings. Hey, too bad: who can love average? Be above average!

RARITY: 3

PUT YOURSELF IN THEIR SHOES

For Exxon's 1979 dealer meeting, staged shortly before the second round of the '70s gas crisis, Ted Simons and John Allen delivered a slick-sounding show with a plot involving a dream sequence and several worthwhile songs. You can't go wrong with some ego stroking:

> *Exxon wants you dealers to know you're*
> *   the best,*
> *You're the best in the business!*
> *Exxon wants you dealers to know they're*
> *   impressed,*
> *You're the best in the business!*
> *All across this nation, you're on the line*
> *   every day*
> *Exxon's firm foundation, that's what*
> *   you are,*
> *That's what you'll stay!*

PETITORS CONSUMERS EXXON RETAILERS COMPETITORS CONSUME RS CONSUMERS PUT YOURSELF IN THEIR SHOES CONSUMERS EXXON PETITORS CONSUMERS EXXON RETAILERS COMPETITORS CONSUME CONSUMERS EXXON RETAILERS COMPETITORS CONSUMERS EXXON PETITORS CONSUMERS EXXON RETAILERS COMPETITORS CONSUME CONSUMERS EXXON RETAILERS COMPETITORS CONSUMERS EXXON PETITORS CONSUMERS EXXON RETAILERS COMPETITORS CONSUME CONSUMERS CONSUMERS EXXON RETAILERS COMPETITORS CONSUMERS EXXON PETITORS CONSUMERS EXXON RETAILERS COMPETITORS CONSUME CONSUMERS EXXON RETAILERS COMPETITORS CONSUMERS EXXON PETITORS CONSUMERS EXXON RETAILERS COMPETITORS CONSUME CONSUMERS EXXON EXXON RETAILERS COMPETITORS CONSUMERS EXXON PETITORS CONSUMERS EXXON RETAILERS COMPETITORS CONSUME CONSUMERS EXXON RETAILERS COMPETITORS CONSUMERS EXXON PETITORS CONSUMERS EXXON RETAILERS COMPETITORS CONSUME CONSUMERS EXXON RETAILERS RETAILERS COMPETITORS CONSUME CONSUMERS EXXON RETAILERS COMPETITORS CONSUMERS EXXON PETITORS CONSUMERS EXXON RETAILERS COMPETITORS CONSUME CONSUMERS EXXON RETAILERS COMPETITORS CONSUMERS EXXON PETITORS CONSUMERS EXXON RETAILERS COMPETITORS COMPETITORS CONSUME CONSUMERS EXXON RETAILERS COMPETITORS CONSUMERS EXXON PETITORS CONSUMERS EXXON RETAILERS COMPETITORS CONSUME CONSUMERS EXXON RETAILERS COMPETITORS CONSUMERS EXXON PETITORS CONSUMERS EXXON RETAILERS COMPETITORS CONSUME CONSUMERS EXXON RETAILERS COMPETITORS CONSUMERS EXXON PETITORS CONSUMERS EXXON RETAILERS COMPETITORS CONSUME

1979 RETAILER CONVENTION

The show is built around a beleaguered dealer named Harry, who in "Harry's Lament" recounts all the problems he has to deal with and admits "this business is giving me gas." Harry's wife stands by her man in "An Exxon Dealer's Wife."

> *I can write up a thousand customer*
> *   follow-up cards while I'm cookin' up*
> *   a lunch,*
> *And I can give up a holiday to pump some*
> *   gas when it comes down to the*
> *   crrr-unch!*
> *And I can cheer up Harry when he comes*
> *   home and his octane's mighty low,*

PUT YOURSELF
IN THEIR
SHOES

LENNY WOLPE

DON ATKINSON

ELLY BARBOUR

DAVID DEARDORFF

ANN HODAPP

BILL LINTON

ORRIN REILEY

CHUCK COOPER

DOROTHY KIARA

> *And I can give him the premium attention*
>   *he needs that makes a man get up*
>   *and go!*
> *What I'm sayin' is, this dealer's wife is a*
>   *full-service island!*

Dealers were encouraged to put themselves in the shoes of consumers, competitors, and even company bigwigs. Consumers predictably want great service, as emphasized in "Once Around the Car" and "We're Gonna Pass You By." Indie competitors gloat about undercutting the "majors" in a song with an impressive Sinatra-esque sound, "Major Surgery."

> *Cuttin' down the majors, cut 'em down*
>   *to size,*
> *Nothin' I like better than to cut down*
>   *bigger guys!*
> *Love to beat 'em, I defeat 'em, I'm*
>   *efficient, you see,*
> *I'm like a surgeon performing major*
>   *surgery!*
> *Operate on Exxon, Texaco, and Shell,*
> *I cut down their profits, and their*
>   *customers as well!*

The opening number, "False Start," involves a mystery. Peppy music and rah-rah lyrics about Exxon's greatness suddenly skid to a discordant halt amidst the screams of the cast. What happened? Did an "OPEC" banner fly in? Neither Ted Simons nor "Harry" (TV and Broadway vet Lenny Wolpe) could remember the visual element. If only Exxon had put themselves in the shoes of future industrial show collectors.

RARITY: 3

1970 HAWAIIAN HULLABALOO

This lively, well-executed show was staged at the 1970 Babson Bros. convention. What do you mean you don't know what business Babson Bros. was in? Does "Surge" mean nothing to you? Hello?

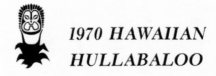

1970 HAWAIIAN HULLABALOO

We couldn't capture the balmy breezes, the majestic mountains or the beautiful beaches but we have recorded some of the excitement and sounds of the 1970 Hawaiian Hullabaloo.

This special album contains all of the original music, created for our Hullabaloo. If you were there, we are sure you will enjoy listening to the music and some of the narrative again. If you were not able to attend, this album brings to you many of the highlights from one of the most interesting and entertaining meetings that Babson Bros. Co. has ever presented.

The accent was on YOU and without you there certainly would not have been a Hawaiian Hullabaloo.

BABSON BROS. CO.

Babson Bros. made milking machines and equipment, including the Surge bucket system. Though Surge business would decline from the mid-'70s and the company would be sold in 1999, in 1970 things were going well enough to fly dealers to Hawaii for a Hullabaloo, which is a native Hawaiian word meaning "pasty middle-aged white guys getting sunburns."

What is the latest from Babson Brothers?
What will it be like a year from now?
Will they still be improving the milking machine,
Or will they redesign the cow?

The Hoyt Jones–penned songs cover topics such as accounting, employee recruitment, operations, and R&D. The sinister-sounding R&D song takes place in an underground lab.

What's that sound, with a sinister laugh?
Shulick's discovered how to milk a giraffe!

What do you mean who's Shulick? Robert Shulick, who patented thirteen dairy equipment improvements while working for Babson? Hello?

RARITY: 1

SURGE...the accent is on YOU

(SURGE)

the challenge of change

ATLANTA - DALLAS - 1971

THE CHALLENGE OF CHANGE

A whole show about birth control! That's got to be worth a listen. Although many of the songs in this 1971 Ortho Pharmaceuticals show aren't original, the uncredited lyrics often rise, or sink, to the level you're hoping for.

The title track was repurposed several times in the late '60s and early '70s, turning up on Oldsmobile and Durkee Foods records with corresponding lyric fixes. It's a cool-sounding, dark song, full of warnings about getting left behind by a changing business world.

> *Hey, Mr. Salesman with your head so high,*
> *Are you quick to change your pitch if the*
>   *doc don't buy?*

An altered "Gonna Build a Mountain," from *Stop the World, I Want to Get Off*, has a heavy-handed message.

> *Gonna reach that druggist, make him call*
>   *me "friend"!*
> *Gonna teach that doctor what to*
>   *recommend!*
> *To other offers, I will answer "no"—I'll say*
> *I'd rather stick around a company that's*
>   *bound to grow!*

A parody of "There's Nothing Like a Dame" from *South Pacific* is marred by murky sound quality and may have been carried over from some earlier project. The lyrics depart quite widely from the original.

> *Women turn to us for reliable*
>   *contraceptive action!*
> *Not to mention healthy female sexual*
>   *satisfaction!*
>
> *Though a married female's problems may*
>   *be myriad,*
> *Thanks to us she can usually expect her*
>   *period!*

Note that she's "a married female." The notion of unmarried women using birth control was still politically incorrect in 1971.

Other tracks include rewrites of "Makin' Whoopee," "Up, Up and Away," and a possibly original "Building a Better Tomorrow Today," which has a credible funky vibe and wailing vocals by the unknown singer who performed the title track.

There's also a bitter passing reference to the 1970 Senate hearing on birth control pills, in which the pharmaceutical companies were lambasted for hushing up side effects and keeping information from women. As a result, the companies were forced to include more information in the packaging and reduce hormone levels in the pills, and the consumer rights and women's movements gained momentum. I had to dig up that information myself; Ortho wisely decided it wouldn't make for a morale-boosting song.

RARITY: 1

ORTHO PHARMACEUTICAL CORPORATION

THE SIZZLE IS THE STEAK

As "Hot Promotions" begins, you might be forgiven for thinking someone slapped a latter-day Blood, Sweat & Tears LP on the turntable instead of the requested *Sundown*, Johnson & Johnson's 1977 show. It's all there: the flatulent cop show horns; a credible rhythm section packed under so much sonic Styrofoam that what should have been a groove sounds more like a slight indentation; the "wailing" electric guitar with just enough distortion to annoy and alienate squares without in any way enticing even the lamest rock types (who could forget the controversy surrounding the fuzztone guitar solo on the Carpenters' "Goodbye to Love," a daring move that sharply divided the band's fan base and ultimately led to the song being credited as the very first power ballad). Replacing the soulful bellow of Toronto's David Clayton-Thomas is a chorus right out of a dinner theater production of *Hair* where they don't even take off their clothes.

None of this is intended as anything but praise, by the way. I've described these aspects of "Hot Promotions" with such seeming derision not as an indication of how far it misses the mark, mainstream-entertainment-simulation–wise, but rather how precisely it hits the bull's-eye as actual entertainment und *zeitspiegel*. In the 1970s, everyone knew it was all bullshit. Everything. Everyone knew it. A culture so off-the-rails goofy that people lined up to buy Pet Rocks, knowing that it was a ripoff and that this was the whole point: "so I'm laughing...so who's a sucker?" Irony, schmirony, this was smiley face Dada triumphant. Already, Steven Spielberg and his ilk were busy ruining it all, but for a few sacred, stupid years unapologetic meaninglessness carried the day.

"Hot Promotions: Big Reward! Hot Promotions: Big demand across the board!" No shoehorned-in hi concept here, no mock-historical tableaux or parodic pastiche, no. This was straight-faced promotion of promotion, set to a deliciously idiotic disco beat. "Comprehensive, intensive promotions/To make you number one!" A song with embarrassing camel toe and oversized mirror shades, its simple message e'er unchanging: "point of sale is just sensational!" I guess the product is suntan lotion or something, but they don't seem too concerned about that, especially...could be ball bearings or baseball caps, for all it matters. Or Pet Rocks. Whatever. Let's just dance...and promote.

—SM

SUNDOWN

We love the sun, the feel, the touch of it,
But there's such a thing as much too
*   much of it.*
True — that's true — but what do we do?

This 1977 sales meeting show introduced
Johnson & Johnson's new sunscreen, Sundown,
at the Camelback Inn in sunny Scottsdale,
Arizona. Sundown was entering a crowded
sunscreen market, as acknowledged in
"Product Confusion."

So many bottles to look at, so many
*   bottles to buy,*
All kinds of sizes and colors and shapes,
Enough to boggle the eye!

So of course the solution to consumers'
anxiety is to introduce another brand. But not
just any brand: the "Sundown Theme" repeats
over and over that it stays on for hours and has
"pleasing smoothness." To jump-start sales,
the company devised "Hot Promotions."

Hot promotions...to entice!
Hot promotions...with a special feature
*   price!*
High gross volume for your customers!
Bright shelf backers for the store!
With the first consumer offering
Cents-off coupons, watch 'em soar!

The songs, by Ted Simons and John Allen,
have a nice '70s sound, with touches of disco
and rock guitar sizzle, but in the end "Product
Confusion" may have been prophetic. A check
of Johnson & Johnson's current product lineup
reveals no Sundown.

RARITY: 1

THE CHANGING
PACE OF
LEADERSHIP

CAMELBACK

NATIONAL SALES MEETING
& NATIONAL INTRODUCTION
SUNDOWN® SUNSCREEN
DECEMBER 5-9, 1977

Johnson & Johnson
HEALTH CARE DIVISION

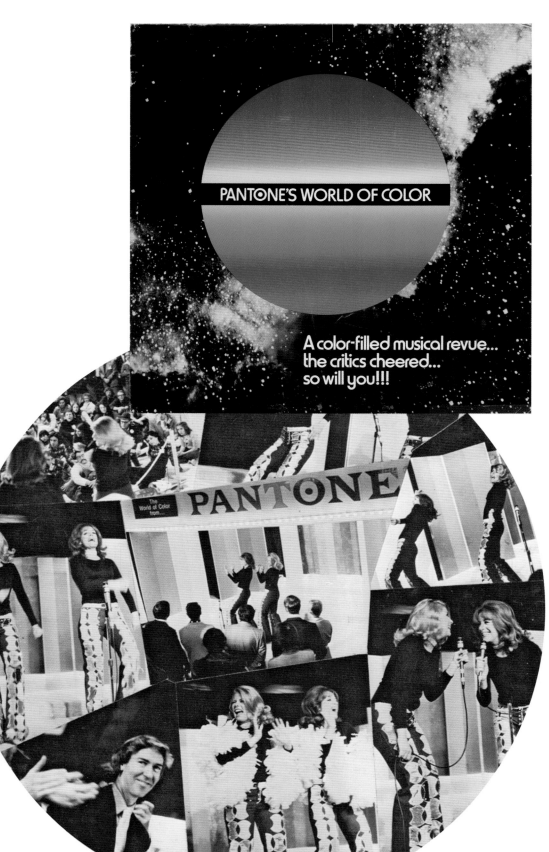

PANTONE'S WORLD OF COLOR

Another example of the subgenre of industrials aimed at potential customers rather than employees, this 1974 two-woman show for Pantone, the color systems company, was performed at the Graphic Arts Show in Chicago a staggering ten times a day for ten days. Whew!

Industrial vet Ted Simons dishes up a one-sided record's worth of xylophone-heavy song parodies. Skeptical about "That's Entertainment" refashioned as an ode to Pantone's newly computerized color matching system? The verve and good cheer of performers Ann Hilton and Vicki Belmonte overcome all objections.

> *The input goes in, there is no need
>   to wait!*
> *The output comes out, not a second
>   too late!*
> *You'll see when we demonstrate*
> *Our delightful densitometer! And
>   spectrophotometer!*

Other songs receiving Pantonization include "In the Mood," "We've Only Just Begun," and "You Are the Sunshine of My Life." The show was a hit, according to review blurbs on the back cover from *Printing News*, *Printing Views*, *Journal of Commerce*, and *American Ink Maker*. Even the *Chicago Sun-Times* took note: "Liveliest Exhibit at Show…theatrical in every sense, professional and colorful: a tuneful, unique pitch—the first of its kind in the graphic arts." It may not be one of the brightest stars in the industrial galaxy, but it must have been pretty entertaining if you walked into the Graphic Arts Show with no expectations.

RARITY: 1

DEARIE, DO YOU REMEMBER?

*We've upped our performance, just check
the brochures!*
That's how we help you—up yours!

Look out, squares—it's 1974 and snarky kids
are invading industrial shows!

This Westinghouse record opens with an
un-hip man talking about the Machine Tool
Forum, only to be interrupted by a gang of
groovy young people: "Hey, man, is this the
studio for the rock session?" "Hold it! You kids
must be in the wrong place. We're recording
highlights from the Westinghouse Machine
Tool Forum!" "The Westinghouse Machine Tool
Forum! Great name for a rock group, right? Why
didn't we think of that?" "It's not a rock group!
It means we're turning on people to what's new
in the machine tool industry!" "Well, it's your

lucky day, Mr. Machine Tool, because we gotta
rehearse anyway, so we'll turn 'em on for ya!"

Because the show was put on for a large,
conservative corporation, the kooky kids aren't
actually espousing anything more radical than

If you were there you saw the introduction of a unique new Programmable Controller. Heard discussions of the metric system, its costs, obstacles and opportunities, and what they will mean to you. Learned how safety and noise standards will affect the industry. Were filled in on emerging technologies: Hot Isostatic Pressing; Hydro-Static Extrusion; Reverse Osmosis—Lube Oil Recovery.

Two days of concentrated listening, pondering, discussing.

But for the first time ever at one of these shop-talk fests came an unexpected break in the formalities. Music! Songs! Comedy!

It's all here. To play back in fond remembrance if you were there—or to hear for the first time if you were unable to attend.

So listen. And enjoy!

not wearing ties. The "rock," a few bars of "Proud Mary," soon gives way to the familiar territory of Broadway parodies. So, yes, it's a batch of uncredited rewrites rather than an original show, but the subject matter is so far out, man, and the attitude is so cheeky that it's a dark-horse favorite.

The kids start by recalling highlights of past Machine Tool Forums, as kids so often do. They then turn us on to details about Westinghouse's new "Programmable Controller," set to melodies from *Gypsy*. In an admission of temporary defeat, long chunks of data are spoken rather than sung. Likewise for the three new breaker features introduced in the brisk march "Vari-Width, Vari-Depth Handle Mechanism," though some of it is sung.

> *One's a handle mech that's mounted on*
> *the flange, boys!*
> *Three's a base mounting solid as can be!*
> *Between the handle and the mounting*
> *it's adjustable,*
> *Oh say, can you see all the possibilities*
> *For the brand-new Westinghouse*
> *flange-mounted*
> *Vari-depth handle mechanism,*
> *cha-cha-cha!*

The parody of "Gee, Officer Krupke" from *West Side Story* is clearly adapted from the version used in the 1969 PPG fiberglass drapes show. Here, it's "Proximity Limit Switch."

> *What a nifty package! It does most any job!*
> *You change the sensitivity with one*
> *adjustment knob!*
> *To use the head remotely, no panel space*
> *required!*
> *And here's the plus, Gus—the head's not*
> *DC wired!*

"Quiet Line Motor," a rewrite of "Steam Heat" from *The Pajama Game*, includes a nice rhyme for the Occupational Safety and Health Administration.

> *It's there where you can see it, it means*
> *we guarantee it,*
> *The distance, the pressure, the power.*
> *You know we're keeping kosher*
> *So you can pass the OSHA rules*
> *For dBA allowed by the hour.*

Yeah, well, I'd like to see the rabbinic certification.

RARITY: 2

GOULD GROOWWING

Here's a discful of uncredited crazy from a company you probably don't know. In the '70s Gould, Inc., made batteries, oil filters, hydraulics, and electrical equipment, only to struggle in the '80s and eventually get bought, liquidated, and broken up. But in 1976, woo-hoo, showtime!

The disco-flavored title track borrows the music of the 1975 hit "The Hustle" to boast

> *Growing, we have sales in the billions,*
> *We bring power to millions and millions!*
> *We've the expertise and resources*
> *To control electrical forces!*
> *We provide the power the world uses,*
> *Store, convert, we even make fuses!*
> *We're that corporation you know as Gould!*

"It's a Wonderful Story to Tell," about the acquisition of rival ITE-Imperial, is a cheery, horns-and-xylophone-heavy version of "On a Wonderful Day Like Today."

OULD GROOWWING

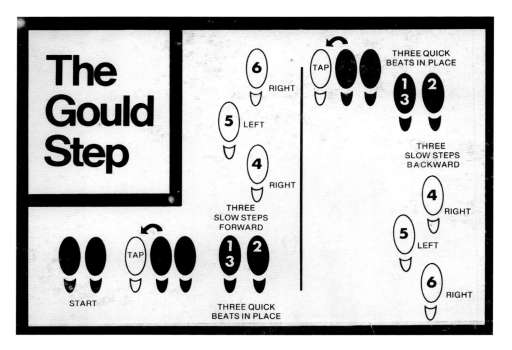

The Gould Step

6 RIGHT
5 LEFT
4 RIGHT

THREE SLOW STEPS FORWARD

TAP
1 3 2

THREE QUICK BEATS IN PLACE

START

TAP

THREE QUICK BEATS IN PLACE

1 3 2

THREE SLOW STEPS BACKWARD

4 RIGHT
5 LEFT
6 RIGHT

ITE, candidly, is a power in power,
Its name and its products are STRONG!
Now acquired by Gould, from that very
first hour,
It's three times bigger, has more vigor,
Moving right along!
Planning for corporate growth,
That's what we plan, but it's bigger
than both!
To customers, shareholders, workers,
this oath:
It's a wonderful story to tell!

"Big Beat 2," set to the tune of "I Believe in You" from *How to Succeed in Business without Really Trying*, is confusing as well as gloriously clumsy. The Beat Big 2 program may have been a plan to overtake GE and Westinghouse.

We know the need…for…good solid
judgment in cost reduction,
And there's the pro…gram's
tre…mendous effect on the old
bottom line.

Oh, we love Beat Big 2, we love Beat Big 2!
And when our costs start rising too fast,
We don't cry, or gasp.
We've got to grab hold of Big 2 mugs and
we take heart, we take heart!
To…end…the…cost…spiral…faster
than you can say Beat Big 2!

Equally befuddling and clunky are "C.O.R.E. Reporting" and "The KMI Program," with lyrically challenged lyrics like "It's a highly specialized key component of operational unity" and "We must maximize the capital with which we have to work." The vocalists and musicians struggle to hold this industrial hot mess together. Overall, so endearingly wrong that it's right.

RARITY: 1

ASTROLINE FOR THE CHALLENGE OF CHANGE

It would be too easy to say this 1971 Brunswick bowling equipment show is a gutter ball. With only one real song, it's certainly not a major entry, but the cover makes an effort at visual interest, and the back has a fair amount of explanatory text and photos of the show, the bowling equipment, and Brunswick executives. The uncredited Astroline song explores the oft-overlooked connection between outer space and bowling.

Set your sight on that new universe of
bowling in space!
Put a solar smile on your face!
Dig it, brother, that vision of Mars,
Look, the answer is in the stars!

Brunswick

1971 National Sales Meeting

Astroline

for the Challenge of change

Astroline was Brunswick's new line of automatic scorers, ball returns, and other equipment. The song never gets more specific than words like "automatic" and "styling," but it's got a skeevy, guilty-pleasure early '70s sound, the audio equivalent of avocado green and harvest gold. Instead of a gutter ball, let's say it's a 7–10 split.

RARITY: 1

KEDS NATIONAL SALES MEETING, PARADISE ISLAND, JULY 1971

KEDS
National Sales Meeting
Paradise Island
July, 1971

SIDE 2   DC82071B

1. RED, WHITE AND BLUES (2:20)
2. WATERPROOF (1:58)
3. WOMEN'S OPENER (3:06)
4. FABRIC GRASSHOPPERS (4:29)
5. FINALE (1:29)

Written by:
Tobias & Lebowsky

not for sale or public performance

This is an extraordinary record. On paper, it looks dismissible as a minor low-budget effort: blank cover, small uncredited cast accompanied by a piano, and several rewrites of familiar songs, which usually means B-list at best. But the performances are strong, the recording is good quality, and the staggering volume of shoe specs crammed into the songs makes for a head-spinning experience rivaled only by a few other hardcore shows.

Writers Stan Lebowsky and Fred Tobias penned several other industrials, including the 1969 Westinghouse show *Perspective for the 70s*. In 1970 they had a short-lived Broadway musical called *Gantry*, an adaptation of *Elmer Gantry*, the Sinclair Lewis novel. Here they kick off the proceedings with the energetic "You're Gonna Have It Better Than You've Ever Had It Before," touting an expanded product line.

You won't do seasonal selling, you'll cover the marketplace!

Build leather volume on your solid canvas base!
More distribution so your sales will rise, profits soar!
You're gonna have it better than you've ever had it before!

Then it's song after song with recognizable melodies but with head-hurting new lyrics explaining shoe features. "The Impossible Dream" becomes "The Possible Dream."

This is their quest, to never say "can't,"
To end all confusion between planning and plant!
And to add further joy to the salesmen's smiles,
There'll be six brand-new stitchdowns and six vulcanized rope sole styles!

The stupefying peak is "Ol' Don Hadley." Invoking the name of a Keds executive, it's a five-minute weirdathon of kids' shoe information set to "Old MacDonald Had a Farm."

Ol' Don Hadley has a line, E-I-E-I-O!
A children's casual footwear line, E-I-E-I-O!
The first is called the New Regatta
The New Regatta you'll sell a lotta
A molded rubber boat shoe
With a two-color sole and foxing too
A round toe last and a wedge heel
The first children's wedge heel
Four colors in durable duck
A natural to make a buck
Children's retail $6.45
For misses it'll be $6.95
Very attractive at that price
The dealer markup's very nice
Ol' Don Hadley's line gets hotter
With the New Regatta!

MY PAL'S NAME IS FOOT FOOT

1. YOU'RE GONNA HAVE IT BETTER THAN YOU'VE EVER
HAD IT BEFORE (2:40)

2. THE POSSIBLE DREAM (1:59)

3. THOSE OLD TIME FAVORITES (5:07)

4. THE CHAMPION (2:12)

5. OL' DON HADLEY (5:00)

"Ol' Don Hadley" is the kind of shop-talk-laden mindbender treasured by hardcore industrialsists. By the specialized aesthetic standards we embrace, little could improve a junk drawer's worth of incomprehensible product particulars set to that most obnoxious of children's songs "Old MacDonald Had a Farm." Yet this number ups the ante with a rare, devoutly admired motif: by-name employee specificity. And that specifically named employee is Don Hadley, a shining star of Uniroyal's sneaker division, Keds.

Hired by Uniroyal in 1952, Hadley obviously progressed into a "shoe dog" of high repute during his long tenure with the firm, capably marketing, as the tune so incessantly reminds us, such styles as the New Regatta and the Javelin. By 1975 he'd become Production Manager of the Grasshopper Line, popularizing the "casual shoe" concept. It's so easy to forget what a revolution the casual shoe set in motion, arriving as it did in a world where there were shoes and there were sneakers,

and never the twain would meet. If it is specious supposition to assert that Don Hadley envisioned a future where no such Maginot Line dividing footwear categories would inhibit broad-based sales growth, then so be it.

It is a matter of record that by 1976 Hadley had achieved the position of National Sales Manager, Branded Footwear and as late as the Reagan era was still carrying high the banner for Keds Espadrilles, a casual shoe accepted eagerly by the buying public despite sneering disregard from those elitist footwear "experts" for whom *couture* trumped comfort and status held precedence over value. Hadley's everyman instincts carried the day, and we who now listen to his namesake song with awe and mounting impatience would do well to glance down at our own casual shoes and recall how, in 1981, Ol' Don Hadley himself told a newspaper reporter: "This has probably been the best year yet for Espadrilles."

—SM

LEATHER AND LACES

What is it about the Kinney "Manager's Song" that seems so pornographic? Other industrial numbers included stripper-jazz sections and leer-ics like "I do my best in my *special* way" and "at times it's not so easy/yet I try to *please*" but seldom does such a palpable triple-X '70s vibe waft into the room, like commingled fumes of Panama Red and Charlie, right off the bat. Considering that Kinney Shoes' TV ads (starring clean-cut entertainer Ken Berry) were memorably wholesome and sleazeless for that ever-randy era, this is an unexpected twist in the ever surprising journey of discovery that is industrials. The dedicated researcher can only absently finger groom his or her real or imagined mustache and wonder, "Hmm…why for, then, this here?"

Hard to tell if it was an intentional saucy wink between Kinney insiders or simply a product of the zany zeitgeist that gave us the Andrea True Connection, Gay Bob dolls, and *Gong Show* pottymouth Jaye P. Morgan. Whichever, I'll defy any listener who was a teenage boy in 1977 to get more than a few measures into the Kinney "Manager's Song" before shooting an alarmed glance at the door and involuntarily shouting, "Yes, Mom, I'm FINE!!! I'll be down in a MINUTE!" (Not a teenage boy in 1977? No problem: listen to this song while watching *The Opening of Misty Beethoven* on mute, and you'll get it…an avocado erotopiphany that's a cinch

to outdo that Pink Floyd/*Wizard of Oz* stunt you tried to talk me into.)

After the manager is done bragging in his oddly androgynous voice about what a dedicated pro he is, he proves it. The simmering strip show tempo comes to a boil o' false funk. A female customer, careful to point out that she's unmarried, insists upon seeing a pair of high-heeled moccasins that are "the color of my bed." Over the alternating burlesque/funk musical motifs, an escalation of increasingly lewd demands ensues from frantic male and female customers, all demanding "more more more" from our man and his big ol' Brannock Device.

Only after we've caught ourselves grasping in vain for a token to ensure another three minutes, then realizing, red-faced, that the song and the 1970s are just plain over, do we really begin to resent Ken Berry, star of *Mayberry R.F.D.*, *The Carol Burnett Show*, and Kinney Shoes' 1970s television ad campaign. For now we know that all his diet-vanilla tap dancing and Disney grins—which we'd naively accepted as the very soul of the "Great American Shoe Store"—was just a smoke screen.

The Kinney manager finally stands revealed as an insatiable satyr, and we've glimpsed past the facade to a shoe-biz Sodom where all was smoked oysters, round waterbeds, and foot fetishism.

Way to keep the fun to yourself, "Captain Parmenter," you heel.

—SM

Were audience members glancing around, silently asking each other *"Is this actually happening?"* *"Couldn't we just get a few pages of handouts?"* *"Did he just rhyme 'wedge heel' with 'wedge heel'?"*

The record has lots of other familiar tunes and heaps of references to leather uppers, crepe color outsoles, units priced for volume, and point of sale display. One odd fact: lyricist Fred Tobias recalled the show as having full orchestration, so the piano-only recorded version may have been a cost-saving measure by Keds. And the savings were passed on to you: only $6.45 for the children's New Regatta!

RARITY: 1

WE'RE TUNED IN TO YOU—YOU MAKE IT HAPPEN

No composer, cast, or production credits, no song titles, no clue as to where this 1977 Kinney Shoes manager meeting show was performed. The only known copy turned up without a cover. It wasn't a big-bucks production: the cast numbers about five and there are only a few musicians. Many of the songs have the feel of generic go-get-'em trunk songs that some producer was reusing. There's an attempt to frame it all with an "Eyewitness News Team" motif, but that mostly disappears after the first couple songs.

Two worthwhile numbers save this one from oblivion. In a song possibly titled "Eyewitness Shoes," the singer advises other women:

> *Look at his shoes, you'll see if he's a*
> *winner*
> *Or if he'll spring for a high-class dinner*
> *Look at his shoes, they tell if he's in*
> *fashion*

> *Look at his shoes, they tell if he's got*
> *passion*

> *Yes, if you want to really score,*
> *Keep your eyes right at the floor.*
> *And if you want a real romance*
> *Just look at what's below his pants.*

The highlight is the song about a Kinney store manager being driven crazy by a building crescendo of customer demands.

> *"I like this style; have you got*
> *it in blue?"*
> *"And is this leather? Do they*
> *use glue?"*
> *"I'd like to see the one with the*
> *strap!"*
> *"Do they deliver? Do they gift wrap?"*
> *"Hey, I'd like to return this pair."*
> *("But they're not Kinney!") "Do you*
> *think I care?"*
> *"I'm looking for a solid work boot!"*
> *"I'm looking for a dress shoe that's cute!"*
> *"What have you got in back-to-school?"*
> *"Have you got sneakers that are really*
> *cool?"*
> *"This shoe's tight!"*
> *"Something that's for night!"*
> *"Something for my boy!"*
> *"No free toy?"*

In the end, the frazzled manager pulls himself together and claims that, despite the madness, it's great to manage a Kinney store. The fun couldn't last forever: Kinney, a fully owned subsidiary of Woolworth, shut down in 1998.

RARITY: 1

WORK REST PLAY KINNEY SHOES/SHAPE YOUR TOMORROW...GET A HEAD START TODAY

Like its '77 show, Kinney's '79 outing is mostly forgettable. The uncredited songs range from disco-inflected to more traditional Broadway and lean heavily on vague "Yeah, we're gonna do it" lyrics. But the existence of both regular and picture disc versions is a unique twist, and a couple tracks deserve mention. The only song I've ever encountered about site selection for stores compares Kinney's expertise to the skill of various sports heroes picking their shots. Another song notes:

Customers find nothing quite so appealing
As a store that really captures a feeling.
Visual merchandising really pays
It makes us beautiful in so many ways!

The four-woman cast is billed as "The Kinney Dazzlers," and they dazzle their way through several songs introducing executives such as Norm from production and Jack from communications. Jack's intro song boasts:

We're gonna TV screen 'em, then we'll
magazine 'em
They'll be breaking down the door to get
into the store!

I'm sure we all remember the panic and civil unrest caused by Kinney's unusually effective 1979 ad campaign.

RARITY: 2 (both regular and picture disc versions)

WITH LYONS MAID YOU'RE LAUGHING

Recorded highlights of the 1973 Marketing Presentation at the Talk of the Town.

Lyons Maid
ICE CREAM

WITH LYONS MAID YOU'RE LAUGHING

One of just a handful of British industrial shows that have come to light, *With Lyons Maid You're Laughing* presents the history and contemporary challenges of an ice cream company. The songs are by Malcolm Mitchell and Denis Norden, and thanks to a letter and show synopsis tucked inside the record jacket, we know that the show had one 1973 performance before an audience of 550 Lyons Maid personnel. Liza Minnelli also attended and had a wonderful time, according to her friend the show producer and director Gillian Lynne.

Nostalgia-heavy side 1 recalls the development of the ice cream business from the Edwardian era up to the early '70s. "The Girl on the Lyons Maid Phone" has a cute premise: an ice cream dealer ordering more than he can possibly sell just so he can keep talking to the lovely saleswoman who calls him. Side 2 kicks off with "Get Behind It and Push," a modern-sounding sales motivator, which pauses for a couplet designed to get a roar from the audience familiar with the executives.

What does Mr. McPherson do
When sales start looking deadly?
He bravely keeps his chin up high
And screams at Bryan Hedly.

"The Tele-Op Blues," performed by Julia Sutton, addresses the problem of the Lyons Maid telephone sales girl, who has to keep calling retailers who can't or won't come to the phone. An odd bit of xenophobia, played for laughs, is her complaint that more and more shopkeepers are Turkish, Indian, Greek, or Maltese. Apparently in 1973, the only kind of intolerance that worried Lyons Maid was lactose intolerance.

RARITY: 2

SUCCESS… AND THEN SOME

McDonald's 1971 show is the record album equivalent of a Big Mac: two all-vinyl patties, special lyric booklet, photos, labels, on a cardboard bun. Quite filling and reasonably tasty, though not exactly gourmet quality.

Much of the two records is devoted to skits about crew training and other management issues, and segments about a stuffy European chef named Alexander who attempts to discover McDonald's secrets. Music is credited to Ray Tait and Al Porth, lyrics are by Marv David. Some of the songs are rewrites: "The Battle Hymn of the Republic" becomes "The Battle of the Rush," and the Beatles' "Back in the USSR" becomes "You Gotta Keep Rolling Along."

If you made the change that made your
*   store look great,*
With the look of quality,
If your operation's really up to date,

THE LYONS MAID STORY

The 1973 Launch Meeting at the Talk of The Town was a unique occasion.

It brought together, for the first time, all 550 members of the Lyons Maid sales team.

It presented the 1973 Programme as a musical review which traced the history of the company from earliest days, through to the present moment.

Joe (Guiseppe Bacaroni) Baker took the role of the ice cream seller through the ages.

Starting in Edwardian times with an offer nobody could refuse and ending up as a dealer in love with a voice on the Lyons Maid phone.

John Witty and Malcolm Mitchell provided the narration that linked the songs and sketches.

Julia Sutton showed just why she's the star of Antony Newley's latest musical, with a show stopping performance of the Tele-Op Blues.

The Lyons Maid story was a show that closed on its opening night but the messages in these songs are living on.

It's getting through to every dealer in the country that with Lyons Maid—they're laughing.

FOR THE RECORD

The music and lyrics were written by Malcolm Mitchell and Dennis Norden. The show was produced and directed by Gillian Lynne. Additional material was supplied by Tom Goldsmith and Finlay McPherson.

Stereo Record. Play at 33½ r.p.m.

SUCCESS... *and then some*

If it's what you know it should be,
You're probably rollin' along!

The modernization campaign comes up again in "Look What's Happened to the Store," with the singers crowing "New roof! New signs!" and how the up-to-date look is "blending right into a modern neighborhood." The jargon-heavy "QSC for 1800" refers to the Quality, Service, and Cleanliness rating system that the restaurants (1,800 at the time) were graded on. A typical customer sings "Never Mind the 8 Billion."

While you watch those billions rise,
I hope and trust you realize,
Who put those billions in the air,
It's guys like me who got you there.
Never mind the 8 billion—it's the one in
*   my hand!*

A conceptual high point is the delicate, pseudo-classical three-woman plea for restroom cleanliness, "When a Lady's Got to Go."

When a lady goes, she really goes, turns
*   the key, urgently.*
But if it's not clean behind the door,
She might wish that she had gone before.
You can bet your life that she'll return
*   nevermore...*
Nevermore...

You'd hope that an iconic corporation like McDonald's would have recorded more shows—Hank Beebe and Bill Heyer wrote several during the '70s—but this is the only one that made it onto vinyl. Quoth the McRaven, "Nevermore."

RARITY: 2

PIZZA HUT '73 ANNUAL MEETING

Pizza Hut, like McDonald's, started with a single location in the 1950s and by the early '70s had spread throughout the U.S. and was expanding worldwide. The 1973 meeting in San Diego had material written by Craig Deitschmann and Jon Shulenberger and featured one of the biggest comedy stars of the day, impressionist Rich Little. Side 1 of the record consists of Pizza Hut radio commercials, with Mr. Little doing impressions of Johnny Cash, Dean Martin, Elvis

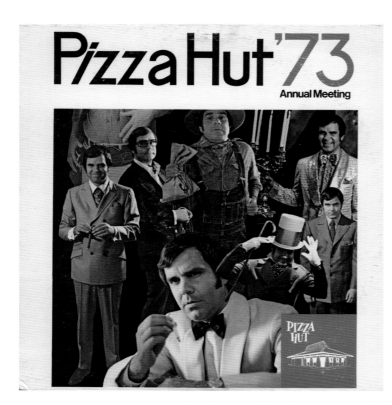

Presley, and Bing Crosby. On side 2 Mr. Little performs an expanded version of the "Pizza Hut Theme" heard in a side 1 commercial, plus an alternate generic version. In "Just Be Yourself," he unleashes a barrage of impressions, such as John Wayne, W. C. Fields, Clark Gable, Ed Sullivan, Humphrey Bogart, and more.

In the end, it's a minor item, but — *humble-brag alert* — I have a copy autographed by Rich Little. Okay, yeah, humblebrags don't get much more humble than that.

RARITY: 2

SIDE BY SIDE 75

Oh thank heaven, "A 7-Eleven Musical." This 1975 show has song parodies credited to Larry Muhoberac (a former Elvis Presley keyboard player) and some satisfying insider details and weirdness. "Ring Them Bells," a

John Kander and Fred Ebb song originally written for Liza Minnelli, becomes the story of a man who travels the world looking for the right business venture, only to find it at the 7-Eleven back in his hometown. Happy ending number one.

Several songs are lifted from Stephen Sondheim's *Company*. That show wasn't about a company, but rather company as in people hanging out together. "What Would We Do without You / Side by Side" is an upbeat portrait, complete with tap dancing, of the partnership between the top brass and the people running the stores, though the executives take some hits for being out of touch. "I'm Not Getting Married" is a rapid-fire tour de force in which a woman who's agreed to manage a store gets cold feet.

I don't like ice cream, I hate cottage cheese,

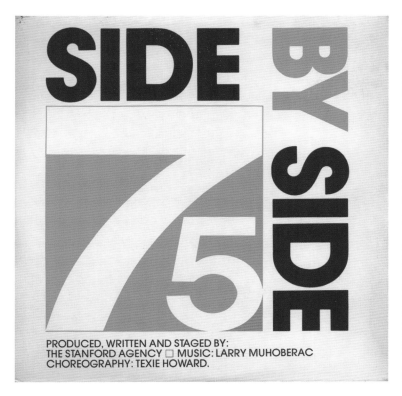

PRODUCED, WRITTEN AND STAGED BY:
THE STANFORD AGENCY ☐ MUSIC: LARRY MUHOBERAC
CHOREOGRAPHY: TEXIE HOWARD.

Just having completed the greatest year in Southland's history, I know you all are looking forward to this new year and its challenges. And "Side By Side" is the best way I know of making it all happen in 1975. I want to thank you and your family for the fine job you are doing.
Sincerely,
Jere W. Thompson

A 7-ELEVEN MUSICAL

1. **OH THANK HEAVEN**...a musical happening!
2. **WHAT WOULD WE DO WITHOUT YOU/SIDE BY SIDE**...this exciting medley of two great musical numbers sets the pace of the show as well as the theme for our 1975 Convention. The two song titles along with the lyrics really do say what we all feel...that we're all in this together. What would we do without each other?
3. **RING THEM BELLS**...a story about a guy who looked all over the world for his niche, a place to do his thing. And after all that searching he found it in the form of a little 7-Eleven store right back in his home town.
4. **I'M NOT GETTING MARRIED**...When we join the **7-ELEVEN** team it's a lot like "getting married". That's what this number's all about.
5. **ANOTHER HUNDRED PEOPLE JUST CAME INTO THE STORE**...a "today" statement about our stores and our company's history. Who would have thought in 1927 that almost fifty years later something like three million people a day would be our friends and customers.
6. **IT'S YOU**...ah, yes. A touch of nostalgia going back to the time when a unique idea turned a neighborhood ice dock into a mighty handy little grocery store.
7. **WE'VE GOT THE WHOLE WORLD IN OUR HANDS**...this really says it. You and I can be what we want to be in this company. It's up to us.

THE STARS OF THE SHOW
☆ Lette Rehnolds   ☆ Dan Truhitte
☆ Nancy Meyers   ☆ Dan Ferrone

RAY BERRY
Western Regional Manager

DON BURNSIDE
South Pacific Division Manager

TERRY DE BARD
Western Pacific Division Manager

KEN SLAUTH
Merchandise Manager

DENNIS POTTS
Merchandise Manager

JIM SHAUGHNESSY
The Stanford Agency

I don't like kids, I hate green peas.
Thank you for the training school,
Thanks a lot, but I'm no fool.
I tell you now, I'm not gonna do it — I'm
*   not gonna do it — you can't make me*
*   do it —*

Of course she does it, prompting church bells and a choir singing "Amen." Happy ending number two.

The jackpot of strangeness is "Another Hundred People Just Came into the Store." It toggles jarringly between rewrites of Sondheim's "Another Hundred People" and the Bobbie Gentry classic "Ode to Billie Joe." The latter's languid, ominous music is paired with lyrics about 7-Eleven's 1927 founding and subsequent growth. Then suddenly we're in Sondheim's urban crush of another hundred people.

I'm coming and going when I change
*   the shift*
We meet at the door,
Then I hired a guy who was born to drift,
Left with half the store,
There's the inventory sheet that's running
*   late,*
Another hundred forms I've really learned
*   to hate,*
But I love the business anyway, now isn't
*   that great?*

Happy ending number...two and a half? Quite a few industrial tunes catalogue the woes of managers or salesmen, then suddenly, unconvincingly, insist that it's all worth it in the end. Understandable; the corporations weren't paying for shows that would send the team into a tailspin of existential despair.

RARITY: 2

which receive mention in the odd opera-style number "The Englewood Opera Company." They're all here: the tea, the egg noodles, the Wishbone dressing, the sauce and gravy mixes, the Knox Gelatin, the Cup-a-Soup, and the Soviet-sounding Lipton Family Drink Mix. Yes, it's very much like bein' a flower in spring.

The mid-range orchestral music plunks along sturdily enough, with an occasional nod to the age of the electric guitar. Music is by Larry Meeks (a former Benny Goodman pianist), with lyrics by Maryruth Weyand. The best song, "Salesman's Sonata," paints a colorful picture of a salesman pitching to a distracted client.

> *You're determined that you get his full*
> *attention!*
> *You consider setting fire to your tie!*
> *Do a dance on his credenza*
> *'Til you learn he never spends a*
> *Single penny 'til the committee says*
> *to buy!*

As with songs for Kinney, J. C. Penney, 7-Eleven, and others, after the catalogue of woes, the song bravely concludes that it's the life we love and we wouldn't have it any other way. Here the vocalist even interrupts the chorus with way-too-insistent interjections such as "I *love* it!" "I'm glad, glad, d'ya hear, *glad!*" Yeah, I hear you, mister. Have a glass of Family Drink Mix and calm down.

RARITY: 2

LIPTON ON THE MOVE

> *It's a beautiful thing to be part of the*
> *Lipton family*
> *Like bein' a flower in spring, or a song*
> *children sing*
> *It's a beautiful thing*

I file this 1972 production under "So-So Shows with Eye-Catching Period Covers and a Few Moments of Charm." The back cover of the 10-inch album shows the range of Lipton products,

PUSHING TEA

In other contexts, the wavy lettering and swirly colors that flo-thru the cover of this album might evoke brisk youthfulness: a spinning hit 45, maybe, or the freedom of "shootin' the curl." Here, they represent a sucking vortex of supermart blandness all the more engaging for its feckless attempt at a "Now!" feel. At the center of the mild maelstrom—its drain trap, if you will—is an image of corporate HQ with giant samples of Lipton's product range stacked on the roof, all of it overseen by the gargantuan godheads of Mr. and Ms. Handsome, ad-dom's idealized proxies for the American consumer.

The surreal image is rendered in a projector-traced clean line style quite widespread at the time, likely in imitation of illustrator Bob Peak's work or such psychedelic imagery as the cover art of Love's *Forever Changes*. Either way, this doesn't quite get there, instead recalling the maplike contours of an unsullied paint-by-numbers canvas. Are you thinking what I'm thinking? Craft project!! With an X-Acto blade, Elmer's glue, and some samples of flocked paper in various fluorescent shades, one could really do a number on this design, creating, with any luck, the uncoolest blacklight poster ever.

—SM

K '71 IT'S A KELLOGG'S YEAR

K '71 IT'S A KELLOGG'S YEAR

Although it's noteworthy for depicting what may be the largest-ever letter *K* formed by humans, there's no original show music on this uncredited 1971 record. A couple tracks on the 7-inch disc are adaptations of commercial jingles, while "The K-71 March" is a rewrite of "Step to the Rear" from the musical *How Now, Dow Jones*.

Sixty-five years we have been pioneers
And that has made us number one.
So—come on, give 'em hell—you can get
*   out and sell*
'cause you're great personnel all the way!

The most interesting track references an early '70s cereal brouhaha. In September 1970 a consumer advocate named Robert Choate Jr. testified to the Senate Select Committee on Nutrition and Human Needs that the majority of America's popular breakfast cereals were fattening but not actually nutritious. The cereal companies denied the charges but lost the PR war and had to put nutrition information on boxes. That controversy is the theme of "Low Noon," a parody of "The Ballad of High Noon" performed by a credible Johnny Cash imitator, who laments poor Tony the Tiger's ambush by busybodies.

A paper tiger's what they call you
And callin' names is far from fair.
Looks like they're fixin' to blackball you
They say nutrition is what you're missin',
It just don't seem they're shootin' square.

Tony's beloved Frosted Flakes have survived, minus "Sugar" in the name and fortified with essential vitamins and minerals. They're grrrrrrudgingly improved!

RARITY: 2

TOM'S 1975 SALES MEETING & FIFTIETH ANNIVERSARY CELEBRATION

Founded in 1925, Tom's started out selling peanuts in cellophane sleeves and expanded into other snack foods and vending machines. The company still exists, though it's been bought and sold and gone bankrupt numerous times. Tom's fiftieth anniversary extravaganza has a very tasty sound with smoky, soulful songs by Phil Kelly and Marshall Riggan. "Takes Brass" is an appropriately brassy retrospective of Tom's history and a look toward the future. Most striking is "How to Make a Machine," in which vocalist Trella Hart explains why a vending machine is her love interest rather than a man.

> *He fills me with cookies, and fills me with cakes,*
> *And toasted peanuts are the love that we make.*

Peanut sex. Ohhh yeahhhh.

RARITY: 1

THINGS ARE CHANGING!

One last gasp of Oldsmobility made it onto vinyl: a marketing conference record from 1970 called *Things Are Changing!*. The 45 rpm record features "Things Are Changing," the same song used by Durkee and Ortho Pharmaceuticals, here with Olds-specific lyrics.

> *Hey you out there, Mr. Oldsmobile,*
> *Are you watchin' where you're goin', have you got the feel?*
> *While you're wheelin' and a-dealin' on your office phone,*
> *Are you missin' any action going on in your zone?*

As always, "Things Are Changing" has a great sound and a hard-hitting message, but with four known uses from '69 to '72, it proves that the more things are changing, the more they're staying the same.

RARITY: 1

THE CHEVROLET EXPERIENCE

For decades the Jam Handy Organization produced training materials as well as shows for many companies, including Chevrolet. In the early 1970s founder Jamison Handy, well into his eighties, helped a lieutenant named Bill Sandy start a successor company that would take over the automotive part of the business. One of only two Bill Sandy shows to make it onto vinyl is 1976's *The Chevrolet Experience*, announcing the '77 models.

There's some serviceable material here, as you'd expect from industrial songwriting veterans Wilson Stone and David Blomquist, but like the '77 Chevys themselves, there's not much to thrill enthusiasts. The faux swanky "Concours" uses imagery of "candles and crystal" and "moonlight and fountains" to introduce the Nova Concours, a crashingly dull midsize model tarted up with plusher seats and extra badges. "Experience" and "Innovation" are slick but generic, with only a couple stray Chevy references. "Fun and Functional," about station wagons, is distinguished mainly by a bizarre high-pitched warbly voice in the mix—maybe the show included a puppet or a robot, or perhaps a cast member got a sequin stuck in his or her throat.

Some of the songs weren't specific to the show. "Now *That's* More Like It!" was the '77 Chevy theme song used in advertising, and "Chevrolet Proud" was a stirring Hank Beebe anthem dating back to 1961.

> *The man who drives that Chevy knows what it's like to be...Chevrolet proud!*
> *The man who engineers it knows what it's like to be...*
> *Chevrolet proud!*
> *The man who builds that Chevy knows what it's like to be...*
> *Chevrolet proud!*
> *The man who sells that Chevy knows what it's like to be...*
> *Chevrolet proud!*

R. E. Cook
General Sales Manager

The shape of the future is clear.

We're in the process of obsoleting 94 million cars on the American road to put us into better alignment with our customers' and our nation's needs. That's the significance of General Motors' five-year, 15 billion dollar redesign program.

People, today, are looking for more than material goods. They're looking for a lift to their life.

Side 2 drifts away from show music entirely, with an Americana concert and skippable remarks by general sales manager R. E. Cook. (No offense to you R. E. Cook fans.)

RARITY: 4

THE MAKING OF A PRECEDENT—TOYOTA, THE CHALLENGE OF THE 70's

Toyota entered the American market in 1965, and by 1970 it was the second-best-selling import trailing only Volkswagen. The 1970 sales meeting of American Toyota dealers predicted great growth and success in the years ahead, and for once the ballyhoo turned out to be absolutely true.

The uncredited material sounds like a film soundtrack rather than a live stage show, and the cover photos may have been from a

THE CHEVROLET EXPERIENCE

THE MAKING OF A PRECEDENT

TOYOTA, The Challenge of the '70s

"The Making of a Precedent" is Toyota's State of the Union message. It's a message of success. And a bright, brassy tribute to the thousands of men who made that success come about.

It's a look at automotive history . . . and automotive precedence. It's the story of how a stranger in a strange land became a friendly and familiar sight. And how that straightforward assembly of craftsmanship, quality and design became that nation's second larg-

est selling imported car in just a few short years.

It is, in effect, the tale of where Toyota has been, where it is today, and where it is going. It is, as we have said, a success story. An unprecedented one.

This album contains the sounds of The Making of a Precedent, a special presentation produced for the Toyota Dealers of the United States, and presented in Dallas, Atlanta, Chicago, New York and Las Vegas during the month of August, 1970.

Besides being a "What's Happening" message, the production of The Making of a Precedent was a glorious excuse to introduce the all new 1970 Toyota Corona and the 1971 Toyota Corolla. Within this album you'll find statements by S. Hattori, President of Toyota Motor Distributors, and James F. McGraw, National Sales Manager, and all the sounds and music that helped to create and breathe life into . . . THE MAKING OF A PRECEDENT.

THE TOYOTA FIRST FAMILY

---

film. The President-Precedent pun inspires some political bits, with the Corona as the "candidate" and the Corolla the "running mate," and reports from supposed conventions and rallies about the ticket's features. Mixed in are executive speeches, interviews with dealers, and narrated segments about Toyota's history and current momentum. There's one cute little song with a typical American industrial horns-and-xylophone sound.

> *The thing about Toyota is the trouble that they go ta,*
> *Is to guarantee that you'll make lots of dough!*
> *Researching and designing it, and testing and refining it,*
> *And making sure your customers will never let it go!*

The Japanese may have been starting to catch up in the automotive world, but I'm pretty sure it wasn't a Japanese lyricist who came up with the *Toyota / they go ta* rhyme. *USA! USA!*

RARITY: 2

VOLKSWAGEN '79

VW was an American institution by 1979, even if it didn't happen to be American. For its U.S. dealer network, the company commissioned a show by the veteran team Wilson Stone and David Blomquist. The show displays a mixture of optimism and cynicism, with the upbeat "VW's Moving" balanced by "VW Does It Again." Fed up with quality problems and an unresponsive bureaucracy, VW dealer Wally Samuels delivers a sarcastic rant.

Volkswagen '79

MUSIC FROM THE '79 INTRO SHOW

The trucks come in — what have they got?
Ten-thousand-dollar campers — oh,
*   those'll be hot!*
Each time that they do it, I just hope I live
*   through it,*
When Volkswagen does it again.

The disco-inflected "Looking to You" reminds dealers that today's sophisticated customers demand quality and value, and "Business Quartet" uses barbershop quartet harmonies to extol a diversified dealership.

Get parts and service, used cars and new,
Then put them all to work for you.
If new cars should falter, don't you panic
*   in grief,*
Maybe parts and service can lend
*   some relief.*

In "Wally's Prayer," Wally asks God for the new American-made Rabbits to be free of the quality control problems that have been plaguing the company. The new Rabbits arrive, and all agree they look good. Except again, the

---

positive is balanced by a negative: because VW's headquarters was in Englewood Cliffs, New Jersey, *spiffy* is rhymed with *Englewood Cliffy*.

RARITY: 3

PORSCHE+AUDI presents

THE MUSICAL SCORE FROM

Born Again

NATIONAL DEALER MEETING
MUNICH 1979

WRITTEN AND DIRECTED BY
EDWARD REVEAUX

MUSIC AND LYRICS
WALTER MARKS

CHOREOGRAPHER
JIMMIE JAMES

A THOMAS CRAVEN FILM CORPORATION PRODUCTION

BORN AGAIN

Another 1979 show, from VW's corporate cousin Porsche/Audi. Composer Walter Marks says this was the last industrial show he wrote, and much about it feels familiar: a plot about a troubled dealer who has a dream and sees a vision of a better tomorrow, and songs that talk about "a bright new day" and the importance of giving the customer personalized care. A jolt of modern sound appears in "4000 Fever," about the hot new Audi model, and "Champ One Day" introduces the "kid brother" of the legendary Porsche 911, the new 924. "The Company We Keep" is a reminder to dealers to keep things classy.

You can't sell to a man who has
*   champagne taste*

4000 FEVER
Oh I feel excitement in the air
People are talkin'
And you can hear it everywhere
The word's out
And it's sweeping the nation
And it's all about
Audi's wonderful car.

4000 fever . . . It's 4000 fever
The Audi 4000 is here
Road and Track voted it
Tops in its class
As the European car of the Year.

Oh, it really handles like a
    dream out on the road
It is everything a car should be
A full-fledged member of the
    Audi family.
It's the sports sedan well
    worth waiting for.

4000 fever . . . It's 4000 fever
That's sweeping the country
    for real.
An international jury of
    motoring journalists
Voted it the Golden Steering
    Wheel. (Dance)

4000 fever . . . It's 4000 fever
That sporty and luxury car
With four triple zero
You'll have a great year, Oh
It's gonna go great and go far.

4000 fever . . . 4000 fever
Catch it now.

CHAMP ONE DAY
There is a new contender
Comin' up through the bunch
Its the Turbo with power
    to spare and a knockout punch.
He's the kid brother of the
    911; the champion,
But they say
That the kid brother of the 911
is gonna be the champ one day.

It's the next generation
In the grand design
In the great tradition
Of the Porsche line
He's got the moves of his
    older brother — but better
In many ways
the kid brother of the 911
Is gonna be the champ one day!

The Turbo is loaded with
    dynamite.
He's got the speed and the
    drive; you can bet
He'll outperform all his
    competition.
He handles with style and
    grace and class
A winner in every way.
He'll be coming in race after
    race in the first position.

When he's really ready
And he's makin his move
He'll take that Porsche image
And he'll make it improve.
When his older brother hangs
    his famous gloves up,
The public is gonna say,
The kid brother of the 911
The kid they call 924
Is champion of the world,
    today. (Dance)

FINALE — musical medley

If you offer him a can of beer.
And you can't sell a guy who wants a
Porsche or an Audi
In a lowdown atmosphere.

Although *Born Again* was performed for American dealers, it was staged in Munich. Is Germany really the place to sing a song dissing beer?

RARITY: 3

REFLECTIONS ON SPORT

A fair-to-middlin' 1977 show for Sports Illustrated on a 7-inch record, with a small cast and a four-piece band dishing out a mild rock sound. The songs were written by Alan Braunstein, and the plot involved a ringer in the audience, a woman who, during banter with tennis great Tony Trabert, reveals that she doesn't like sports. The rest of the show consists of the other cast members trying to change her mind, while also pointing out the appeal of *Sports Illustrated*.

Songs include "Sport Is Booming," with statistics about how many millions of Americans are into sports, and "P.E.," in which sports hater Elaine recalls the humiliation of school gym class. In "I Did It," the others recall their athletic accomplishments, and even sad sack Elaine finally has her breakthrough when she remembers a wonderful time riding a horse with her grandfather. "I've never been an athlete, but I've known the thrill of sports."

The one song that gets into familiar industrial territory is the finale, "*Sports Illustrated*," which assures potential advertisers:

And with sixteen million readers,
naturally
Sports Illustrated is the authority
They'll respond to your ad, because
they're in a mood
To listen, to everything from corporate
messages,
To liquor and fine cars.
All your sporting equipment, travel near
and far.

I don't read *Sports Illustrated*, but it turns out that I *am* in a mood to listen to corporate messages.

RARITY: 2

ONE FOR THE MONEY

The love of Money is the root of good!

This 1982 *Money* magazine show for advertisers was written by Nathaniel Lande, Rod Warren, and Jerry Powell (veteran of the '60s shows *All About Life* and *Flush Left Stagger Right*). The cast includes our storyteller John Russell, performing under the name Peter Shawn. The general outline is similar to the '60s media shows: you've got the tried-and-true vaudevillian back-and-forth in "Money Talks."

Say, Mr. Kelly! — Yes, Mr. Hayes?
I am looking for innovation, and fresh
*   modern ways,*
We're reaching out a helping hand,
To help our readers understand
And to feel secure, know what to do
When money walks in and talks to you.

Other perennial musical styles appear
in "The Money Tango" and "Money Helps,"
featuring barbershop quartet harmonies.

When the wolf's at your door, and the
*   door has no lock,*
When your ship has come in, but it sank
*   at the dock,*
When you're hit on the head by a Piece of
*   the Rock,*
That's when Money helps.

REAGANOMICS (TRICKLE DOWN)
Randall Easterbrook, Pamela McLernon, Scott Ellis, Maureen McNamara, Peter Shawn

There's the song praising *Money*'s
enviable circulation numbers and readership
demographics, a couple tongue-in-
cheek "current events" songs, such as
"Reaganomics," and a dizzying list song, "Mad
About the Ad," which presents a cavalcade
of companies ("From Apple to Xerox, that's
roughly A to Z") that advertise in *Money*. But
what's the deal with a female cast member
singing "Give me Dictaphone, give me Wang"?
Oh, never mind, now I get it.

RARITY: 3

EB: A SOMEWHAT IRREVERENT HISTORY

My dream is to gather all the knowledge that's worth knowing
To arrange it alphabetically for showing
With engravings and an index in the back.

As someone who's trying to gather all the knowledge worth knowing on one strange topic, I have to salute the efforts of the Encyclopedia Britannica USA people. In 1978 they'd just reached $100 million in fiscal year sales for the first time and were also celebrating the five-year anniversary of their new corporate entity, EBUSA (pronounced "Eh-boo-sa"). Six hundred attendees at the Boca Raton meeting witnessed a history of the company told through "irreverent" (read "cringe-inducing") uncredited sketches and songs.

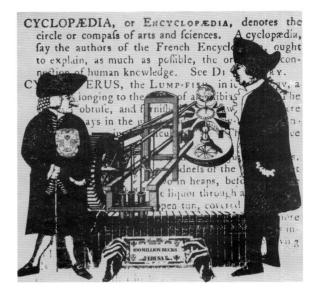

It's not all terrible. The bluesy "Advertisin'" has a decent guitar solo and tosses around phrases like "discounted price," "limited quantity," and "free bookcase offer." An uncomfortable bit involving General Custer and

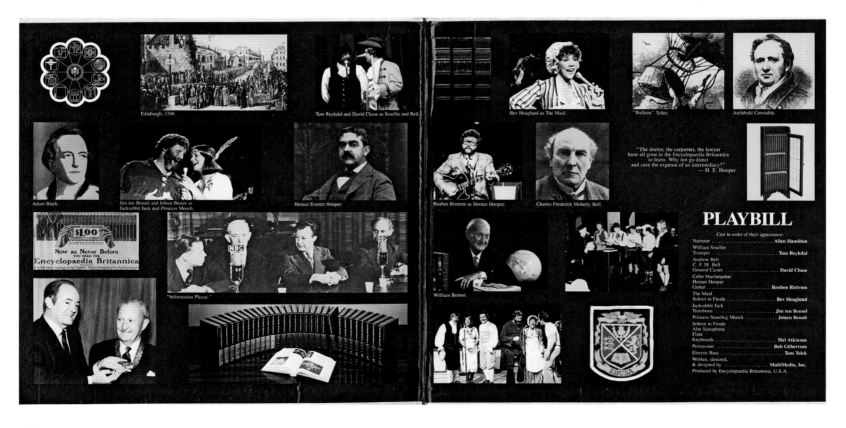

Edinburgh, 1768.

Tom Reykdal and David Chase as Smellie and Bell.

Bev Hoaglund as The Maid.

"Balloon" Tytler.

Archibald Constable.

Adam Black.

Jim ten Bensel and Joleen Benoit as Jackrabbit Jack and Princess Mooch.

Horace Everett Hooper.

Reuben Ristrom as Horace Hooper.

Charles Frederick Moberly Bell.

"The doctor, the carpenter, the lawyer have all gone to the Encyclopaedia Britannica to learn. Why not go direct and save the expense of an intermediary?"
— H. E. Hooper

Now as Never Before — YOU NEED THE — Encyclopaedia Britannica

"Information Please."

William Benton.

PLAYBILL

Cast in order of their appearance:

Narrator	Allen Hamilton
William Smellie	
Trumpet	Tom Reykdal
Andrew Bell	
C. F. M. Bell	
General Custer	David Chase
Colin Macfarquhar	
Horace Hooper	
Guitar	Reuben Ristrom
The Maid	
Soloist in Finale	Bev Hoaglund
Jackrabbit Jack	
Trombone	Jim ten Bensel
Princess Standing Mooch	Joleen Benoit
Soloist in Finale	
Alto Saxophone	
Flute	
Keyboards	Hal Atkinson
Percussion	Bob Gilbertson
Electric Bass	Tom Tolck
Written, directed, & designed by	MultiMedia, Inc.

Produced by Encyclopaedia Britannica, U.S.A.

Princess Standing Mooch yields a parody of the Barry Manilow hit "Copacabana."

Britannica, oh, Britannica
The very best encyclopedia
Britannica, oh, Britannica
Who needs a college when all of that
knowledge
Can be found in...Britannica.

Okay, it's not so great, but the payoff is interesting: a phone rings, and the narrator says, "Hello, narrator here. Yes, Mr. Manilow, I understand. If we use any more of your songs, we'll have to pay a royalty." Or maybe you can buy him off with a free bookcase.

RARITY: 2

ENTER BILLENIUM

The discovery of this 1985 Encyclopedia Britannica show raised high hopes in the tiny industrial show fan community. Some of the songs were credited to the writer of the killer 1969 American-Standard show *The Bathrooms Are Coming!*, Sid Siegel! Sadly, we were let down.

"Billenium" apparently refers to the milestone of a billion dollars in sales, which EBUSA had just hit. Although some of the Sid Siegel music sounds a bit like his high-quality *Bathrooms* material, the lyrics are almost entirely bland fluff in the "new day is dawning, together we'll succeed" vein. I've impetuously decided to blame the other credited writers: Charles Ernst, Dave Hayes, Jeff Siegel, and TMC Musical Productions.

The only interesting track is "How Did You Get to EBUSA?" Though Encyclopedia Britannica had branched out during the '70s to selling at malls, state fairs, and bookstores,

ENTER BILLENIUM
Nassau, Bahamas

Original Soundtrack Recording

Phil Masterton (L) and Leah Green

Dan Frick (L) and Gene Weygandt

Bonnie Sue Arp

Betsy Randle

"In Billenium Almost Anything is Possible"

"Enter Billenium"
Encyclopaedia Britannica, USA
National Sales Meeting
Nassau, Bahamas
October 25-28, 1985
Executive Producer **Jeff Siegel**
Co-producer **Motivation Media**, Glenview, Illinois
The Mighty EBUSA Players

Photographs by **Marcia Fenton**
Design by **Margery Hall Graphic Design**
EBUSA Field Communications
Jeff Siegel, Tom Panelas, Rick Santangelo, and **Marcia Fenton**
The producers greatfully acknowledge the support of **Peter Norton, Robert L. Baseman, Barbara Camillucci, Bonnie Pletcher, IVI Travel, Inc.,** and the more than 100 people who directly and indirectly made Billenium a reality.

Studio Media, Evanston, Illinois. Midwest Record Pressing. ©1985 Encyclopaedia Britannica, Inc. All rights reserved

Side 1	
Intro Narration: Larry Moran	.35
Enter Billenium Lyrics: Dave Hayes Music: TMC Music Productions, Inc.	3:04
What Would the World Be Lyrics: Sid Siegel Music: Sid Siegel	3:01
The Man From Britannica Lyrics: Dave Hayes Music: TMC Music Productions, Inc.	2:10
Movin' Up Lyrics: Sid Siegel and Dave Hayes Music: Sid Siegel	2:56
How Did You Get to EBUSA? Lyrics: Sid Siegel and Dave Hayes Music: Sid Siegel	2:56
Side 2	
E.B.U.S.A. Lyrics: Jeff Siegel Music: Charles Ernst	3:07
Be All You Can Possibly Be Lyrics: Sid Siegel Music: Sid Siegel	3:22
We Make the Difference Lyrics: Dave Hayes Music: TMC Music Productions, Inc.	3:26
Enter Billenium (Instrumental) Music: TMC Music Productions, Inc.	6:12

the door-to-door salepeople were still a big part of the business. The lyrics reflect a surprising range of backgrounds that EBUSA field reps might have come from.

I was a plumber with no pipes to fix,
I was a bookie with all the wrong picks,
I was a dancer who couldn't keep up with
   the beat,
I was a waiter, made wonderful tips,
I was a stripper, and I used my hips,
I was a hooker, so glad to be back on
   her feet!
And now, we're with EBUSA, EBUSA!

Unfortunately, due to the rise of the Internet, the hooker's now on her back again. In 2012, Encyclopedia Britannica discontinued the print edition.

RARITY: 1

TAKE IT FROM HERE—1971

This 1971 Xerox show by Wilson Stone and David Blomquist is largely copied, er, adapted from the much more common '63 version as well as from other Jam Handy productions. "Take It from Here," "Xerox's the Name," and "Dream of Destiny" are reprised from the earlier version, with minor changes to the lyrics. "Understanding" is from the '66 Coke show, also with revised lyrics. "New World Opening Up" was in the '67 Chevy show, and possibly others as well.

In the eight years since the earlier *Take It from Here*, Xerox had greatly expanded, going global and moving into computers. In "Bit by Bit," there's a prescient glimpse of the coming information superhighway.

It grows and grows, bit by bit
Flows on an electronic avenue,
Building information, that is what we do,
Bringing tomorrow to you.
Plug-in computers and copy devices,
Words and pictures combined
Graphics plus optics, reduplication,
Xerox is stretching your mind!

The liner notes generously refer to "Bit by Bit" as "a rock and roll song," thanks to a restrained electric guitar amid the horns and some young people singing harmony. Conservative production company Jam Handy was trying to get hip. "We Want to Get the Facts" has whispers of wah-wah guitar, and Charlie the Xerox salesman demands to know "what the hell's going on." Careful, Jam Handy: it's only a short step from rudeness and rock and roll to snorting toner.

RARITY: 2

Produced for the
Xerox Corporate Staff by
The Jam Handy Organization

Music and Lyrics
Wilson Stone

Book and Additional Lyrics
David Blomquist

Musical Direction
Maurice Levine

Orchestrations
Arthur Harris

Featuring
Mace Barrett as
Charlie Powers

Columbia stereo records can be played on today's mono record players with excellent results. They will last as long as mono records played on the same equipment, yet will reveal full stereo sound when played on stereo record players.

The action stops momentarily as the Xerox philosophy is stated . . . a commitment to help improve the quality of life through the application of better communications. This thought is presented musically in a modern ballad titled The Good Life

Charlie now presents the concept of The Architecture of Information. "Yes," he says, "information can be built like a house." With the entire cast joining him, he sets forth this concept in a rock and roll song — Bit by Bit

Now that he is beginning to get the "Big Picture," Charlie calls on the legal department to discuss some of his ideas. In a mock musical treatment, he is gently rebuffed in The Legal Madrigal

"But Xerox does so many things. How can I describe it?", asks Charlie. He is given the answer in a rollicking country style song. "There is one word that sums it up," he is told and the word is Communications

Charlie now understands the whole world of Xerox. He realizes that what is going on in the company today and what will continue through the 70's is part of a continuing dream. He sings the finale A Dream of Destiny

DO YOU COPY?

There are many here among us who feel that even second-tier sunshine pop is still a pretty darn good thing, and unlike many other permutations of rock, for which that will o' the wisp called "authenticity" is coin of the realm, it seems to actually improve in proportion to the very crassness of its commercial intentions. By way of illustration, imagine that Peppermint Rainbow's "Will You Be Staying After Sunday" (a magnificent record already, it's a given) had been created to promote the Days Inn motel chain. It would then be even better than it really is…maybe even better for that than first-tier work like the Association's "Along Comes Mary."

By those lights "Bit by Bit," composed solely to motivate the worker bees at Xerox toward revenue streams yet undreamed, is some kind of third-tier sunshine apotheosis. Musically, it touches on genre conventions like the stacked horn section buildups of "Love, American Style" and the faux-reflective-bridge-to-further-punch-the-sugar-rush-chorus device of "Up, Up and Away." The optimism overload of its performance is positively Stepfordian, with a humdrum spoken section that lifts the piece into corporation-cult nerdvana.

But, smirk as we might, the lyric forecasts the impending 1970s in visionary terms that indeed became strangely accurate reality…by the 1990s. Of course, by then all that Brady Kids bubblegum had long been scraped off culture's shoe, with the appetite of the masses demanding nothing less than the instant crack-pipe thrill of grunge's yarling angst and hip-hop's vulgar braggadocio. According to ever morphing authenticity-inversion theory, then, these vastly profitable genres are suspect, and the obscure efforts of industrial show composers representative of something more innocent…more genuine. What a tangled web we weave.

—SM

221

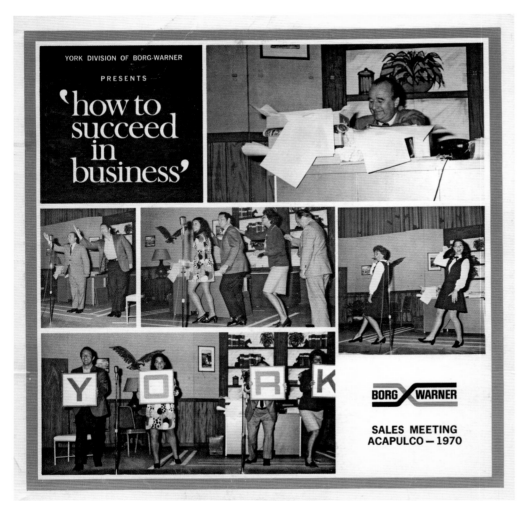

YORK DIVISION OF BORG-WARNER
PRESENTS

'how to succeed in business'

BORG WARNER

SALES MEETING
ACAPULCO — 1970

JOHN C. BECHER—"GEORGE"

DENA DIETRICH — "JANE"

CHARLES KAREL — "DON"

JANA ROBBINS—"LIL"

HOW TO SUCCEED IN BUSINESS

The plot of this uncredited 1970 York air conditioner show concerns a bumbling York dealer named George who didn't win a trip to the Aruba meeting because poor record keeping and financial disorganization hurt his business. His brother-in-law Don, a more successful York dealer, teaches him in song about cash flow projections, budgeting, and effectively running a service department. The songs appear to be mainly parodies, including "Southeast Corner of the Sheet," a song about profit and loss set to "Raindrops Keep

Falling on My Head"; "I'll Never Learn It on My Own," set to "I'll Never Fall in Love Again"; and "Trouble," set to "Ya Got Trouble" from *The Music Man*.

> *I'd say you've got trouble, my friend,*
> *In your service department!*
> *And that's a capital T and it rhymes*
> *   with B,*
> *And your service is bad!*
> *No system, no dispatcher, it's no wonder*
> *That your customers keep calling you*
> *   a cad!*
>
> *You'll learn the way to figure out your*
> *   service costs,*
> *Like overhead, like tools, and shop*
> *   expense!*
> *You'll learn the way to handle purchase*
> *   orders!*
> *Such benefits, they really are immense!*

There's also "Venezuela," a tease about the upcoming 1971 luxury getaway and sales meeting for dealers who stayed on top of all the baffling small business problems. So far, no '71 record has turned up. Maybe I just haven't found it yet, or maybe so many York dealers were screwups in '71 that York didn't bother with a Venezuela meeting after all.

RARITY: 2

ALL IN THE YORK FAMILY

Industrial shows can be a window onto trends of the day: musical styles, the state of the economy, or in this case what's hot on television. In 1972 *All in the Family* had just become a national phenomenon, and York hopped on the bandwagon with its own air-conditioning-themed version of Archie, Edith, Mike, and Gloria—as well as a "Mr. Harris," who appears to have been a York dealer mentoring new salesman Mike.

Some of the uncredited songs are parodies, such as "Baby It's Hot Inside," with Archie brushing off Edith's pleas for air-conditioning, and "You Gotta Have Plans," a rewrite of "(You Gotta Have) Heart" from *Damn Yankees*. There's also a version of the *All in the Family* theme song, "Those Were the Days." The high-energy "Sales Training" appears to be an original.

Now you can fully explain heat loss
*   and gain*
Air distribution too!
And you have learned design and you
*   do fine*
On load estimating, cost calculating,
*   salesman super-do!*

Mike's learned to write proposals,
He presents them very well.
Our tools and our materials he knows just
*   the way to sell.*
Selling techniques Mike has learned,
Including one called "close,"
That's lots of facts and plans, and Mike
Has mastered all of those!

As with the previous York shows, the band sounds great, with swinging horns and the occasional dollop of modern wah-wah guitar. "Makin' Profits" verges on religious ecstasy.

With administration, it's up to us
Plan and do budgeting, with no fuss.
Control the business! Use all means!
I'll say it once again! (Hallelujah!)
Makin' profits is up to us, amen!

YORK DIVISION OF BORG-WARNER PRESENTS

'all in the YORK family'

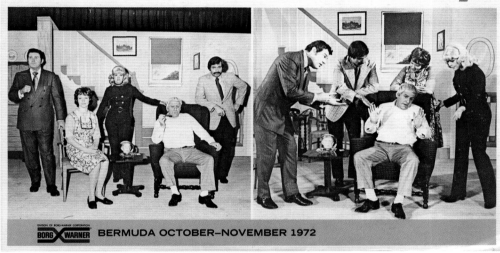

BORG WARNER   BERMUDA OCTOBER–NOVEMBER 1972

Amen, York Division of Borg-Warner. Even if no other shows ever come to light, you've given us plenty of red-hot songs about selling coolness.

RARITY: 2

FEATURING AN

ALL-STAR CAST

JAMES HARDER — "ARCHIE"

CHARLOTTE FAIRCHILD—"EDITH"

CHARLES BRASWELL—"MR HARRIS"

GIL GERARD—"MICHAEL"

DORTHEA ALFRED — "GLORIA"

OUR FUTURE'S NOW!

More air-conditioning show tunes! This time it's the Trane Company, with a good-sounding 1971 song parody show credited to Bob Williams. The Burt Bacharach–Hal David classic "Alfie" gets a makeover from the baffled wife of a Trane dealer named Ralphie.

And just what is DDP, Ralphie?
Is it Dealer Development Plan?
Then there's CDD and a TCC, Ralphie,
Am I wife to an alphabet man?

Other rewrites include "If I Were a Wise Man," with lyrics about hiring and training more personnel, and "Trane Comfort Corps" to the tune of "Aquarius / Let the Sunshine In."

An odd highlight is a bit called "Dis-Comfort Corps." Apparently the Comfort Corps technicians had been complaining about the coveralls: raising one's arms caused a painful binding in the crotch. The live demonstration gets one of the biggest laughs on industrial show vinyl. Ouch.

RARITY: 1

THE SIMPSON "COMMAND PERFORMANCE"

This uncredited 1972 Simpson washing machine show is so far the only nonautomotive Australian industrial to turn up, and it's charming enough. There are no song titles listed, so we can only guess that "Perfectly Average" is the name of the number sung by a housewife.

I'm perfectly average in every way,
Spending a typically average day.

She goes on to mention her "friend," her balky twenty-year-old washing machine. In "Show Me the Washer" she admits that Simpson's new models could tempt her to make a change.

Please, show me the washer that lets
*   me decide*
If I want to wash perma-press clothes,
One whose controls are so simple to use,
That's the thing women want, heaven
*   knows!*
All that I'm praying for, all that I'm saying is
Show me the washer that puts me in
*   command!*

There's a song about the new advertising campaign and point of sale displays possibly titled "Something to Cheer About," and others with vague morale-boosting messages. Beyond a couple of okay songs, the fun lies in the weird cover and the breathless inside material, which includes the adrenaline-boosting claim: "The Simpson 'Command Performance' campaign is the biggest washer advertising launch to hit Australia in recent years." No argument here.

RARITY: 2

THE SIMPSON
'COMMAND PERFORMANCE'

GOING PLACES WITH GLIDDEN...IN '72

This 1971 Glidden Paint show is a decent second-tier specimen, with original music by George Hill, Richard Whetstone, and Henry Schneider and lyrics by the memorably named Frank X. Fatsie. There's a plot about Glidden salesman George Grandley, who's about to go to the sales meeting but worries that Glidden doesn't really understand what he's up against in the field. He falls asleep and is visited by ghostly messengers who explain to him that Glidden does understand, has prepared new ad campaigns and sales aids, and values his work. In a brilliant cost-saving move, the ghostly messengers are all played by Glidden executives!

A small bass-heavy combo with a chintzy-sounding organ backs the two singers through numbers such as "Salesman Song."

A salesman, a salesman, a salesman travels alone.
You're a long way from the home base,
And the company's a voice on the phone.

Grandley makes a grandiose point in "Advertising."

If you're selling paint, tell 'em paint is what it ain't.
Get their eye upon the donut, not the hole.

Sell them, sell them, sell sell sell
Tell them, tell them, tell tell tell
That painting is the way to save your soul.

Grandley's wife, Doris, sings about the dreariness of being stuck at home while George is on the road. "Problems" finds Grandley grappling with complaints about shortages and quality control issues, "Greed" is about an incentive prize program, and "Jamaica" is a tease about next year's getaway for top sellers. There's even — wait for it — a message from Glidden general manager Gary Bechtel!

RARITY: 1

MAKIN' SURE IT'S MASONITE!

There's something a little different about this 1975 sales meeting record: the frequently clunky song parodies were written and performed by Masonite employees, not hired-gun professionals.

Masonite was founded in the 1920s in Laurel, Mississippi, by William Mason, who developed a way to convert wood waste from sawmills into a high-density fiberboard that became a popular building material. The '75 sales meeting at the Laurel headquarters featured a five-piece in-house band playing uncredited Masonite-specific versions of the tunes "Wabash Cannonball," "Danny Boy," "I Saw the Light," and more. From "Coating Foreman Blues":

Well, the soles on my shoes are worn out
*   from*
Walking around the coating lines.
I check on safety hazards, quality, and
*   production,*
And so far we're doing fine.
That's my job to see that when our
*   products leave me*
They're the finest in the world.
That our customer receives beauty and
*   durability*
To rival the rarest pearl.

The fiddle player is pretty solid and the singer has a fair set of pipes, but the rhythm occasionally falls apart and the rickety lyrics don't always rhyme. Not bad for amateurs, and actually no worse than some of the lame "professional" shows that didn't really merit preservation on vinyl. One other check in the "plus" column: the inside gatefold has forty photos from the four-day meeting, makin' sure we never forget all the fun.

RARITY: 2

Sunday
arrival…reception…
revival of old friendships.

Wednesday
seminars…
Ira Hayes…Denver's Super…
words from Sam Greeley.

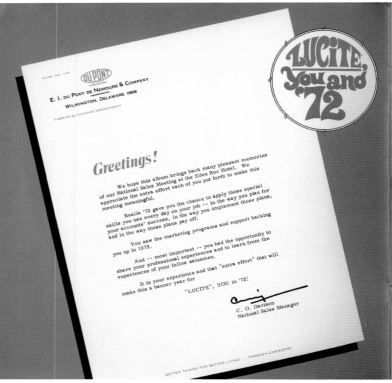

LUCITE, YOU AND '72

The packaging is the main attraction of this 1971 show for Du Pont's now defunct Lucite paint line. The cover opens into a sixteen-page booklet, allowing the recipient to relive the seven days' worth of hijinks in Miami Beach through dozens of photos, speech highlights, and sample lyrics. It's a musty, faintly rancid feast for anyone who enjoys gawking at 1971 men's fashions or executives at podiums.

As for the record, it's another so-so live recording heavily reliant on song parodies, with a few numbers that might be original. The title track scrounges up a couple rhymes for *paint*.

When it comes to house paint or
wall paint
Ceiling paint or floor paint — or to all paint
Jump up and sing like a saint,
Sing it loud, and without restraint.

You might be thinking, "Okay but what does 'Lucite, You and '72' *really mean*?" In the booklet, one executive put it this way: "So if you plan, I think that you will succeed, as I said, and I think you will also be free. At least that's what Lucite, You and '72 means to me."

Maybe. To me, *Lucite, You and '72* means another ultra-rare, subpar show that's redeemed by its fantastic presentation.

RARITY: 1

THE KICK-OFF

Sunday—November 28th

"LUCITE" Cheer

From East to West—
"Lucite" Paints are the best!

From coast to coast—
"Lucite" Paints are the most!

Give me an   L

Give me a   U

Give me a   C

Give me an   I

Give me a   T

Give me an   E

What have you got?
"Lucite"—"Lucite" Paints!

1972 SALES PROGRAMS

Thursday—December 2nd

"The organization that not only understands but solves retailers' problems will be the organization that will succeed. It is our objective to continue to provide you with facts that enable you to better understand your retailers' problems and, therefore, be better equipped to solve them. Our continuing marketing objective will be to assist you as much as possible in your jobs of being truly expert merchandisers of paint."

"So summing up, as a paint consumer, I've got to be impressed with the way we look at our products and packages as the consumer sees them, and then do the things that are necessary to provide maximum purchase motivation. Du Pont is continually working to satisfy my paint needs both from the standpoint of convenience of use and the basic quality and functionality of the products."

One final point that I would like to leave with you. This is not just another line of brushes and rollers. It is a complete consumer-oriented program that will bring your retailers more satisfied customers and more paint sales by making available to the consumer high quality application tools specifically designed for use with "Lucite" Paints so that maximum satisfaction with the painting results is achieved."

LEADER—C. A. RILEY	**GROUP LEADER—W. S. CULLITON**	**GROUP LEADER—C. A. STANLEY**	**VISITING TEAMS**

—13—R. A. Repetto, Counselor

	Zuchowski, J. J.
an, C. P.	Goffinet, E. O.
W.	Otey, J. S.
M.	

—14—R. D. Atkinson, Counselor

J. A.	Ekerberg, A. E.
J. S.	Phelan, L. B.
a, G. H.	Elliott, R. P.
J.	

—15—W. Faulkner, Counselor

e, E. J.	Glover, C. S.
er, J. J.	Bell, A. C.
ur, W. K.	Williams, D.
s, R. K.	

—16—H. Judd, Counselor

rg, E. D.	Stout, J. W.
s, W. E.	Lord, H. P.
M. F.	Garza, S.
J. A.	McKeel, G. M.

—17—W. E. Heifner, Counselor

man, E. H.	Driscoll, J. J.
n, P. B.	Cooke, C. L.
e, J. B.	Reinhardt, J. H.
s, P. A.	

—18—W. G. Moore, Counselor

J. A.	Falk, F. J.
ond, F. M.	Rommel, G.
ell, G. J.	Jensen, K. M.
, P. G.	

Team #19—G. C. Haney, Counselor

Whitman, R. J.	Henry, D. A.
Perry, S. G.	Snyders, J. R.
Chalk, A. B.	McGrath, J. P.
Ivey, G. E.	

Team #20—R. W. Gordon, Counselor

Richardson, A. P.	Mohr, R. A.
Fahlstrom, C. G.	Austin, M. C.
Schmidt, G. F.	Wierson, S. M.
O'Leary, C. H.	

Team #21—T. J. Leonard, Counselor

Williams, S. R.	Metzger, D. W.
Williams, G. F.	Pappalau, D.
Miller, T. E.	Horgan, E.
Brown, J. T.	

Team #22—R. P. Cox, Counselor

Tallant, T. M.	Darnell, F. G.
Boon, L. W.	Dorsey, W. H.
Claussen, J. B.	Moree, J. E.
Lefebvre, J.	

Team #23—W. D. McAvoy, Counselor

Novicki, C. A.	Drake, D. M.
Guinup, R. K.	Guenveur, J. C.
Robinson, J. B.	Mahaffey, A. I.
Solge, J. F.	

Team #24—J. D. Fultz, Counselor

Garvin, A. L.	Jordan, H. M.
Walker, J. F.	Telscher, S. R.
Swift, C. R.	Sisbarro, F. D.
Tucker, D. A.	

Team #25—V. E. Belvo, Counselor

Victory, W. O.	Beach, E. W.
Copeland, C. W.	Moran, T. J.
Gregg, R. C.	Senge, E. A.
Rafferty, J. H.	

Team #26—R. F. Porter, Counselor

Rust, G. B.	Jones, R. B.
Quade, W. J.	Henderson, J. C.
Thomas, W. C.	Richardson, T. W.

Team #27—C. E. Moss, Counselor

Doyle, T. M.	DeLuca, J. B.
VanAlstine, R. T.	Bilancioni, A. W.
Lynch, T. H.	Hampton, W. D.
Moore, D. L.	

Team #28—R. H. Dunn, Counselor

Robins, S.	Milstead, K. D.
Geyer, D. W.	Joyce, J. M.
Roberts, S. R.	Floyd, R. E.
Rhodes, J. W.	

Team #29—E. J. Napoleoni, Counselor

Manssuer, J.	Combs, P. S.
Kolumbus, J. S.	Warther, J. M.
Wolford, R. E.	Gisler, T. J.
Munson, W. B.	

Team #30—W. S. Levan, Counselor

Stirri, G. L.	Shea, E. L.
Rengers, J. D.	Littlefield, G. L.
East, W. V.	Keyler, E. G.
Royal, P. A.	

Team #31—R. H. Hughes, Counselor

Wellman, H. S.	Reynolds, J. B.
Swajeski, J. S.	Sawdey, D. J.
Burger, R. J.	

Team #32—C. J. Hanna, Counselor

Sikkel, P. L.	Smith, C. D.
Wileman, L. H.	Truschsess, H. F.
Saegebarth, K. A.	Cranmer, C. B.

Team #33—F. S. Nicoll, Counselor

Tjernell, S. F.	Montelius, K. L.
Joyner, J. B.	Sutton, J. N.
Washington, S. R.	

ALTERNATE COUNSELORS

| J. A. Lyons | C. D. Racine |
| H. A. Weibel | |

"The in-store merchandising aids I've shown you today are only the beginning of an all-out effort to improve our merchandising at the point-of-purchase. Before 1972 is over, you'll see even more improvements than you've seen today. The in-store paint department is where the action is—and that's where we'll be in 1972."

"The 1972 LUCITE advertising program is designed to attract customers to your retailers. It approaches your business through the eyes of the consumer. It can't do the job alone. But it will reach consumers . . ."

". . . With a new, unique and powerful approach that will assist you and your retailers in increasing Du Pont paint sales. That's what Advertising/'72 can, and will do, for LUCITE, You and '72."

"It is now our job, the job of the sales force, to communicate plans to our customers in such a way that we increase our sales volume with our present retailers and that we add substantial new distribution and sales volume. Considering this, I think it is appropriate that I am able to announce our 1972 New Account Program which I believe is a most outstanding new policy in over a decade."

HBP SUPERSTARS

Like its 1967 predecessor, this 1972 Owens-Corning Home Building Products show is a live recording with uncredited song parodies and comedy bits. What it lacks in originality or quality it makes up for in energy and good humor, sort of.

The three-woman cast (including a pre-*Cheers* Shelley Long) praises "those handsome men from HBP" to the tune of "I'd Like to Teach the World to Sing." Other rewritten favorites include "The Age of Aquarius" and "Cabaret." "Corning — An Opera" is a screechy, nearly unlistenable opera parody, but the spoken introduction is awesome.

The scene opens in a mobile home factory, as our fiery heroine Corning complains to her friends about the low insulating standards in many coaches and manufactured homes.

An executive named Allan Rudolph is brought on with "Allan R, Superstar," while a version of "Those Were the Days" strikes a melancholy note.

Those were the days, my friend, we
*   thought they'd never end,*
We sold those ceiling panels, 2 by 8.
We sold a box or two, that was the best
*   we'd do,*
Was it too early or were we too late?

I'm not qualified to say what was wrong with the timing but, yes, those certainly were the days.

RARITY: 1

A MAN NAMED BROWN

This 1970 Brown-Forman Distillers show is not very good, though I find it more enjoyable after I've had a few belts of Old Forester. It's notable mainly for the involvement of Raymond Scott, a popular composer and bandleader from the 1930s to the '50s whose music has often been used in cartoons. According to the Raymond Scott historian Irwin Chusid, the music for this show appears to have been Scott's final commercial project.

Brown-Forman, purveyor of brands such as Jack Daniel's, Early Times, and Southern Comfort, commissioned a "stage and screen production" to mark its hundredth anniversary and celebrate company founder George Garvin Brown. The songs are bland orchestral numbers with the occasional foray into rock, or "rock." Dick Stern's lyrics extol Kentucky, the city of Louisville, and how nice it is to enjoy a drink at the end of the day. In an unusual move for an industrial show, the vocals were handled by students from the University of Louisville. There's nothing about selling and barely

Brown-Forman Distillers Corporation

A Man Named Brown

IN HONOR OF THEIR 100TH YEAR, BROWN-FORMAN DISTILLERS CORPORATION PRESENTS THE ORIGINAL CAST RECORDING OF THEIR STAGE AND SCREEN PRODUCTION - A MAN NAMED BROWN

anything about the product. From "Bourbon, Bourbon":

Bourbon is a friend of man, other drinks
*   are also-ran*
Water pure from streams of old, makes it
*   smooth,*
Smooth as gold.

Where are the detail-packed lyrics about merchandising schemes and increasing market share? That's what makes a booze industrial smooth as gold!

RARITY: 3

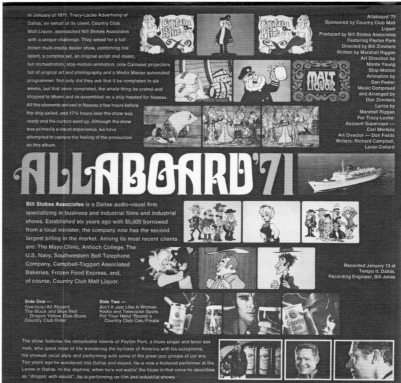

ALL ABOARD '71

Staged in Nassau, the Bahamas, this elaborate multimedia 1971 Country Club Malt Liquor show must have impressed the sales force. Unfortunately, the record doesn't really do the show justice. There are several long, semi-incoherent narrated segments that must have been much more rewarding with the animated visuals.

However, the songs by Don Zimmers and Marshall Riggan are appealing, ranging from the funky "Spinning Wheel"–esque "Country Club Rider" to the gently psychedelic title track. Combining Mamas & the Papas–style harmonies and a lyrical theme reminiscent of "Magical Mystery Tour," "All Aboard" summons the attendees to

Take a trip of a different kind (all aboard)
And leave your hassles all behind
 (all aboard)
The passengers and crew are signed
For an odyssey within the mind
All aboard, all aboard
Why don't you climb all aboard (all aboard)
The Country Club Malt Liquor Magical
 Cruise.

A magical odyssey within the mind! Take that, hassles!

RARITY: 3

232

40 DAYS AND 40 NIGHTS

Ahoy, mateys! Who's that blue-hued sea captain puppet posed before a cracking lightning bolt? The central ghost of some kids' Hallowe'en TV special? The robotic host of a "Journey to Davy Jones' Locker" ride at Kings Dominion amusement park? Nay, ye landlubber, he's Captain Blue, a-sailin' the bounding main to promote the promotin' of malt liquor. *Arrrr.*

Malt liquor: the basis for sweet pseudo-cocktails sold by the bottle as "hard lemonade" and "spiked tea" and the kitschquaff perennial Champale…notorious as the high-test contents of the low-rent "40" so celebrated by rappers. Simply unscrewing the cap and taking a swig will magically give you a mullet and a Bad Company tattoo. But Country Club had classier things in mind back in the '70s, when it offered the stuff as a maverick alternative to all that bitter, gassy beer we'd been choking down for centuries. Plus, as the TV spots said, it was "a lot to drink without drinking a lot" (guess the slogan "gets you drunker, quicker" wouldn't have the same panache).

What better way to stir company pride in this delicious, wholesome product than to load your execs onto a slow boat to Nassau and then subject them to "live talent, a complex set, an original script and music, full orchestration, stop-motion animation, nine carousel projectors full of original art and photography and a Media Master automated programmer." From the looks of things on the back cover, it was one corker of a presentation, with animation by accomplished Dallas designer-artist Dan Peeler, who later designed the characters on *The Swamp Critters of Lost Lagoon* (an odd kiddie show created by "Watching Scotty Grow" chartmaker Bobby Goldsboro) and oversaw the 1990s redesign of pizza arcade mascot Chuck E. Cheese.

And if the thought of Chuck E.'s pizza threatens to make you "heave to," then by god don't imagine yourself stowed away in a Bahamas convention hall, sipping malt liquor with a boatload of salesmen.

Ad men tell no tales. *Yarrrr.*

—SM

The show features the remarkable talents of Payton Park, a blues singer and tenor sax man, who spent most of life wandering the byroads of America with his saxophone, his unusual vocal style and performing with some of the great jazz groups of our era. Ten years ago he wandered into Dallas and stayed. He is now a featured performer at the Levee in Dallas. In the daytime, when he's not wailin' the blues in that voice he describes as "drippin' with mould", he is performing on film and industrial shows.

233

THE GREAT GET TOGETHER

Much of the bombastic Coke = America spirit from the '61 show is still in evidence in this big budget 1979 Coca-Cola show, with broadly similar songs such as "Coke Goes with America" and "Whatever America Wants" waving the flag. Others, like "We'll Build Our Road Together" and "Coke Keeps Moving On," are rich-sounding but vague and generic.

A few of the uncredited Larry Grossman and Hal Hackady tracks are worthwhile. "That Certain Something" unspools a long, clever Cole Porter–ish list of things that have an indefinable X factor, of which Coke is one. And "Smile, It's a Great Business" joins the Kinks' "Lola" as one of the few songs that attempts to rhyme *cola*.

*Those cherries life's supposed to be a
    bowl 'a
Are back in season—what's the reason?
    Coca-Cola!*

The real sugar-and-caffeine musical kick comes from "That Big Bottling Plant up in

the Sky." Like the '76 Exxon song "Dealers' Heaven," it imagines an afterlife in which you're still working for the company, although with improvements.

*In that big bottling plant up in the blue,
Every shipment arrives the day it's due!
The trucks are always loaded right,
And strikes get settled overnight!
And there's no such a thing as IOU!*

The song eventually winds up in a place Coke bottlers may have fantasized about but wouldn't want to say in public.

*Every route man is bright and as strong
    as a Turk,
Dotes on hard work—just loves hard work!
And there's no IRS to drive you berserk!
And they send the guys from OSHA
    straight to hell!*

If you're already dead and working in a Coke bottling plant, no industrial accident can kill you again, so sure, why not?

RARITY: 3

1986 PEPSI ADVERTISING PREMIERE

1986 PEPSI ADVERTISING PREMIERE

Pepsi's 1986 show is the end of the line — the latest show record in my collection. The songs by Ted Simons and Donald Epstein have the classic big-bucks industrial sound, dressed up with a bit of electric guitar and futuristic effects. Why was Pepsi splurging on an extravagant show, plus a record with a fancy mirror-reflective gold cover, this late in history? Two words: New Coke.

For years Pepsi had been gaining on perennial top dog Coke, and by the early '80s Coke decided to act. A reformulated, sweeter version was tested and found to be preferred by most people. But Coke, as it later admitted, underestimated how strongly some people would react to changing an icon. "New Coke" was introduced in April 1985. The backlash was quick, and by July Coke had reversed course and brought back the old Coke as "Coke Classic." Pepsi watched the fiasco unfold and took out full-page newspaper ads crowing "The Other Guy Blinked." The needling continued at the convention with "In the Blink of an Eye."

First there was old Coke, that seemed as good as gold Coke,
But no one said "Leave well enough alone."
So some Atlanta smarty came up with New Coke,
A hardly tried-and-true Coke,
And made believe it was a Pepsi clone.
But no one else agreed, so back now came Old Coke,
A welcome-to-the-fold Coke,
While New Coke simply sat there on the shelves.
And in the press they shouted, "Aren't we the bright ones,"
"Our two Cokes are the right ones,"
While privately they tried to kick themselves.

Other songs include "Any Way You Slice It," about Slice fruit-flavored soft drinks; "Pepsi Everywhere," about Pepsi's success in vending and food service and its "take home sales"; and "A Nice Old-Fashioned Business," a tongue-in-cheek look at technology with references to microchips, bar codes, "modulated chromatrons," and "digitated modal valves." Pepsi pitchman Michael J. Fox made an appearance, probably in conjunction with the song "Back to the Future."

Get ready to wave to Mars,
'Cause we're heading back to the future
And you can bet that future's bright,
'Cause Pepsi leads the way
Back to the future — today!

Lyricist Donald Epstein says the space theme originally was to have been a much bigger part of the show. Just days before the convention the space shuttle *Challenger* exploded and the creative team did a frantic rewrite.

RARITY: 3

THIS IS CLARKMANSHIP

Gather 'round, you fat cats,
We're gonna shake and groove!
'Cause Clark's trucks for '70
Are really on the move!

First I'll give you fat cats a moment to digest that cover. Okay, now look away before that eye makeup permanently traumatizes you.

This 1970 Clark Equipment show has lyrics by Paul Nash and music by Norman Paris, who arranged many Michael Brown industrials and was married to Broadway star Dorothy Loudon, who was in Michael's 1960 Singer show.

Paris's only known example of industrial show composing is this show about forklifts, which boasts a nice horn-driven orchestral sound as well as a generous dose of details about model numbers and drivetrain systems and such.

We've seen the long-suffering wife as a theme in *Diesel Dazzle* and Exxon's *Put Yourself in Their Shoes*. Here we have wives singing "My V.I.P. — Tribute to Salesmen."

Yes, we're those things called salesmen's
  wives,
We gave up living when we chose our lives.
But one truth stands, it will always be,
We love those men, our V.I.P.s.

Sweet…and depressing. Other highlights include the unusual "Hooray for Human Engineering," sung by human bones in praise of the more comfortable B-Model series, and "It Pays to Advertise," a burlesque number in which, once again, product advertising is compared to women showing off their assets. The winner may be "Big Six," a swingin' tribute to the new Clark IT-60 heavy duty truck.

"See the IT-60," the Clark man said.
"It's designed for mud or washboard beds.
Got mighty wide tires to carry loads
  so great,
Got big rear axles that articulate!"

The song presents the IT-60 as the ideal replacement for legendary construction worker "Big Stosh" who has just disappeared in the deep mud of a job site…interesting and, once again, oddly depressing. No wonder the woman on the cover doesn't look radiantly happy about "Clarkmanship."

RARITY: 3

SHOW BOOK BY:
Tom Hubbard

MUSIC BY:
Norman Paris

LYRICS BY:
Paul Nash

CHOREOGRAPHY BY:
Elaine O'Donnel

PRODUCED BY:
Bartlett Film Services, Inc.
DETROIT, MICHIGAN

PRODUCER:
RICHARD STRANE

DIRECTION BY:
WAYNE KNIFFIN

TECHNICAL DIRECTION:
GORDON LAWTON

ASSOCIATE PRODUCER-VISUALS:
CHUCK LONDON

ART DIRECTION:
TERRY SANTRY

ASSOCIATE WRITER:
PAUL NASH

COSTUMES BY:
MARCI HANEY

ENTIRE PRODUCTION CONCEIVED AND PRODUCED BY:
TOM HUBBARD
EXECUTIVE PRODUCER

this is Clarkmanship

WE HAVE THE POWER

A sad ending to the mighty run of Hank Beebe–Bill Heyer industrials on record: eight years after 1966's immortal *Diesel Dazzle*, GM's Detroit Diesel division (now called Detroit Diesel Allison) decided it wanted another show. But the company didn't want to spend much money or invest the time and energy working with writers to figure out new songs that would resonate with the concerns of the 1974 sales force. They wound up recycling the old *Diesel Dazzle* material in a new production called *We Have the Power*, with slightly altered lyrics and one new Beebe-Heyer song, the title track that sounds like it was cranked out in a hurry. It's a pallid, eerie, unsatisfying revival that makes you realize how dazzling the original was. Fun cover, though.

RARITY: 2

A WORLD OF WINNERS

Toto, I don't think we're in Radio City Music Hall anymore.

Few industrials aspired to the blowout extravagance of the '64 Ford Tractor show. But the cover of 1977's *A World of Winners* illustrates how vastly different the tractor show experience could be. On a muddy patch of ground outside Orlando, Massey-Ferguson dealers sit on bleachers as giant machines rumble past. There's a stage and a handful of inert-looking cast members, but the music is canned, coming out of speakers that must have struggled to compete with the roaring engines. Yet there's some charming, even A-list material here.

A World of Winners was produced out of Cedar Rapids, which saw a fair amount of agriculture-related industrial show activity.

The show songs take up only one side of the record, with radio commercials on the other side. The well-crafted music (uncredited, but by Sue Tucker) has a banjo-and-fiddle flavor, a far cry from the cosmopolitan orchestra of Ford's Radio City show.

The M-F 60 is new this year!
A super backhoe topping Case and Deere!
New harrows, plows, and cultivators —
    chisels too!
New sales opportunities for you, you, you!

Consumer products mean extra dough!
Those mowers and blowers can help
    you grow!
Fifty percent of a winner's net
Comes from parts and service, and
    don't forget
While cheaper parts may have a
    certain attraction
M-F parts mean satisfaction!

The centerpiece is a "why we do what we do" song, a tribute to the tractor dealer as the man without whom life as we know it couldn't exist. With a kick-ass spoken vocal by lyricist Bob Cook, backed by a soaring chorus, "We're Massey-Ferguson" tells the M-F faithful:

You're the man that says "Yes I can"
And you handle the best in the field,
And you're the man that stands behind
The man with the record yield!
You handle the North American king,
And you service it with pride.
But with all the work, the thing that counts
Is what you feel inside.
Do you feel it? THAT'S PRIDE!
(Yes, we're Massey!)
Yeah! We're number one!

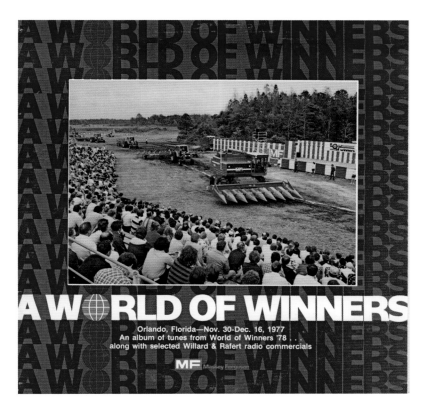

A WORLD OF WINNERS

Orlando, Florida—Nov. 30-Dec. 16, 1977
An album of tunes from World of Winners '78 . . .
along with selected Willard & Rafert radio commercials

MF Massey-Ferguson

Selected Willard & Rafert radio commercials . . .
along with tunes from World of Winners '78

Willard & Rafert

(We believe in Massey, Massey-Ferguson!)
Do you believe it? Sing it!
(We believe you're the man with the
power in your hand!)
So stand up proud and say it loud!
(We're Massey-Ferguson!)

Wow. I've never been on a tractor in my life, but I *do* feel it. Sometimes when nobody's looking, I stand up proud and say it loud: "We're Massey-Ferguson!"

RARITY: 3

FOLLOW THE ROAD

This 1975 show is a puzzle. No composer or performer credits, no leads or tips, no nothing. But this record's loopy delights earn its anonymous creator(s) a spot in the Industrial Show Hall of Fame.

Dominion Road Machinery, a Canadian manufacturer of motor graders, only made motor graders, as it reminded its sales force in the song titled "They Only Make Motor Graders." Competitors bemoan the fact that Dominion isn't distracted by other product lines.

They don't make coal haulers
They don't make off-highway trucks
Here's how they make their bucks:
By only making motor graders!
So when they build them, you can bet
they build them good!
They're motor grader masters, from
what's outside to what's under
the hood!

Follow the Road has some of the most hardcore technical specifications ever squeezed into song lyrics, and it's also over the top in several ethnic directions. "Quality and Economy" has a Scottish flavor, with data about the new Champion 700 series delivered in a heavy brogue.

Their operatin' costs are cheaper than
any you can name,
And where the stress points are the
highest, they overlap the frame!
Low-maintenance bearings are their latest
claim to fame!

Our drive axles are the floatin' kind,
and laddie,

DOWNGRADING

Unusually for an industrial album, an elegiac atmosphere pervades the cover of *Follow the Road*. Dawn? Dusk? The end of another hard day or the beginning of a new one? Six of one, half dozen of the other, when all you know—all you'll ever know—is the endess absurdity of toiling to draw bare sustenance from this rutted wasteland that surrounds you. Sure, follow the road; heave a weary sigh and follow it all the way to nowhere, as the shadows swallow every vestige of hope your benumbed soul ever held. Ah, the hell with it; let's consider the type.

The show's title is set in Potatostamp, a casual font popular in the 1970s for Christian Youth Group concert programs and antidrug brochures. It customarily signals a homespun message of sincere tedium, here offset—or complemented, depending upon the nature and degree of your despair—by two other alternating type styles.

The irksome faux elegance of Junquemail Italic, designed specifically for must-ignore wedding invitations, lends a note of irony to the words "Highlights from the…" and "…Dominion Road Machinery Announcement Meeting" as if an event with such an unwieldy subtitle could possibly yield anything any sane observer would call a "highlight." The year, 1975, and the strangely gigantic, all caps "IN TORONTO CANADA" are presented in Logan's Run Sans Serif, favored by progressive rock bands for their self-released concept LPs about future dystopias in which rock is outlawed.

This potentially jarring combination of dismal imagery and dissonant typography improbably produces an effect of peacefulness and eccentric charm, thereby negating negation, a feat of graphic transubstantiation that can only be regarded as the fruit of genius, a promise borne out by the eclectic enchantment captured on the vinyl.

—SM

PRP 242

Follow The Road

SIDE TWO
5 STANDARD EQUIPMENT
7 THE SONG OF THE WISE MAN
8 OPTIONS
9 THE BULLWOOD PLANT IN THE BLUEGRASS STATE
10 FOLLOW THE ROAD (REPRISE)

SIDE ONE

Produced by the Geo. P. Johnson Company

And you will know him by his dual-flow
    hydraulic system!

Bafflingly, after ninety seconds, the song switches gears from ersatz Asian to a horn and bass driven–soul sound. Maybe it made sense live on the stage.

Follow the Road has one more bogus ethnic card to play. A swirling klezmer-style clarinet signals two songs as being "Middle Eastern." "The Harem Song" features female singers, who must surely have been wearing veils and shimmering whatnots as they sang.

Our lord and master is a Champion dealer,
So of course we live in style and luxury,
And once he starts to sell the 700s
Then life will simply be sheer ecstasy!

Technologically, the 700s
The finest motor grader ever known!
The 720s, 40s, and the 60
Could make up quite a harem of their own!

The exotic Orientalism continues in "Standard Equipment," a staggering four-minute blast of data.

Open half-cab with insulated floor mat
Grab handles and safety steps
Fully adjustable two-passenger seat
With folding arms and back rest!

Power-assisted oil disc brakes
For each of the four wheels,
Grader controls for sitting or standing
Depending how the operator feels!

And on and on. And on. And on. OMG, as the kids say. (Do the kids still say that?)

RARITY: 1

That's the best!
The machine can keep on runnin'
Though the axle be distressed!
We can pull out our transmission without
    pullin' out the rest!

In "The Song of the Wise Man" the weirdness hops the globe to land on a mystical Far East style.

For in the motor grader manual it is
    written,
A Champion shall appear and change a
    big Cat to a kitten,
None will resist him,

Musical Highlights of The Timken Company's
1972 MARKETING CONFERENCE
at The Greenbrier

DIMENSIONS 72

This 1972 Timken Bearings show, the final record with a Jam Handy Organization producer credit, is a Frankenstein monster. Jam Handy sent veteran musical director Maurice Levine out to the old show graveyard, and he came back with a hearse-load of songs from other industrials, some dating back almost ten years. Crudely stitched together with simple lyric tweaks and brought to a semblance of life, it's an impressive recycling project but not a significant show.

"We Want to Get the Facts" is from the '71 Xerox show; "New World Opening Up" is from the '67 Chevy show; "Flexibility" is from the '65 Chevy show; "Proper Planning" is from the '66 Coke show; and "Timken's the Name" and "The Timken Company" are adapted from the '63 Xerox show. "The Metric System" and "People Make the Difference" aren't from any other show that's come to light, but let's just say I'm skeptical about their freshness.

Sadly, there's practically no mention of the bearings business, but there is one encouraging detail. In a nod to the changing

times, one song includes a female salesperson. As Frankenstein's monster would say, "*Rrr,* sexual discrimination bad!"

RARITY: 1

FLY CESSNA

A sturdy example of a big-budget, later period industrial, this 1979 show has a full orchestra and a slick Broadway sound. Wilson Stone and David Blomquist, industrial collaborators since the '60s, had the formula down pat by now, turning out songs reminiscent of others in their VW, Coke, Xerox, and Chevy shows. Although it

doesn't make the industrial top tier, *Fly Cessna* occasionally soars.

> *A hundred thousand airplanes in the sky*
> *Have got to impress ya!*
> *A half million seats, and that is why*
> *Nobody but nobody beats Cessna!*

"One of a Kind" is a cousin of Cole Porter's "You're the Top" (and of the '79 Coke show's "That Certain Something").

> *What a young Jim Zorn is, what a Dixie*
> *   morn is,*
> *What a unicorn is, Cessna is: one of*
> *   a kind!*

Male cast members sing "The Business Travel Blues," with the ladies providing the answer in "Cessna Can Do It," touting the flexibility of airplane charters and rentals. "Growing Pains" is a sarcastic look at the company's problems.

> *I call up Cessna at quarter to two,*
> *The computer is down so I don't get*
> *   through.*
> *But what's the difference? Everyone there*
> *   is new!*
> *And nobody knows who I am!*
> *The latest product brochure sure was*
> *   great,*
> *Too bad all the info is now out of date.*

> *The name's obsolete and the picture's not*
> *   straight.*

Near the end, a whiny dealer complains "Who Cares About the Dealer," only to have the whole cast explain that the entire show has been to honor him, and that he should know "The Star Is You." Cool. From now on I'm going to look at my local Cessna dealer with more respect.

RARITY: 1

JCPENNEY 1974 MANAGEMENT CONFERENCE

A poignant swan song for industrial show regulars Skip Redwine and arranger-conductor Norman Paris, this Penney show is baffling at times but has some lovely moments. There definitely was a plot, or possibly plots, involving an idyllic small town named Calico Falls ("short hair, clean air") and people working at a JCPenney store (the new streamlined version of the name), or possibly a JCProudfoot store.

The Skip Redwine songs display traces of his International Paper and York air conditioner panache, and the arrangement and recording are honey sweet. Some numbers have no apparent Penney content, but elsewhere there's enough retail detail to satisfy the industrial show nerd. "Form a Committee" takes a sardonic look at company bureaucracy.

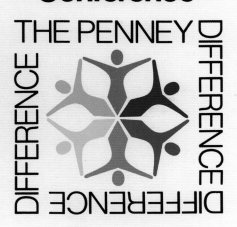

JCPenney
1974 Management
Conference

THE PENNEY DIFFERENCE

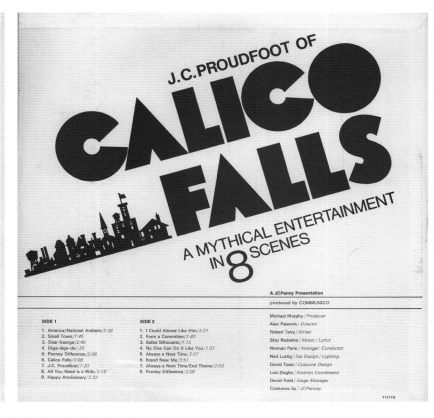

J.C.PROUDFOOT OF

CALICO FALLS

A MYTHICAL ENTERTAINMENT IN **8** SCENES

A JCPenny Presentation

produced by COMMUNICO

SIDE 1
1. America/National Anthem/2:38
2. Small Town/1:45
3. Dear George/2:40
4. Diga-diga-do/:25
5. Penney Difference/2:08
6. Calico Falls/3:08
7. J.C. Proudfoot/1:20
8. All You Need is a Wife/2:19
9. Happy Anniversary/2:33

SIDE 2
1. I Could Almost Like Him/2:21
2. Form a Committee/2:40
3. Ballet Silhouette/1:15
4. No One Can Do It Like You/1:21
5. Always a Next Time/2:57
6. Brand New Me/3:51
7. Always a Next Time/End Theme/2:03
8. Penney Difference/2:08

Michael Murphy / *Producer*
Alex Palermo / *Director*
Robert Terry / *Writer*
Skip Redwine / *Music / Lyrics*
Norman Paris / *Arranger: Conductor*
Ned Lustig / *Set Design / Lighting*
David Toser / *Costume Design*
Lois Ziegler / *Fashion Coordinator*
David Gold / *Stage Manager*
Costumes by / *JCPenney*

4121F6

*If you think that you'll sink in the
     company sea,
Don't have self-pity — form a committee.
Once you slip, lose your grip on the
     company tree,
Don't leave the city — form a committee.
Committee means the one to blame, they
     calm all your fears,
A complicated problem can be studied
     for years!*

"Happy Anniversary" finds a store manager bickering with the company's balky ten-year-old computer system, each blaming the other for late deliveries and bad data. In "I Could Almost Like Him" a store employee yearns for her boss to notice her.

*I'd melt if I really felt we had half as much
     rapport*

*As he has for that display by the door...
     what's more...
He gives so much of his love away,
To the Boys Scouts and the YMCA...hey,
Doesn't he know some girl would prize
Sharing some of that light that floods
     his eyes
When some new advertising notion
     strikes him
Even I could almost like him.*

Love comes at last in the duet between employee and boss, "No One Can Do It Like You." The classical-style violins push the song to the brink of cheesiness, but odd details help save it.

*No one else stores ten gyro gliders
With your great know-how,
Who else hangs five harpsichords
Without a wrinkled brow?*

*I've seen how you sparkle
When you tag a snorkel,
Racking, stacking egg shampoo,
No one can do it like you.
I love the way you tag those paper
    dresses!
And the way you bag those gas
    drill presses!
I find it so elating, that verve when
    you're uncrating
Backyard swings — my heart sings!*

Skip Redwine worked on a Cole Porter revue in the mid-'60s, and flashes of Porteresque wit and phrasing are in evidence here as well as in his other shows. Skip died young, according to his colleague Michael Brown. I'm pleased to help his industrial work live on.

RARITY: 2

'79 FEVER

Good morning, dance fans, and welcome again to '79 Fever — the world's first sales meeting with a disco beat! There's not one other office furniture manufacturer that hustled through 1978 the way we did! No wonder we've got '79 Fever!

This is it: the smoking gun. This is what killed disco.

The three-day January 1979 meeting of Westinghouse ASD (Architectural Systems Department) is summarized in the remarkable "Three Days in Eight Minutes," with music by Kevin Gavin and lyrics by Ken Peters. Side 2 is the same music without the meeting content.

"And here to start it all off, wearing the shiniest dancing shoes in San Diego, our National Sales Manager, Don Sullivan!"

*Here's Don to tell you what's going
    down here!
He'll lead the band now, he'll wear the
    crown here!
He's got the fever!*

Executive introductions, speech summaries, the credentials of a motivational speaker, descriptions of meals and recreational outings: it's all set to the inescapable *'79 Fever* theme music. Sometimes the theme drops out briefly to make way for a bit of a Fran Tarkenton speech or a different musical intro (one unfortunate guy was brought on to Randy Newman's "Short People"), but the disco music always comes back. It cannot be stopped. At least not for eight minutes. Actually, eight minutes and twenty seconds.

'79 Fever is a truly stunning piece of corporate and cultural ephemera. In trying to decide whether it's the worst thing in the world or the best thing in the world, I have to conclude: both.

RARITY: 1

'79 Fever
In San Diego, California, at Vacation Village, in January of 1979, the Westinghouse ASD sales force convened for its annual meeting.
That meeting was, well— unique.
Naturally, it featured some terrific speeches, great seminars, dinners and so forth, but the theme was disco, and the participants *literally* danced their way through three exciting days.
This album features many of the special speakers' introductions and the original music written and arranged specially for the occasion.
So sit back, relive the excitement and catch '79 Fever all over again.

Don Sullivan
National Sales Manager
Westinghouse ASD

'79 Fever Production Credits
Marsteller, Inc., Pittsburgh PA
Producer: Ken Peters
Writers: Ken Peters, Steve Alber
Art Director: Bob Sands
Song: "We got the Fever"
Music: Kevin Gavin
Lyrics: Ken Peters
Sound System and Recording: Norm Cleary, Bob Bradford, Audio Innovators, Pittsburgh PA
Visual Sequences and Special Effects Production: The Presentation People Division of Gateway Studios, Inc.
Lighting: Michael Doherty
Choreography and Staging: Don Brockett Productions
Photography: Gateway Studios, Inc.
Album Cover Design: Bob Sands
ASD, Grand Rapids
Special thanks to Alan Zimmerman, Tom Sanford, Don Sullivan, Mike Ferrara, Pat Taylor, and the Boss: Jack Cooper.

AGAIN WITH A.... *John Russell* "INDUSTRIALS" ANECDOTE!

BELIEVE YOU ME, IT WASN'T ALL CHEERS & CURTAIN CALLS IN THE CONFERENCE ENTERTAINMENT GAME! IN HIS OWN WORDS, JOHN, OUR INTREPID "WITNESS TO HISTORY" RECALLS AN "UN-CONVENTIONAL" CASE OF **WHEN VEEPS ATTACK!**

PANASONIC'S VICE PRESIDENT OF MARKETING CAME OUT ON STAGE. USUALLY THESE THINGS ARE **PEP TALKS**. YOU KNOW: "YOU'RE DOING **GREAT!** GO OUT AND SELL SOME **MORE!**"

WELL, THIS GUY JUST GOT OUT THERE & SAID: YOU **WORTHLESS** PIECES OF GARBAGE.

YOU'VE JUST ABOUT **DESTROYED** THIS COMPANY!

UNLESS YOU DOUBLE YOUR SALES **IMMEDIATELY**, YOU'RE GONNA BE **FIRED!** THANK YOU.

THEN THE MUSIC STARTS AND WE COME OUT, DANCING AND SINGING: **HEY!** ISN'T IT GREAT!! PANA-SONIC!!

AND THE AUDIENCE...

WHITE AS SHEETS...

THEY DIDN'T KNOW WHAT HIT THEM.

The End of the Golden Age

The last thunderous notes of the finale ring out, then fade away. The tonearm lifts from the closing track, then clunks as it returns to its rest. Or the needle just hisses in that last groove until you put the arm back manually. Either way, the souvenir album titled *The Golden Age of Industrial Musicals*, on the Pretentious Metaphor label, has ended.

Technology, economics, and a natural evolutionary process brought the curtain down by the end of the 1980s. What was new and thrilling in the '50s and expected in the '60s was starting to feel old hat in the '70s. The shows might still entertain and educate but they no longer surprised. And with difficult economic times in the '70s, fewer companies wanted to spend the money for a big show. Large casts were rarer and rarer; it became common to use prerecorded music and lip-synching rather than a live orchestra and vocals.

New technologies allowed companies to entertain an audience without paying for expensive writers, composers, and performers. A few laser lights zapping, a recyclable prerecorded audiovisual module with a vague "let's achieve excellence" message—maybe it wasn't a fabulous theatrical experience but it was cheap. Also, the new MTV generation of salespeople and executives had little attachment to musical theater. By the early '80s composers such as Hank Beebe and Wilson Stone noticed that the calls had stopped coming. Younger composers who created rock-themed industrial shows continued to work for a few more years, but by the late '80s even these shows were disappearing.

Elliott Delman, one of the composers of the 1979 B.F. Goodrich show who's still in the corporate meeting business, says that in the past twenty years not only is there no appetite for original music and lyrics, clients no longer even want song parodies. The younger generation just wants the songs they already know and love. Any attempt to offer an original number is met with suspicion: "Is that a *real* song or did *you* write it?"

A 1986 *New York Times* story on industrials noted that car introduction shows had come back from a dip, but shows for other industries were languishing. The *Times* also mentioned the trend of production companies working up elaborate show presentations "on spec." Producers were expected to audition a miniversion of a show, created at their own expense—wasted money if the client selected a competitor. More and more producers decided it wasn't worth the trouble. The article also described the casting process for a Chase Bank show—but, tellingly, only dancers were needed, not singers. For many performers, a great way to make money and hone skills was disappearing.

Though the golden age of industrial musicals is long gone, we can console ourselves with the fact that surely more examples will turn up. Speaking of which, if you have an industrial show souvenir record not mentioned in this book, I'd very much like to know about it. Drop a line to steve@industrialmusicals.com. Meanwhile, the cream of the crop is available for your listening pleasure at industrialmusicals.com.

In conclusion, it'll be a great year if you use the product knowledge and selling tools explained in those peppy show tunes! Now, get out there and sell—for yourself, for the company, for America!

WELL, WELL... YET ANOTHER... *John Russell* "INDUSTRIALS" ANECDOTE!

JOHN, IN A REFRESHINGLY CANDID CONFESSION, SHOWS HOW EVEN THE MOST WELL-PREPARED PRO CAN "BUNGLE ONE" EVERY NOW AND AGAIN! IN OUR LAST "MINI MEMOIR" WE RELIVE THE ANXIOUS MOMENT WHEN OUR MAN **ZONED!**

I WAS GREAT AT MEMORIZING THINGS QUICKLY. BUT SOMETIMES I GOT **TRIPPED UP.**

THIS WAS AT **FORD'S** ENORMOUS 75th ANNIVERSARY SHOW IN 1978 IN DETROIT...

(WHICH WE ALSO PERFORMED 1 WEEK LATER FOR THE LINCOLN-MERCURY PEOPLE, WITH **CHANGES** TO THE LYRICS AND THE PRODUCT INFORMATION.)

I WAS THE MASTER OF CEREMONIES AND THERE I WAS, INTRODUCING THE 1979 MERCURY **ZEPHYR**...

Ladies & Gentlem Tonight,

DELIVERING A SPIEL FULL OF "Z" WORDS...

In our zeal to zing the competition and zoom to the very Zenith of the market, with Zero doubt in the Zest of our

...AND WHEN I GOT TO THE **END** OF THE SPEECH,

I COULDN'T REMEMBER THE **NAME** OF THE CAR.

I give you...: **THE 1979...** ...UM...

I JUST **STOOD** THERE, IN FRONT OF **2,000** PEOPLE.

I **LOOKED** AT THE SIDE OF THE CAR,

BUT IT WAS A MOCK-UP, AND THE NAME **WASN'T ON IT.**

FINALLY, I JUST SAID

..the 1979...

...car.

I WAS **SO** HUMILIATED.

BUT NOBODY CARED.

WHEEE! EVREKA! YIPEE! O HOORAY! WHOO! YAY! YEAH! FA KUDOS! BRAVO! YAY! YEAH! YEE-HAW! AH-OOO! HUZZAH! HIP-HIP! THREE CHEERS

CLAP CLAP CLAP AP CLAP CLA

Acknowledgments

The authors would like to thank:

Laura Lindgren and Ken Swezey, publishers of Blast Books, who had the right vision for this book and carried it through in a way that surpassed our dangerously high hopes.

Our wives, Samantha Shubert and Shelley Murphy, and our children, Rebecca and Hannah, and Alex, Lily, and Miles, for their patience during our work on the book, and for the years of nodding politely as we feverishly presented our latest discoveries.

Jon Ward and Don Bolles, fellow collectors who loaned irreplaceable records.

Folks from the industrial show world who generously took time to recount their experiences: Hank Beebe, John Russell, Michael and Joy Brown, Wilson Stone, Sheldon Harnick, the late Lloyd Norlin, Ted Simons, the late John Allen, Fred Albitz, Donald Epstein, Herb Kanzell, the late Bob WeDyck, Arnold Midlash, Fred Tobias, the late Claibe Richardson, Ed Nayor, Julian Stein, John Kander, Walter Marks, the late Sonny Kippe, Elliott Delman, Marshall Riggan, Bob Cook, Sue Tucker, Ernie Cefalu, Don Logay, the late Maurice Levine, Lenny Wolpe, Georgia Creighton, SuEllen Estey, Buff Shurr, Hal Linden, Florence Henderson, Bill Hayes, Tedd Determan, the late Jim Harder, Chuck Green, Diane Findlay, Lew Gluckin, Willi Burke, Bob Brooks, Anne Hilton, Vicki Belmonte, Virginia Sandifur, Ron Young, Bill Sandy, the late Haford Kerbawy, Joyce Nolan, Todd Jackson, David and Joan Marshall, Joan Beugen, Jana Robbins.

Otis Fodder, for his enthusiastic expertise applied to the website industrialmusicals.com.

For various help, advice, support, good karma: the late Helen and Seamus Murphy, Pete and Ellen Young, Alan Young, Sherlee Shubert, Irwin Chusid, the late Don Brockway, Jim Roseland, Eric Swedberg, Jim Robinson, Bruce Yeko, Jello Biafra, Brad Bennett, Todd Ruel, Wayno, Gregg Turkington, Dave Letterman, Rachel Ross, Dr. David Eldridge, George Regis, Cheryl Levenbrown, Linda Bonvie, Steve O'Donnell, Paul Major, and Don Kennison.

Our special thanks to Len Janke, plant manager, Dick Kruizenga, Vice President, and the entire staff of the Grand Haven Factory for helping make this sales meeting a success.

I WOULD LIKE 1☐ 2☐ TICKETS FOR THE 5:00 P.M. COCKTAIL SHOW

I WOULD LIKE 1☐ 2☐ TICKETS FOR THE 11:00 P.M. SUPPER SHOW

☛ SPECIAL ☚

FOR THOSE AMONG THE FIRST TO CHOOSE THE 11:00 P.M. SUPPER SHOW, 1☐ OR 2☐ TICKETS ARE AVAILABLE FOR A BROADWAY HIT, WHICH WE HAVE SELECTED FOR YOUR ENTERTAINMENT. CURTAIN AT 8:40 P.M.

_____ _____ _____
NAME   STORE   TITLE